THE CREDOS OF EIGHT BLACK LEADERS

Converting Obstacles into Opportunities

John J. Ansbro

University Press of America,® Inc.
Lanham · Boulder · New York · Toronto · Oxford

University Press of America,® Inc.
4501 Forbes Boulevard
Suite 200
Lanham, Maryland 20706
UPA Acquisitions Department (301) 459-3366

PO Box 317
Oxford
OX2 9RU, UK

Library of Congress Control Number: 2004109755
ISBN 0-7618-2742-0 (clothbound : alk. ppr.)

CONTENTS

Acknowledgements

Acknowledgement is gratefully extended for permission to refer to the following:

The Frederick Douglass Papers, Series One: Speeches, Debates, and Interviews, 1841-1895, five volumes, edited by John W. Blassingham et al.; Yale University Press, 1979-1992. Copyright © 1979, 1982, 1985, 1991, 1992 by Yale University. Used by permission of Yale University Press.

The Marcus Garvey and Universal Negro Improvement Association Papers, nine volumes, edited by Robert A. Hill et al.; University of California Press, 1983-1995. Copyright © 1983-1995 by The Regents of the University of California. Used by permission of University of California Press.

Marcus Garvey: Life and Lessons, A Centennial Companion to the Marcus Garvey and Universal Negro Improvement Association Papers, edited by Robert A. Hill and Barbara Bair; University of California Press, 1987. Copyright © 1987 by The Regents of the University of California. Used by permission of University of California Press.

Philosophy and Opinions of Marcus Garvey, two volumes, by Marcus Garvey, edited by Amy Jacques-Garvey; Atheneum, 1969. Copyright © 1923, 1925 by Amy Jacques-Garvey. Used by permission of Simon & Schuster.

Black Reconstruction in America, 1860-1880 by W.E.B. Du Bois; Atheneum, 1992. Copyright © 1935, 1962 by W.E.B. Du Bois. Adapted by permission of David Graham Du Bois.

W.E.B. Du Bois Speaks, Speeches and Addresses, 1890-1919, Volume One, edited by Philip S. Foner; Pathfinder Press, 1970. Copyright © 1970 by Philip S. Foner and Shirley Graham Du Bois. Used by permission of Pathfinder Press.

W.E.B. Du Bois Speaks, Speeches and Addresses, 1920-1963, Volume Two, edited by Philip S. Foner; Pathfinder Press, 1970, Copyright © 1970 by Philip S. Foner and Shirley Graham Du Bois. Used by permission of Pathfinder Press.

The Souls of Black Folk, The Dusk of Dawn, Essays and Articles by W.E.B. Du Bois in *W.E.B. Du Bois Writings,* edited by Nathan Huggins; Library of America, 1986. Copyright © 1986 by Literary Classics of the United States, Inc. Adapted by permission of David Graham Du Bois.

W.E.B. Du Bois: The Crisis Writings, edited by Daniel Walden; Fawcett Publications, Inc., 1972. Copyright © 1972 by Fawcett Publications, Inc. Adapted by permission of David Graham Du Bois.

By Any Means Necessary: Speeches, Interviews, and a Letter by Malcolm X, edited by George Breitman; Pathfinder Press, 1970. Copyright © 1970, 1992 by Betty Shabazz and Pathfinder Press. Used by permission of Pathfinder Press.

The Last Year of Malcolm X: The Evolution of a Revolutionary by George Breitman; Pathfinder Press, 1967. Copyright © 1967 by Pathfinder Press. Used by permission of Pathfinder Press.

Malcolm X on Afro-American History, Second Edition, edited by George Breitman; Pathfinder Press, 1970. Copyright © 1967, 1970, 1990 by Betty Shabazz and Pathfinder Press. Used by permission of Pathfinder Press.

Malcolm X Speaks, edited by George Breitman; Grove Press, 1966. Copyright © 1965, 1989 by Betty Shabazz and Pathfinder Press. Used by permission of Pathfinder Press.

Malcolm X: The FBI File by Clayborne Carson, edited by David Gallen; Carroll & Graf Publishers, Inc., 1991. Copyright © 1991 by David Gallen. Used by permission of Carroll and Graf Publishers, Inc.

Malcolm X, The Final Speeches, February 1965, edited by Steve Clark; Pathfinder Press, 1992. Copyright © 1992 by Betty Shabazz and Pathfinder Press. Used by permission of Pathfinder Press.

Malcolm X Talks to Young People: Speeches in the U.S., Britain, and Africa, edited by Steve Clark; Pathfinder Press, 1991. Copyright © 1965, 1970, 1991, 2002 by Betty Shabazz and Pathfinder Press. Used by permission of Pathfinder Press.

Malcolm A to X: The Man and His Ideas, edited by David Gallen; Carroll and Graf Publishers, Inc., 1992. Copyright © 1992 by David Gallen. Used by permission of Carroll & Graf Publishers, Inc.

Malcolm X: The Last Speeches, edited by Bruce Perry; Pathfinder Press, 1989. Copyright © 1989 by Betty Shabazz, Bruce Perry, and Pathfinder Press. Used by permission of Pathfinder Press.

A Call to Conscience: The Landmark Speeches of Dr. Martin Luther King, Jr., edited by Clayborne Carson et al.; Warner Books, 2001. Copyright © 2001 by the Estate of Martin Luther King, Jr. Used by permission of the Estate of Martin Luther King, Jr., c/o the agent, Writers House.

A Knock at Midnight: Inspiration from the Great Sermons of Martin Luther King, Jr., edited by Clayborne Carson and Peter Holloran; Warner Books, Inc., 1998. Copyright © 1998 by the Estate of Martin Luther King, Jr. Used by permission of the Estate of Martin Luther King, Jr., c/o the agent, Writers House.

Martin Luther King, Jr.: The FBI File by Michael Friedly and David Gallen; Carroll & Graf Publishers, Inc., 1993. Copyright © 1993 by David Gallen. Used by permission of Carroll & Graf Publishers, Inc., 1993.

The Papers of Martin Luther King, Jr., Volume I, *Called to Serve,* January 1929-June 1951; Volume II, *Rediscovering Precious Values,* July 1951-November 1955; Volume III, *Birth of a New Age,* December 1955-December 1956; Volume IV, *Symbol of the Movement,* January 1957-December 1958, edited by Clayborne Carson et al.; University of California Press, 1992, 1994, 1997, 2000. Writings of Martin Luther King, Jr., Copyright © 1992, 1994, 1997, 2000 by the Estate of Martin Luther King, Jr. Used by permission of the Estate of Martin Luther King, Jr., c/o the agent,

Jr. Renewed by the Estate of Martin Luther King, Jr. Used by permission of the Estate of Martin Luther King, Jr., c/o the agent, Writers House.

A Testament of Hope: The Essential Writings of Martin Luther King, Jr., edited by James M. Washington; Harper & Row, Publishers, Inc., 1986. Copyright © 1986 by Coretta Scott King. Renewed by the Estate of Martin Luther King, Jr. Used by permission of the Estate of Martin Luther King, Jr., c/o the agent, Writers House.

Nelson Mandela Speaks: Forging a Democratic Nonracial South Africa, edited by Steve Clark; Pathfinder Press, 1993. Copyright © 1993 by Nelson Mandela and Pathfinder Press. Used by permission of Pathfinder Press.

Nelson Mandela: Speeches 1990, edited by Greg McCartan; Pathfinder Press, 1990. Copyright © 1990 by Pathfinder Press. Used by permission of Pathfinder Press.

How Far We Slaves Have Come: South Africa and Cuba in Today's World, by Nelson Mandela and Fidel Castro; Pathfinder Press, 1991. Copyright © 1991 by Pathfinder Press. Used by permission of Pathfinder Press.

Long Walk to Freedom: The Autobiography of Nelson Mandela by Nelson Mandela; Little, Brown and Company, 1994. Copyright © 1994, 1995 by Nelson Rolihlahla Mandela. Used by permission of Little, Brown and Company.

No Easy Walk To Freedom by Nelson Mandela; Heinemann Educational Books, 1965. Copyright © 1965 by Nelson Mandela. Used by permission of Harcourt Education.

The Struggle Is My Life by Nelson Mandela, Second Edition; Pathfinder Press, 1990. Copyright © 1990 by Pathfinder Press. Used by permission of Pathfinder Press.

Crying in the Wilderness: The Struggle for Justice in South Africa by Desmond M. Tutu, edited by John Webster; William B. Eerdmans Publishing Company, 1982. Copyright © 1982 by Desmond Mpilo Tutu and William B. Eerdmans Publishing Company. Used by permission of the Continuum International Publishing Group Ltd.

The Words of Desmond Tutu, selected and introduced by Naomi Tutu; Newmarket Press, New York, 1989. Text copyright © 1989 by Desmond Tutu. Selections of quotations copyright © 1989 by Newmarket Press. Adapted by permission of Newmarket Press.

No Future Without Forgiveness by Desmond Mpilo Tutu; Doubleday, 1999. Copyright © 1999 by Desmond Mpilo Tutu. Used by permission of Doubleday, a division of Random House, Inc.

No Future Without Forgiveness by Desmond Mpilo Tutu; Rider, U.K., 1999. Used by permission of The Random House Group Limited.

The Rainbow People of God: The Making of a Peaceful Revolution by Desmond Tutu and John Allen, editor; Doubleday, 1994. Copyright © 1994 by Desmond Tutu and John Allen. Used by permission of Doubleday, a division of Random House, Inc.

The Rainbow People of God: The Making of a Peaceful Revolution by Desmond Tutu; Hodder & Stoughton Publishers, U.K., 1994. Used by permission of Hodder & Stoughton Publishers.

INTRODUCTION

For several years, I wrote articles on the credos of these leaders for the Journal of the Southern Christian Leadership Conference, *SCLC*. I have expanded these articles for this book. The credos have been designed to include their central convictions. My other articles for *SCLC* presented examples of how these leaders recognized the power of the negative. In researching their books, essays, articles, editorials, speeches, debates, and interviews, I discerned that they had understood how the principle of the power of the negative operated in the historical process, their campaigns for civil rights, their lives, and nature. Each chapter of this book contains applications of this principle that can be viewed as parts of their credos.

The power of the negative means that an opposing force—whether we must regard it as an obstacle or we originate it—at times, can be utilized to help produce a beneficial outcome. Paradoxically, positive thinking is required in order to harvest the power of the negative. Consider how our nation did react to the assaults on September 11. They had been diabolically devised to destroy the national spirit, but the nation responded by generating extraordinary unity, self-sacrifice, generosity, and patriotism. Moreover, within three weeks, a new level of international cooperation emerged when many nations joined the coalition to combat terrorism.

For numerous examples of the power of the negative, we can reflect on the history of sports—especially the Olympics.

Many athletes have explained that they have attained their
goals because they used their handicaps to develop additional
discipline which enabled them to enhance their achievements.
Lance Armstrong revealed his awareness of the power of the
negative when he contended that he would not have won the
Tour de France a third time if he did not have to battle cancer.

The most vigorous proponent of the power of the negative in
ancient Western thought was the philosopher Heraclitus, who
affirmed that growth emerges only through struggle and that a
productive harmony in material and spiritual life results from
a conflict between opposing forces. In the nineteenth century,
Hegel acknowledged Heraclitus' contribution to his logic and
developed a dialectic in which a thesis, a position in history
or thought, is challenged by an antithesis, a negative position,
and together they produce a synthesis, which can be a better
position with more truth or justice or both.

W.E.B. Du Bois studied the Hegelian dialectic at Harvard
University. Martin Luther King, Jr. explored philosophies at
Morehouse College, the University of Pennsylvania, Harvard
University, and Boston University, where he received a Ph.D.
in systematic theology. Having studied some of Hegel's major
works for a seminar, he asserted that Hegel was his favorite
philosopher. King's books and articles contain applications of
the Hegelian dialectic. His courses in theology, scripture, and
church history increased his appreciation of the power of the
negative as he encountered many examples of the principle,
"The blood of martyrs is the seed of faith." In his studies,
Archbishop Desmond Tutu also examined the efficacy of this
principle. To inspire his followers to make sacrifices, Marcus
Garvey made several references to the Christian martyrs.

The statements in the chapters are not quotations. They are
my formulations, each of which is documented by references to
one or more primary works listed in the "Sources" section. This
method has allowed for a more inclusive presentation and has
helped ensure that I not use an isolated statement by a leader
which conflicts with several of his other statements in the same

period. A person's philosophy should not be defined only on the basis of a passionate and momentary reaction to a perceived injustice.

In presenting the credos of these leaders, I preserved the terms they used to refer to African-Americans. Although they were contemporaries, Malcolm X preferred the term "black" and criticized the use of the term "Negro" whereas King often referred to the "Negro" to demonstrate his opposition to black separatism. Since some of these leaders were not egalitarians, I used their references to the "Negro male," "man," "men," and "mankind."

This book focuses mainly on the mature thought of these leaders and includes the early convictions they retained. It is necessary to indicate this approach because some of them did radically change their views. Chronological references have been added where necessary. This introduction will refer to significant evolutions in their philosophies, strategies, and tactics for social reform and to some of the obstacles they had to encounter.

Frederick Douglass (1818-95), as a fugitive slave, lectured against slavery but explained that his belief in the value and necessity of Christian love caused him to denounce war as a method of social reform. By appealing to the minds and hearts of the slaveholders, he tried to persuade them to free their slaves. Yet, when the Civil War erupted, he approved of it as a means to abolish slavery and to prevent slaveholders from further undermining the nation's institutions.

For several years, Douglass criticized the Constitution of the United States as a proslavery instrument. Persuaded by the arguments of the abolitionist Wendell Phillips, Douglass had pointed to how the Constitution included the "three-fifths compromise," empowered Congress to suppress insurrections, tolerated the importation of persons by the states, specified the obligation to return escaped laborers, and emphasized the responsibility of the federal government to respond to the request of a state government to suppress domestic violence.

He would not vote under a constitution supporting slavery.

But after examining arguments for a contrary interpretation of the Constitution from other abolitionists, Douglass decided to declare that it was an anti-slavery document. He cited the intentions of the Founding Fathers, several of whom regarded slavery as an evil, as well as the wording of the Preamble— "We the people," "justice," "general welfare," and "blessings of liberty." He emphasized that the Constitution had omitted the words "slave," "slavery," and "slaveholding" and that the Fourth Amendment had affirmed "the right of the people to be secure in their persons." He cited the prohibition against the suspension of the writ of habeas corpus in peacetime. With a reverence for the Constitution as designed to promote liberty and equality, he called upon all Americans to respect it as the fundamental law of the land. As a result of this interpretation of the Constitution, while still affirming the need for moral suasion and agitation for social reform, he began to propose the necessity of using the ballot as well as political coalitions and compromises as long as they did not require the sacrifice of one's moral principles.

One of Douglass' main concerns was the rights of women. For several decades, he contended that women should have the same rights as men, including the franchise. In the first issue of his paper *The North Star*, he affirmed, "Right is of no sex." Of the thirty-seven men at a convention for equal rights in July 1848 at Seneca Falls, New York, he was the only one to vote for a resolution for woman's suffrage. On the day of his death, he attended a conference of the National Council of Women.

Booker Taliaferro Washington (1856-1915), founder and president of the Tuskegee Normal and Industrial Institute, did change his public stand on segregation. In his 1895 Atlanta Exposition Address, he had proclaimed that in purely social activities blacks and whites could be as separate as fingers, but in all activities necessary for mutual progress, they could be as one as the hand. For two decades, he did not publicly condemn several forms of racial segregation. But in an article in *The New Republic* on December 4, 1915, he denounced the attempt to retain residential segregation. While he delayed his public opposition to segregation, his correspondence reveals that he had long been involved in private campaigns against segregation and disfranchisement.

Apart from this significant change in his public position on segregation, Washington was quite consistent in his emphasis upon the value of discipline to build character, the dignity of manual labor, self-help, economic advancement, race pride, interracial cooperation, education that coordinates industrial with academic training, service to the community, and active love for humanity.

Marcus Mosiah Garvey (1887-1940) appealed to American blacks to work toward unity with other blacks throughout the world. This unity was the principal objective of his Universal Negro Improvement Association (UNIA). He did exhort all blacks to liberate Africa and establish a nation there for their protection. His constant message was that blacks should take pride in the achievements of their race in ancient civilizations and in its crucial military and economic contributions to the preservation of democracies. In order to maintain their racial purity, they had to avoid miscegenation. They should develop their self-reliance and focus on obtaining economic power— the necessary means for the acquisition of political and social rights.

In pursuing several goals, Garvey had to encounter many obstacles, some of which did enable him to utilize the power of the negative. Federal law enforcement agencies opposed his agitation and for several years monitored his activities to secure his deportation or imprisonment. He was shot by a disgruntled creditor. Some white and black newspapers were critical of him and his Movement. He charged that W.E.B. Du Bois, by challenging his rhetoric as well as business methods, "sabotaged" his enterprises—the UNIA, the Negro Factories Corporation, the African Communities League, and the Black Star Line. He had to abandon his program for transferring the

UNIA headquarters to Monrovia, Liberia for the seat of his government because President C.D.B. King did not fulfill his promise to provide the UNIA with the land for colonization and development.

There were conflicts among Garvey's officials, and he had to dismiss several of them for disloyalty or corruption. He felt that some of his associates wanted his position. Some of the staff on the ships of the Black Star Line were negligent and incompetent. Because of dishonest or indifferent employees, he had to close many businesses of the African Communities League. In 1925, he was imprisoned for mail fraud on the basis of what he regarded as insufficient evidence. After two years and five months, President Coolidge did commute his sentence, but he was deported to Jamaica. His 1929 campaign for a seat in its colonial legislature was interrupted when he was charged with contempt of court by the Jamaica Supreme Court and was sentenced to three months' imprisonment because he had condemned several judges for taking bribes and had called for their impeachment and imprisonment. For financial reasons, he had to stop the publication of his daily paper, *The New Jamaican*. Many members of the UNIA joined Father Divine's Peace Mission and other black religious sects. Some of these obstacles restricted the growth of the UNIA but they could not extinguish Garvey's determination to proclaim his principles and to work for the "salvation" of his race.

William Edward Burghardt Du Bois (1868-1963) graduated from Fisk University, studied two years at the University of Berlin, and was the first black to receive a Ph.D. at Harvard University where he had studied psychology, philosophy, and history. He taught at Wilberforce University for two years and was the professor of sociology at Atlanta University for thirteen years. In 1905, he helped to establish the Niagara Movement that demanded universal male suffrage, freedom of speech, equality of education, and the abolition of all caste distinctions based on race. He severely criticized Booker T. Washington's policies as perpetuating racism.

In 1909, when the Niagara Movement came to an end, Du Bois and his colleagues launched the National Association for the Advancement of Colored People (NAACP). He was its director of research and editor of its journal, *The Crisis*, for twenty-four years. Because he contended that blacks could be liberated only through their separate economic, social, and political institutions, he was forced to resign his editorship. In 1944, he did return to work at the NAACP but later was dismissed for some views which were considered radical. His activities included lecturing, writing, and organizing several Pan-Africanist conferences. He was the author of twenty-one books, edited fifteen, and published more than one hundred articles.

Initially, Du Bois was opposed to World War I but partly because of the influence of NAACP leaders, he supported the war and then felt very close to being a full American. He was confident that because blacks did participate in the war, there would be an expansion of democratic rights and a reduction of social injustices after the war. He also thought that the war would foster the independence of the former German African colonies.

Du Bois had to change his thinking on how racial prejudice could be overcome. His early belief was that ignorance was the main cause of this prejudice and that once the scientific truth was presented, racial hatred would disappear. But when he saw that barriers created by racial prejudice had remained for decades, he realized that blacks had to confront not only the conscious racist decisions and customs of some whites but their conditioned reflexes and subconscious reasoning. His conclusion was that it would take organization, sacrifice, and patience for a lengthy struggle to overcome such entrenched irrationality.

After World War II, Du Bois did develop his concern for economic justice not only for blacks but for poor whites, and continued to investigate the nature of institutional racism. For several decades, he had been studying the interconnections of racism, imperialism, and colonialism with capitalism. Having taught the philosophy of Karl Marx, he came to believe that capitalism ought to be rejected. While condemning what he judged as the imperialism and militarism of the United States, he praised the Soviet and Chinese Governments. He called for peaceful relations with the Soviet Union. Having endorsed the slogan "Peace—No More War," he helped found the Peace Information Center that campaigned against the Korean War and distributed the Stockholm Peace Appeal.

Malcolm X (1925-65) had numerous negative experiences: the violent death of his father, the Reverend Earl Little, who was an organizer for Marcus Garvey, the extreme poverty of his family, the weak emotional state of his mother, a crushing discouragement from a teacher, the dangers and hardships of his life as a hustler, his years of imprisonment, his agonizing disillusionment with his idol, Elijah Muhammad, the attacks on him in the press, and the death threats that hounded him in his last year. Although his life was filled with suffering and he described the plight of blacks in America as a "nightmare," he was optimistic about the nation's potential for reform. This can be inferred from his willingness to sacrifice for social justice. His optimism caused him to initiate several negative actions and to utilize some arduous situations that he had to confront in order to further the liberation of blacks.

After serving as a spokesman for the Nation of Islam (NOI) for more than a decade, Malcolm X left the organization and founded the Organization of Afro-American Unity (OAAU). He indicated that on his pilgrimage to Mecca, he had learned that the religion of Islam called for the equal treatment of all, regardless of race, and that he had met with several white Muslims who did practice their belief in full equality toward him. These experiences caused him to revise his judgment of whites and to reject the notion that all whites were devils. He no longer denounced interracial marriage. Neither did he still urge blacks to form rifle clubs. After rejecting the restricted perspective of the Nation of Islam, he decided to advocate a

Pan-Africanist worldview and attempted to internationalize the OAAU. He even expressed a new eagerness to cooperate with other black leaders in civil rights activities.

Martin Luther King, Jr. (1929-68) applied the principles of nonviolence in all of his campaigns. In the Montgomery Bus Boycott, he and his colleagues believed that they had a moral obligation to oppose the system of segregation and to secure respect for the passengers from the drivers. He explained that Christ had provided the spiritual motivation for the boycott while Gandhi furnished the method. His training in the Black Church and his acceptance of the philosophy of Personalism with its emphasis on the dignity of the person had intensified his awareness of the evil of segregation.

Because of King's nonviolent resistance at Montgomery, Albany, and Birmingham in order to achieve desegregation, he was awarded the Nobel Peace Prize in 1964. In subsequent campaigns, he asserted that if blacks were to have the power to overcome racism and improve their condition, they had to have the right to vote and economic justice. Eventually, he came to realize that, whatever the costs to his Movement, the spiritual and practical ideal of nonviolence also required him to condemn the Vietnam War.

In his last days, King participated in a march in Memphis to support a strike by sanitation workers and was planning a multiracial Poor People's Campaign that would send 3,000 trained cadre to Washington, D.C. They would commit civil disobedience by means of sit-ins at federal offices to attempt to persuade Congress to produce an Economic Bill of Rights for the Disadvantaged that would provide jobs, income for those unable to work, housing, and aid to ghetto schools.

In challenging racism, materialism, and militarism, King was seeking to fulfill the objectives of the Southern Christian Leadership Conference—to save the soul of America and to help establish the "beloved community." Members of such a community would regard every person as created in the image of God and would allow the spirit of *agape*, unconditional love, to direct all social, political, economic, educational, and religious relationships. Though King knew that the ideal of the "beloved community" could not be achieved in its fullness due to the imperfections of human nature, he was convinced that it could serve as a standard to inspire and measure the moral direction of the nation.

Nelson Rolihlahla Mandela (1918-   ) on several occasions demonstrated his capacity to revise his strategies and tactics, when necessary. In 1947, as a member of the African National Congress Youth League, he became concerned that communists and Indians, due to their extraordinary education, experience, and training, would assume control of the African National Congress (ANC) and thereby weaken the concept of African Nationalism. Therefore, he voted for a resolution stating that "members of political organizations" should resign from the ANC. Nevertheless, when the national conference rejected the resolution, he accepted its decision and began working with those communists and Indians whose organizational skills he admired. But, in his writings, he did stress his opposition as a Christian to communism due to its philosophy of materialism and its antipathy to religion.

When Mandela joined the ANC Youth League, he believed in a narrow and exclusive form of nationalism. However, the example of the All-India Congress and experience convinced him and his colleagues of the necessity of understanding their own struggle as nonracial and within a global context. The ANC would need military training and weapons from other nations as well as an international coalition for the imposition of sanctions on the Pretoria regime.

The recalcitrance of the government caused Mandela and his colleagues to change their methods. For thirty-seven years until 1949, the ANC had engaged in a constitutional struggle, submitting demands and resolutions, and sending delegations to the government in order to discuss grievances and pursue political rights. In 1949, after these activities had no impact on the government, the ANC concluded that it should use its disciplined volunteers to protest against apartheid legislation by civil disobedience, strikes, peace marches, boycotts, and mass demonstrations.

Since these nonviolent tactics proved ineffective to change the methods of the government, which included assaults on nonviolent strikers even in their homes and imposing virtual martial law, Mandela and his colleagues determined in 1961 that the ANC had a moral duty to resort to sabotage involving the destruction of power plants and interference with rail and telephone communications. He quoted an African proverb, "The attacks of the wild beast cannot be averted with only bare hands," and affirmed that self-defense is quite compatible with being a good Christian. On August 7, 1990, after several reforms by President F. W. de Klerk, the ANC suspended its armed struggle. In 1993, Mandela and de Klerk were awarded the Nobel Peace Prize.

When Mandela moved from nonviolence to adopt violence, did he believe that he was rejecting a principle? In the 1952 Campaign for the Defiance of Unjust Laws, he explained that he regarded nonviolence not as an inviolable principle but as a tactic demanded by that situation. His contention was that if the demonstrators had employed violence in that campaign, the government would have crushed them. In his writings and speeches, he frequently referred to the apartheid laws in order to convey their cruelty and scope.

Mandela's different views on the nationalization of natural resources and several industries again showed his readiness to alter his tactics. In 1990, he reaffirmed that the 1955 Freedom Charter expressed the ANC's economic policy. In accordance with its Preamble which proclaimed that South Africa should belong to all its inhabitants, the Charter maintained that the people as a whole in a new nonracial society would become owners of the unmined mineral wealth, banks, and monopoly industries and that those who had worked the land would own it. However, foreseeing that he had to secure the participation of the white minority in a democratic government, in his 1994 autobiography, *Long Walk To Freedom* (page 153), he did refer to a "possible nationalization."

President Mandela ruled a democracy with a constitution and bill of rights that renounced racism, embraced equality, and guaranteed all South Africans broad freedoms of speech, movement, and political activity. Much of his success has derived not only from his iron will but also from his renewed commitment to nonviolence. That commitment has been quite evident in his spirit of generosity and forgiveness toward his former oppressors and in his support for the work of the Truth and Reconciliation Commission.

Archbishop Desmond Mpilo Tutu (1931-   ) has retained his early theological convictions and social philosophy. His books, sermons, speeches, and interviews indicate that the suffering of black South Africans produced by apartheid did severely test his belief in Divine Providence, but also that his faith in God's love only increased through all the persecution. In 1984, he was awarded the Nobel Peace Prize on the basis of his spiritual leadership in the nonviolent struggle against apartheid. His demands that the government end apartheid, his call for economic sanctions, his numerous appeals to both sides to avoid the path of bloodshed, and the moral impact of his courageous example were significant contributions to the ultimate peaceful solution.

Presiding over the Truth and Reconciliation Commission, Archbishop Tutu listened to agents of apartheid, applying for amnesty, testify on how they committed torture and murder. The acts described were so brutal that he repeatedly had to bow his head and weep. In *No Future Without Forgiveness*, a title that has captured his principal message, he referred to testimony that a police officer shot an African man and four other officers burned the body on a pyre—turning it several times for seven hours. Meanwhile, they enjoyed a barbecue a few feet from the pyre.

While condemning the horrendous actions under apartheid, Archbishop Tutu frequently stressed the need for restitution, forgiveness, reconciliation, and peace. He explained that the Commission did not seek to punish but to heal. The justice it aimed to achieve was not retributive but restorative. He asked the relatives of the victims to attempt to understand that these police had intensive cultural and psychological conditioning. The system had taught them to treat black persons as things and therefore had dehumanized these police as well as their victims. He did contend that they also needed compassion. When they asked for forgiveness and were willing to provide restitution, Christians could not be expected to forget their atrocities but had to forgive them and hope that they would repent and change. He was able to report that nearly all the victims' relatives who testified were able, despite their grief, to follow the imperatives of forgiveness and reconciliation— imperatives because there is "no future without forgiveness."

These credos can contribute to our understanding of values and virtues while the testimonies to the power of the negative can encourage us to look for an opportunity in every crisis we experience. I trust that this exploration of the thought and lives of these inspirational leaders will stimulate the reader to study some of their books, articles, and speeches as well as the books listed in the *Selected Bibliography*.

I am indebted to the officers of the Ford Foundation, the American Can Foundation, and the Samuel Rubin Foundation for providing travel grants for my research on Dr. King. That research sparked my desire to examine in depth the lives and philosophies of these other leaders who helped determine the objectives, strategies, and tactics of the struggles for civil and human rights.

1

FREDERICK DOUGLASS

When I was thirteen years old, I experienced the need for God to be a Father to me and to protect me. The sermons of a white Methodist minister, the Reverend Hanson, aroused my religious aspirations and convinced me of human sinfulness. A Negro, Charles Johnson, told me what to pray for, and after weeks of doubts and fears, I developed a faith in Jesus Christ as my Savior and a change of heart that allowed me to love all mankind, including slaveholders.

I attended prayer meetings with a Negro, "Father" Lawson. He told me that the Lord had a great work which He wanted me to do and that He would make it happen in His own good time. He advised me to trust in the Lord and that if I asked Him in faith for my freedom, He would give it to me.

Before I knew how to read or heard about a free state, the abolitionists or moral laws, I believed that Negroes would be free—but not in my lifetime. Most slaves shared this belief.

No activity gave me a deeper satisfaction than conducting Sunday schools for my fellow slaves in the woods and then at the house of a free Negro. How intense was their desire to learn to read! If we were detected, the penalty could have been forty lashes from Christian masters who did not want us to read even the holy Bible.

As a fugitive slave, I became convinced that my only earthly hope for emancipation was not the state or the Church but the American Anti-Slavery Society. Abolitionists in the Society acted toward me as a human being, challenged ignorance and prejudice, called for obedience to God rather than a morally blind conformity to the slave laws, and were willing to endure mob violence for the cause.

My allegiance to God necessitates that I repudiate whatever negates human rights and prevents human progress. I pleaded the cause of the slave by condemning slavery as a diabolical system that destroyed souls and bodies and aimed to corrupt our political institutions, churches, and national character.

Truth and the spirit of love are the essential requirements and the only secure foundation for obtaining right results in every human enterprise. The power of God expresses itself in truth. The Scriptural text, "You shall know the truth, and the truth shall set you free" (John 8:32), must be applied to this world as well as to the world to come.

It is an everlasting truth that the human soul is created with a right to be free. No political institution can survive if it tries to abrogate this fundamental right.

To understand the enormous evil of slavery, a person must realize that the slave was formed in the image of God, born with the right to liberty, and equipped with spiritual powers, passions, and affections. But slavery was used to attempt to extinguish his spiritual identity—even threatening him with eternal punishment for disobedience of the master.

In order to gain absolute control over the slave, the master aimed to diminish his reasoning power and distort his moral judgment. The objective was to convince the slave that his master's will was the highest law—God's will for him—and that his master was entitled to all his earnings.

The masters taught their slaves that it was God's will that they be slaves. But the Bible assured me that He cared about my rights and that Jesus came to deliver the captive.

Slaveholders used the Bible to justify slavery and defend their brutality. One of my masters, Thomas Auld, known as a pious reader in the Methodist Church, did pray three times a day. I witnessed him whip one of his young female slaves, my cousin, until the blood flowed and then attempt to justify the deed by quoting the Gospel which warned that the slave who knew his master's wishes and did not prepare to fulfill them would be beaten with many stripes (Luke 12:47). Auld had no understanding that the Bible, filled with faith, hope, and charity, taught that the duty of the strong is not to oppress but to assist the weak.

Cruelty was necessary for slavery, a system of blood and murder. Because the slave naturally desired his freedom, the instruments of terror were indispensable to keep him under the yoke of bondage—whip, thumbscrew, handcuffs, chain, gag, cat-o'-nine-tails, branding-iron, bloodhound, dungeon, pillory, gibbet, bowie-knife, pistol, and starvation. The main principle was that slaves had to be given severe punishment for minor offenses to discourage their commission of major offenses. When a slaveholder did not want to resort to the instruments of torture, he could threaten the disobedient slave that he would sell him to a slaveholder who would use them.

From my own experience, I understand that the slaveholder had to be barbarous to turn a man into a slave and to keep him as a slave. When I was whipped daily, my only thought was to preserve my life, but when I was with a slaveowner who did not want to have me whipped and did not threaten my life, I thought only of my liberty.

I recall being dragged to the auctioneer's block and sold like a beast. My soul still suffers from the tortures of slavery. In my youth, I was deprived of the benefits of an education in religion and morality. Having deprived us of an education, the slaveholders argued that we did not have the intelligence to be free.

How destructive slavery was to the sacredness of marriage and the family! The master decided when and whom a slave would marry and when husband and wife would be separated and torn from their children for the auction block. If female slaves attempted to defend their dignity against assaults by their masters, they were liable to be put to death.

Slavery was sinful because it was opposed to God's will that every man have a right to his own body, violated the law of justice, disobeyed the First Commandment to worship only God, and ignored the fact that Christ died also for the slave. Slavery denied the distinction between the personality of a slave and a thing, promoted lust, disfigured creatures of God by branding and other practices, and spurned the benevolent precepts of the New Testament.

The black slaves were not the only victims of slavery. The slaveholders plundered the white laborers who were forced to compete with the black slaves. The slaveholders blinded these poor white laborers to this competition by encouraging their prejudice against the slaves as men.

I would contend that slavery, the greatest curse, crime, and scandal, was a greater evil to the master than to the slave. In spite of my experiences with nearly all its physical horrors, I would be very willing to suffer these horrors again rather than change places with the haughtiest and wealthiest slaveholder. In attempting to exercise total control over human beings, he corroded his conscience, knew no security, and ultimately had to submit to the divine judgment.

Once I was free, I resolved to work for the emancipation of my brothers and sisters in bondage. I remained faithful to this resolution.

To actualize our spiritual potential, we cannot rely solely on the development of culture in our lives. We must devote our energies also to some noble purpose—religious, patriotic, or philanthropic—that will elevate and nourish our souls.

Slaveholders dominated the South, dictated its legislation, corrupted its moral standards, and propagated their distorted interpretations of the Bible, the Declaration of Independence, and the Constitution. They enforced limitations on freedom of speech, religious liberty, and education, degraded labor as the task of slaves and even prevented other whites from becoming legislators.

Although our nation has professed to be Christian and the

message of Jesus called for peace on earth and good will, it has elected many slaveholders and warmakers to high office, including the presidency.

As a fugitive slave, I learned how the influence of slavery could permeate the rest of the nation. Even though I was in the free state of Massachusetts, it conceded—as would any of the free states—the right to a slaveholder to come there and capture me.

In speeches on the horrors of slavery, I included the names of my former overseers even though I ran the risk of being returned to bondage. As God's instrument, I did this for the sake of humanity and to help hasten the day of deliverance for three million of my brethren.

Since I do love the pure, peaceful, and holy religion of our blessed Savior, I have hated the corrupt, violent, and sinful "religion" of slaveholders and their supporters. Because of its man-stealing, woman-whipping, and cradle-plundering, this hypocritical perversion of the sacred doctrine of Jesus has served the devil, not God.

At the beginning of our republic, the Methodist Episcopal Church, the Baptist Church, and the Presbyterian Church had been in the forefront of the anti-slavery movement. In 1780, the Methodist Episcopal Church stated that slavery violated the laws of God, man, and nature and contradicted the true religion and the dictates of conscience.

But ministers in these churches in the South later did prove to be the boldest and the most uncompromising defenders of slavery as they argued in their sermons that it was a system consistent with the Bible. They were morally responsible that their sanctions of slavery contributed so much to its public acceptance. Had these ministers denounced slavery—as did the religious authorities in the West Indies—they could have caused its early abolition.

How could a Christian minister be morally consistent if he preached that everyone ought to love his neighbor and still approved of the system that kept another in bondage? How could he invite his listeners to search the Scriptures for truth and support the system that in Louisiana imposed the penalty of death for a second attempt to teach a young slave to read? How could a Christian minister own slaves?

What a perversion of Jesus' doctrines of love and justice it was to have the church bell and the auctioneer's bell chime together and to use the profits from the sale of men, women, and children to build churches, support ministers, and buy Bibles! How Christian was it to deny slaves the right to read and to use the profits from their labor to send missionaries to foreign lands to teach people to read?

In order to safeguard liberty, the Free Church of Scotland separated from the Established Church but then lowered the standard of Christianity by sending representatives to receive contributions from American slaveholders. By thus forming a fellowship with slaveholders, the Free Church allowed them to profess that they were Christians even though they were thieves and murderers. The slaveholding ministers cited the Free Church to defend their brand of Christianity. Through this alliance, the Free Church created another obstacle to the work of the anti-slavery movement.

What a moral contradiction for slavery to exist in its worst forms in America—a nation that had rejected bondage under England, proclaimed the principle that all men are created equal, denounced the tyrants of Russia and Austria for their invasion of Hungary, and called for liberty for Ireland!

Despite their inconsistencies, the patriots of the American republic—Washington, Jefferson, Franklin, Adams, Madison, Monroe, and others—acknowledged that slavery was evil and looked forward to its overthrow.

Even before my English friends purchased my freedom on December 5, 1846, I gave lectures in England, Ireland, and Scotland on the evils of slavery with the hope of shaming America to abandon this brutal practice. I thought then that America by itself did not have the moral power to abolish this evil.

The American Colonization Society has been one of the most hostile adversaries of our freedom movement. Created by slaveholders in the South and haters of the Negro in the North, it promotes the emigration of free Negroes to Africa. By teaching that Negroes cannot achieve peace or freedom in America, it has supported prejudice and slavery.

The plight of the supposedly "free" American Negroes has been so desperate that I had to plead that Negroes who fought and bled for this country be treated at least as well as those who fought against it and that we who have proven our love for this country be treated as well as those who hate it.

Capital punishment is not ethical because it is revenge. It descends to the level of the criminal, is diametrically opposed to the natural moral law and the substance of Christianity, and undermines respect for the sacredness of human life. Reason, conscience, and revelation demand the end of this barbarous practice.

We do not choose our race and color. They come from the Almighty. I do not discern a superiority or inferiority in race or color. Although we may take pride in our achievements and be ashamed of our failures, neither race nor color ought to be the source of pride or shame. The devil of race pride in some white people cannot be overcome through promoting the devil of black race pride. The latter encourages the former.

Convinced that to improve the character of Negroes in the North was one of the most efficient ways to emancipate the slaves in the South, I have worked for the moral, religious, social and intellectual elevation of free Negroes. I advocated the emancipation of my race in my speeches and writings.

While the federal government and our white friends can and should assist us to achieve assimilation, nevertheless, our destiny, as Negroes, remains mainly in our own hands. We have to aim for higher ethical standards, agitate for our civil and political rights, and strive for self-reliance by becoming educated and working to accumulate money and also property. Property will provide us with leisure which makes possible the thought, invention, and progress that will generate respect for us.

The riches, intelligence, wisdom, economy, and virtues of others will not be able to rescue those who choose to remain poor, ignorant, foolish, wasteful, and lawless.

To maintain that I am a "self-made man" is only partially correct. In accounting for the success and joy in my life, I must acknowledge that I had the moral laws of the universe on my side and I must give some credit to my special white and black friends and very favorable circumstances. Without these friends and good fortune, I might have spent most of my life eking out a living on the wharves of New Bedford.

My early view of the Constitution of the United States did interpret it as containing provisions that favored slavery. I felt that it gave my former master the right to capture me. In the morally blind actions of the branches of the government, I believed I found confirmations of this interpretation.

My later judgment is that the Constitution does not contain guarantees for slavery, but, in letter and spirit, is anti-slavery. It does not use words such as "white" and "black" but rather its Preamble proclaims, "We, the people of the United States, in order to form a more perfect Union, establish justice, insure domestic tranquility, provide for the common defense, promote the general welfare, and secure the blessings of liberty to ourselves and our posterity...do ordain and establish this Constitution for the United States of America." The Constitution was not designed to perpetuate slavery and is quite consistent with the Declaration of Independence.

Because of my early interpretation of the Constitution as obliging citizens to support slavery, I had refused to vote in such a system. But when I changed my interpretation, I came to realize that the ballot could be a means to abolish slavery and protect the Negro.

In a 1853 speech at the American and Foreign Anti-Slavery Society in New York City, I maintained that as long as there were Negro slaves, no Negro could be truly free. Every day, discrimination reminded the nominally free Negro in many ways of his identity with the slave, his brother. The destiny of the free Negro was one with that of the slave.

The Supreme Court of the United States in its Dred Scott Decision of 1857 judged slaves to be property and denied that they had any rights which should be respected. Nevertheless, an even higher power than the court is the Supreme Court of God Who has decreed that the freedom of every person is a natural right. The U.S. Supreme Court cannot reverse God's decision and change the essence of the person.

The divine government presides over nations not less than persons. Consequently, the continual flagrant violations of the laws of God bring national shame, misery, and death. The Civil War was His response to slavery.

Because revolutions usually have targeted despotisms and clearly aimed at the expansion of liberty, they have secured the sympathy of mankind. But the rebellion of the South was quite antithetical to the spirit of most revolutions. Driven by hatred of free speech, free schools, and free society, it aimed to preserve and bequeath to future generations the diabolical system of slavery.

In 1861, I protested the refusal by the government and the majority of Americans to admit that the real cause of the war was slavery even though they knew it was. Were it not for slavery—not for any other economic or political condition—the North and South could have lived together in peace.

In 1862, as we waited for the Emancipation Proclamation, I warned that it would take more than a generation to remove the profound effects of slavery. In several ways, the slave would remain a slave and would not easily conquer his sense of inferiority. The master would retain his pride, arrogance, and love of power and would not readily relinquish his sense of superiority. Law would abolish slavery but not prejudice against color. An intensive education would be required to achieve harmony among all classes.

The Emancipation Proclamation did free the slave, but it

had even greater significance for the nation and the world—promoting the cause of truth and justice for the entire human family.

Why did slavery last so long in our nation? Men decided that only prosperity—not humanity, Christianity or justice—determined what was right conduct.

The government issued the Emancipation Proclamation but left blacks free to starve, without shelter, and at the mercy of the wrath of their former masters who interpreted the act of emancipation as an act of hostility toward them. In its 1861 Emancipation Edict, even despotic Russia distributed land to the serfs.

In my extensive experience as a lecturer in this country and Europe, I never met a man with a more godlike nature than President Abraham Lincoln. In his second inaugural address, he sounded as if the souls of all the Hebrew prophets inspired his soul. Although the Union meant more to him than the freedom of the Negro, he did hate slavery. If he had placed the abolition of slavery above the salvation of the Union, he would not have had the cooperation of a powerful class and then the rebellion of the South would not have been crushed.

President Lincoln called for charity towards all and malice towards none. I have attempted to speak and act in accordance with this principle. Individuals demonstrate their intellectual and cultural superiority when they do not allow their political and religious differences with each other to disrupt society or their friendships.

People estimate their worth partly on the basis of how they are treated by others. If a group is labeled unfit for a certain type of work, then that group tends to act in accordance with that label. When you want a group to make contributions to society, you have to make it known that you presume that it will.

When a white man wishes to eliminate his race prejudice, he ought to begin to act as if he were not prejudiced by doing good to a Negro, and he will soon discover that he has a new perception of the Negro.

In an 1866 letter to President Andrew Johnson, my friends and I affirmed that peace between the races could be achieved only by promoting justice among all—not by empowering and honoring one race while continuing to deprive and debase the other.

The written history of the anti-slavery movement should include the substantial contributions of talented women such as Lucretia Mott, Lydia Maria Child, Abby Kelley, Elizabeth Cady Stanton, Susan B. Anthony, Harriet Beecher Stowe, Antoinette Brown, and Lucy Stone. They possessed deep moral convictions and were endowed with clarity of thought and the power to persuade.

I am proud to be designated as "a radical woman's rights man." Opposed to oppression in all its forms and having seen the intense devotion and effectiveness of the woman's rights movement in denouncing slavery, I have, for several decades, supported this movement and its just demands for personal freedom.

It took courage to launch the woman suffrage movement. Other movements aimed to challenge the obvious sources of suffering such as war, intemperance, and slavery. But most men perceived the woman suffrage movement as an attempt to make an unnecessary change in the established and quite acceptable order of things.

Elizabeth Cady Stanton convinced me of the wisdom of the cause of woman suffrage. A woman is entitled to vote no less than a man since the Declaration of Independence proclaims that governments derive their just powers from the consent of the governed and also that taxation without representation is tyranny. A woman must obey the law even though she has no role in enacting it. If she can be subject to its penalties, why can't she be the recipient of its privileges, such as the right to vote. No man can state when, where or how women agreed to be denied a role in government.

The main principle of the woman suffrage movement is

that a woman should be the owner of herself even as the main principle of the anti-slavery movement was that every man ought to be the owner of himself. Her rights as a person are equal to the rights of a man as a person. Woman's claim to participate in government has the same basis as man's claim. Because she too does possess the powers of mind and will, a capacity to distinguish good from evil, and her own interests to preserve, she has the natural right to vote and select those who create the laws she must obey.

There is another reason why women should have the vote. After hearing men and women speak on the wrongs done to women, I concluded that a woman can feel these wrongs as no man can and that she knows what is needed to correct them. Through her vote, she can serve as an effective representative of her needs.

Why should the government be denied the benefits of the wisdom and virtue of women? Through their vote and their governance, women could endow the government with their moral sensitivity, a more active concern for children, and an abhorrence of war. Their involvement could counteract the primitive practice of extolling might over right.

In preparing for our 1853 Rochester convention, the leaders of the woman's rights movement and I developed a number of questions about the rights of women which we would submit to the New York State Legislature for its consideration. We believed that women should be paid according to the quality of their work, have access to the higher paying jobs, and be entitled to their own earnings. Widows should be the legal guardians of their children. Women should have the right to vote and equal rights concerning the ownership of property, inheritance, and the administration of estates.

Despite the fact that by nature a woman has the capacity to occupy as lofty a position as a man, her self-appointed master has often treated her like a piece of furniture—revealing his turpitude and lack of understanding.

I advised members of the woman suffrage movement that

when they would work to correct the denial of their rights and attempt to enlighten and elevate humanity, they would have to confront ignorance and malice.

At a 1866 Equal Rights Convention in Albany, New York, I warned the participants of the danger of focusing only upon woman's rights. I urged women to support the Negro cause so that we would not suffer disfranchisement and additional mob violence.

At a convention of the American Equal Rights Association in 1869, although I believed that the rights of woman should be respected as the rights of man, I did maintain that it was more urgent to secure the vote for Negroes than for women. There would have been an equal urgency if white women were constantly insulted, if their children were not allowed to enter schools and were killed, and if women were being lynched from lampposts.

The most effective way to safeguard republican institutions is to extend the right of suffrage to all irrespective of color or sex and without any educational or property test.

In 1888, I predicted that even as the young, mindful of our fundamental political principles, could scarcely comprehend how slavery ever existed here and how the pulpit, press, and state ever defended it, so too when women would attain the suffrage, men would wonder at all of the stupidity and malice which so long delayed this right.

I have learned the value of assuming and seizing my rights whenever I can get them. My continual exercise of my rights has been wearing out the prejudice against my color. I have recommended that women seize their rights, particularly those that are most strongly contested—for example, by heroically entering fields from which they have been excluded.

The leaders of the woman rights movement have exhibited greatness in their talents for administration and organization, and in their ability to discover truth. Hence, it is reasonable to expect that, with these powers, ultimately this movement will achieve its goals.

If I believed that human nature is totally depraved or is more evil than good, I would be opposed to the participation of the masses in government. But because I believe that men and women are more inclined to truth and goodness than to evil, I advocate the expansion of the right to suffrage and the involvement of the masses to improve the moral quality of the government.

In 1879, I was gratified when the Fourteenth Amendment did declare the Negro a citizen and the Fifteenth Amendment gave him the vote. Nonetheless, the next year I had to protest that these Amendments were not implemented in all the Gulf States. In Louisiana and Mississippi, Negroes were banished from the ballot box, and, for only minor offenses, were put in chain gangs so that they would work under the lash on the farms of their former masters.

In 1883, I contended that the Negro was half-free and half-slave. Numerous public schools were caste schools. The Negro did not have equal access to the ballot. His rights to become a lawyer, to serve on juries, and to have a fair trial and a just verdict were not universal. Often, he did not have the right to learn or practice a trade or become a member of a trade union. The American people had yet to judge the respectability of a person on the basis of character and not of color.

The salvation of our race and the other races in this country consists not in isolation and in forming a separate nationality or political party but in making the common interests of the nation our interests. Assimilation promotes life. Separation is a form of death.

Since I have witnessed men in many conditions, I have no reason for being narrow and harboring race prejudice. I regard myself as a man and a member of the human family more than as a member of one ethnic group such as Anglo-African.

The resentment I feel because of the oppression of my race and myself will end when the oppression ends. But I do not want to hold children responsible for the sins of their fathers.

Some predict that the Negro, like the Indian, will die out as the Anglo-Saxon race progresses. They fail to understand the difference between the attitude of the Indian and that of the Negro. Whereas the Indian withdraws before the advance of civilization, takes pride in his isolation, and dies of a broken heart, the Negro—in spite of the physical and psychological torture—survives, embraces American civilization, and wants to teach lessons on the sacredness and perfectibility of human brotherhood.

As we commemorate the victories of liberty over tyranny, we should not restrict our exultations to what has occurred in our quarter of the globe. Whenever there is progress in liberty anywhere, we should embrace a principle that was proclaimed by William Lloyd Garrison, the pioneer in the anti-slavery movement, "Our country is the world—our countrymen are all mankind."

My sympathy is with every oppressed people. I empathize with the suffering Hebrews and Chinese. But, while I hate all oppression, I have never hated the oppressors—not even the slaveholders.

For men of conscience, the predominant motive is duty. Duty has influenced all the actions of my life. My sense of duty has been the source of courage that enabled me to face howling mobs and now to accept with charity verbal assaults from my own people who oppose me. I derive consolation from the thought that all these foes should be my friends.

Negroes are victimized by many types of violence, but I believe that God will provide that truth, justice, and liberty will eventually prevail and our righteous cause will triumph. Given human nature, however, it may require a century to remove the traces of a former bondage.

THE POWER OF THE NEGATIVE

My master, Hugh Auld, inadvertently intensified my desire to learn to read. When he stopped his wife from teaching me to read and warned that my learning to read would render me discontent, unmanageable, and unfit to be a slave, he thereby inspired me to develop the determination to learn to read.

Hearing the tales of woe in songs of the slaves has always depressed me and frequently caused me to weep. Still, those songs served to deepen my hatred of slavery and to provide me with my initial understanding of some of its dehumanizing effects.

When I was sixteen, I was hired out to Edward Covey, the "Negro Breaker," to conquer my rebellious spirit. It was only when I defended myself against his physical attacks that I was able to revive my self-respect, self-confidence, sense of my own manhood, and determination to be free. My willingness to risk death by this encounter made me a free man in fact even though I was still a slave in form.

When I boarded a ship in England in 1847 to return to America, I was denied access to the main dining area and was confined to the stern. Nevertheless, the incident proved to be productive because the London *Times* and some other leading journals condemned this discrimination and did secure equal treatment for me.

In certain moral situations, irritation and counter-irritation are necessary for productive change. Because the conscience of the American public was so comfortable with slavery, I persisted in producing the required irritation until it would totally reject this evil.

Whenever I have challenged the predominance of injustice in America—the violations of the principles of liberty and humanity enunciated in the Declaration of Independence—I believe that I have been fulfilling my obligation to be a true patriot. A person can demonstrate his love for his nation by rebuking its sins, such as slavery, that are a reproach to its people, and by summoning it to repentance and righteousness.

Although I have often been critical of the ways in which certain Christian churches supported slavery, no one should consider me an enemy of the Church. I offered the criticisms for the purification and salvation of those churches as well as for the liberation and redemption of the race. I have been in fellowship with anti-slavery churches.

In order to advance the struggle for freedom, I have readily endured physical assaults, insults, distortions, and slanders from the haters of my race. When one seeks systemic reforms, one can anticipate such forms of opposition. At times, I have even been energized by them. But the indifference of my own people in the North to this struggle has drained me of some of my enthusiasm and natural force.

In his youth, John Brown saw how his friend, a slave boy, was subjected to a brutal beating with a shovel for a trifling offense. Brown was so shocked by this cruelty that he swore his hatred of slavery, and forty years later, conducted a raid on Harper's Ferry to challenge slavery's assault on human rights. This incident reminded me of the beating of a Hebrew bondman by an Egyptian that helped create a Moses.

Any slaveholder who claimed that he had a conversion to Christianity should have demonstrated his acceptance by God by freeing all his slaves. His unwillingness to release them to conform to the will of God revealed that his conversion was not authentic.

The 1850 Fugitive Slave Law was promulgated to uphold slavery, but it rendered positive service to the anti-slavery movement. Because it publicized the horrors of slavery and coerced Northern states to enforce it, this law caused many to support the abolitionists. Moreover, it provoked a spirit of resistance among the hunted which gained them sympathy and respect.

While the Fugitive Slave Law aimed to deaden the moral sentiment in the North against slavery, every fugitive slave who was captured increased the opposition to slavery in the North. This law not only denied the human rights of the slave but defied the principles of free states.

The Fugitive Slave Law turned citizens into bloodhounds hunting down the slave and thus violated the Constitutional Amendments requiring the preservation of the right to a trial by jury and of the right to due process of law before being deprived of life, liberty or property. The Fugitive Slave Law violated also the Gospel which called for justice and mercy. Genuine Christians decided to demonstrate their allegiance to the Gospel by disobedience of this law.

In 1856, an assault in the U.S. Senate upon Senator Charles Sumner of Massachusetts, a champion of our movement, by Congressman Preston Brooks of South Carolina assisted the North to understand the barbaric spirit of slavery. This caning helped expose the determination of the proponents of slavery to dominate or destroy.

Other attempts to oppose the anti-slavery movement served as fuel for the fire by unintentionally imparting new strength to its members, viz., the demonstrations against free speech, the display of pistols and plantation behavior in the Congress, the demand by the government that England return the slaves who attained their freedom at sea, the annexation of Texas to increase the number of slave states, the cold-blooded Dred Scott Decision, the repeal of the Missouri Compromise, the armed effort to force slavery upon Kansas, and the summary manner in which John Brown was hanged. The enemies of freedom have, in effect, contributed to its development.

In 1846, because my Christian belief had filled me with the spirit of love for all mankind, I engaged in a holy war against the slaveholders—using appeals to their minds and hearts. In 1849, however, I stated that I would rejoice over a slave insurrection because in violating the principle of individual liberty, slavery directly violated God's government. In 1861,

I did approve of the war because it could abolish slavery and stop the rebel slaveholders from destroying our democratic institutions.

It was my conviction that the war would provide necessary lessons for the slaveholders. It would certainly correct their interpretation of Northern patience as cowardice and would teach them to respect the rights of Northerners and make them fear us.

I derive immense satisfaction from the fact that only a few years after achieving my freedom, I was speaking in favor of the resolution for woman suffrage. I escaped from slavery for myself; I have worked for the emancipation of the Negro; but because my support for the rights of women has been selfless, I have found in it a degree of nobility.

Because Abraham Lincoln had to grapple with hardships in his youth, he could develop the manly and heroic qualities required for his mission. The severe conditions of his early life, that would have devastated lesser men, only invigorated his spirit.

To evaluate accurately the mettle of a man, you must see how he functions under turbulent conditions. If you find him calm, courageous, and absolutely determined to do his duty in such conditions, you may revere him as a hero. I observed that Abraham Lincoln was such a man in the darkest days of the war.

It may have been necessary for Jefferson Davis and his colleagues to resort to arms for the nation to know the danger of tolerating the power of slaveholders in the government.

The proud and irrational attitude of the South that refused to consider any concessions by the North may have proved to be the salvation of the slave and the nation. If the South had accepted these concessions and had not seceded from the Union, the power of the slaveholders probably would have continued to dominate and demoralize the country.

Rather than be a total calamity, the presidency of Andrew Johnson did contain a blessing. It illustrated the foolishness of tolerating one-man power in the government and proved the need to revise the Constitution to curtail the power of the president.

Article I, Section 7 of the Constitution, which empowers the president to veto legislation passed by Congress, should be abolished. This anti-democratic article assumes that one man, surrounded by his cliques, will be more knowledgeable and patriotic than almost two-thirds of the representatives in the Congress who are in contact with their constituents and to whom they are directly responsible. One-man government is antithetical to the spirit of our free institutions.

The Constitution should not allow the president to have two terms. Otherwise, as soon as he is first elected, he will start scheming for his second election. Aiming for another term, he will be serving also his political party rather than unselfishly devoting his energies to discharging the duties of his office on behalf of the nation.

Nor should the president have the power to grant pardons. With this power, a president could participate in a conspiracy to revolutionize the government and, if it fails, could pardon the conspirators. For the protection of the nation, this power should be given to a committee composed of senators and congressmen.

Sweat, tears, agony, and blood have helped make possible our awareness of truth and our freedom to live in the light of truth. Political truths that we regard as self-evident, such as the principle that every man belongs to himself and the right to freedom of worship, have been purchased with enormous bloodshed and suffering.

The transformation from slavery to freedom, from political deprivation to political equality, and from abject dependence to autonomy has rarely been accomplished without suffering. What has occurred in the West Indies and Russia could be expected to occur here to some extent.

A people that snatches its freedom from the reluctant hand of the tyrant—like the thousands of Haitians who did endure horrendous tortures to win their freedom—will hold it more securely and exhibit it more grandly than a people to whom freedom is given. The sufferings and dangers in the struggle for freedom endow the character with strength and endurance that empower it to stand firm in the midst of adversity.

Shared pleasures can produce friendships. But I can testify that shared anxiety and sufferings in precarious situations can produce stronger and more lasting friendships.

History teaches us that if there is to be progress in liberty, there must be a resistance which is moral or physical or both. The privileged in power have never conceded anything unless it is demanded, and never will. To obtain our full freedom, we Negroes have to struggle against our oppressors, and, when necessary, sacrifice our lives and the lives of others.

Harriet Tubman, the former slave, made nineteen journeys into slave territory to rescue 300 men, women, and children, and was a military scout and nurse for the Union army during the war. In a letter to her, I explained the difference between my service to the cause and hers. Whereas most of what I did for the cause was in public and I received encouragement from a multitude, what she did was in private and witnessed by those trembling souls whom she helped to escape on the Underground Railroad. Apart from John Brown, no one has endured more suffering and danger for the cause than Harriet Tubman.

An urgent and pinching necessity often is required to sting a man into an extraordinary exertion that will reveal to him his hidden powers and resources. Only when his life and limb depend on it will he know the strength of his grip. But when necessity does not challenge a man, and he is surrounded by ease and luxury, he usually will do the minimum for himself and become helpless.

Where can we find the highest types of American physical and intellectual manhood? Not in the delightful latitudes but in the coldest parts of New England where snow and ice cover the ground for six months of the year, and gardeners blast rocks with gunpowder to find places to plant potatoes.

Self-made men attain knowledge, power, and position often in open defiance of the forces of their circumstances and the attempts of society to deny them success.

Having seen the effectiveness of Father Theobald Mathew and Father John Spatt in persuading thousands in Ireland to take the temperance pledge, I have urged Negroes to abstain from alcohol in order that they can gain a moral eminence and command a greater respect.

Woman—like the Negro—has to struggle for her freedom. She must be willing to work for the cause, sacrifice self, and relinquish popular approval in order to achieve justice.

Lucy Stone never intentionally provoked opposition by her many lectures advocating woman suffrage and the abolition of slavery. She did not calculate her influence by the resistance she experienced. But I think that sometimes the resistance one encounters can be a reliable indicator of one's progress.

When the Methodist Episcopal Conference declared that it had no right or desire to support the abolition of slavery, it actually helped the abolition cause. In 1888, fifty years later, this same organization denies woman a voice and a vote in its ecclesiastical assemblies. When the enemy of reform reveals himself, we can deal with him more effectively.

In estimating the success of the woman suffrage movement, rather than emphasizing the distance it has to go to reach its goal, we should reflect on the results it has achieved and the formidable obstacles it has overcome.

Some kind of labor, either physical or mental, is necessary to produce and retain the great, good or desirable. There can be no acquisition without exertion, no polish without friction, no knowledge without labor, no progress without action, and no victory without conflict.

We take the locomotive, sewing machine, printing press, and telegraph for granted. Nevertheless, how much patience, persistence, mental effort, and labor have been required to produce these marvelous and necessary inventions!

From understanding the many calamities that have occurred

at sea, we can expand our knowledge of navigation and naval architecture, enhance safety, and fashion our minds more in the likeness of the divine mind.

What is the source of the strength and unity of a republic? Not the number of her citizens nor her grand achievements but rather the love of her citizens for the institutions that govern them and the willingness of men to die in her defense.

I would question the sincerity of any individual who never disagrees with me. Such uniform agreement lacks integrity. Human minds differ in their operations. Hence, I will consider a difference of opinion because sometimes, like a discord in music, it can generate a beneficial harmony.

If we were wise enough to learn from criticisms, we could often be as much indebted to enemies who concentrate on our imperfections as we are to friends who praise us. Detraction, properly received, can pave the way for the very qualities it denies.

In judging Negroes, whites should think in terms of the depths from which Negroes have come and the obstacles they continue to encounter—the educational, economic, religious, and political discrimination as well as terrorism. How long will Negroes be compelled to suffer until Congress provides the appropriate legislation for the adequate enforcement of the Thirteenth, Fourteenth, and Fifteenth Amendments of the Constitution?

How shall we interpret the systematic efforts to deprive us of the vote, to exclude us from respectable railroad cars and hotels, and to draw the color line against us even in religious organizations? One could interpret all the resistance and the persecution we experience as convincing evidence of our real progress.

There are rights held in reserve for us but we must continue to agitate to secure them. Because our cause is just, it will be victorious.

2

BOOKER T. WASHINGTON

My major goals have been to promote cooperation between the races in the South and to prepare Negro men and women for usefulness.

Being well aware of the ambitions of Negroes throughout this country, I can affirm that it is not their desire to mingle socially with whites when they are not invited. Nor do they have any desire to dominate the white man in politics. They desire equal justice in the courts and the protection of their families and property by those who administer the laws.

In all purely social activities, whites and Negroes can be as separate as the fingers but in all activities necessary for mutual progress, we can be as one as the hand.

It would be the most extreme folly for my race to rely upon only political agitation in seeking social equality. We will secure privileges principally by a constant struggle to develop our economic strength. It is hardly possible for us to achieve educational and religious growth or political freedom without constructing an economic foundation.

Whites should continue to cast down their bucket among the millions of Negroes, who have enriched the South by their labor and have demonstrated their fidelity and love, rather than looking to those of foreign birth for the prosperity of the South. Whites could then have confidence that they would be surrounded by the most patient, unresentful, law-abiding, and loyal people in history.

To those Negroes unaware of the importance of cultivating friendly relations with the white man, I would assert that the Negro has as many good friends among Southern whites as he has anywhere in the world. As we manifest a love for whites, we can teach the world how two races can live in harmony.

After the Civil War, Southern whites returned to devastated plantations and then were asked to train four million of their former slaves for citizenship—in education, economics, and politics. Negroes should realize the magnitude of this burden upon whites and continue to cooperate in the struggle against poverty, ignorance, and crime.

In all of history, when was a race as generous with service and substantial aid in assisting a race of a different color as the white race in this country has been in educating Negroes?

Negroes can derive encouragement from the fact that there are many courageous whites in the South as well as the North who want to help our race receive justice in all areas of life, including the opportunity to elevate ourselves. We should not do anything that would embarrass them or ourselves.

William Lloyd Garrison and his colleagues in the forefront of the abolitionist movement were not only the leaders in the emancipation of Negroes but helped to liberate many whites from racial prejudice.

The time has come for the Southerner to forget that he was the conquered and that the Northerner was the conqueror. So too, the Negro should forget that he was enslaved, and that the white man was the slaveholder. We should all unite with hand and heart to establish a just society.

It is dangerous and even suicidal for any Negro to condemn all whites. We must learn to differentiate between our friends and our enemies. Let us exalt the white man who provides us with guidance and practical aid and treats us with justice while we pity the white man who retards our progress and is himself only half-free. We should talk less about our white enemies and more about our white friends who help Negroes build churches and obtain an education and property.

In my youth, I resolved that I would no longer let any man narrow and degrade my soul—make me less than a human being—by causing me to hate him. I have no hostile feeling toward Southern whites and am as happy rendering a service to them as to members of my own race. A white man is as near to my heart as a black man. Let us respond with love to any white man in any part of the country who would hate us. When he is cruel to us, let us show mercy toward him. If he pushes us down, let us push him up.

I recall that, as a child, I was lying in a bundle of rags on the dirt floor of a slave cabin and my mother was praying over me that Abraham Lincoln would succeed in freeing us. When he signed the Emancipation Proclamation, he converted pieces of property into American citizens. I am indebted to him not only for the freedom of my body but for the freedom of my soul that can live a life without any sectional and racial hatred.

All of us should learn to think in terms of humanity, not in terms of race, color, language or political boundaries. In our schools, we must teach that a person who relinquishes a race narrowness for a love of humanity could experience sublime happiness. The divine commandment is "Love thy neighbor as thyself."

As we stress the need to educate the masses of Negroes, we must emphasize also the necessity of educating poor whites if racial harmony is to be achieved. In all my experience in the North and South, it is the poorly educated white people who demonstrate contempt for the Negro, while the educated and prosperous white man is inclined to treat the Negro in the way one man treats another.

After the end of slavery, I watched a young Negro reading a newspaper to a group of Negroes. They did revere him almost as if he were a god. His ability to read gave him such power. I wanted to develop that ability so that I could experience that power.

The most valuable part of my education was the training that I received when I was a houseboy for a noble white woman,

Mrs. Viola Ruffner, who had been an English teacher and a school principal. She taught me the values of truthfulness, work, thoroughness, promptness, cleanliness, and thrift, gave me books, and encouraged me to form my own library.

When I worked as a houseboy and later in the coal mines and at the salt furnaces, I did derive extraordinary satisfaction from giving these tasks my best effort. My experiences with manual work led me to decide to study at Hampton Institute because it offered industrial as well as academic training.

Hampton Institute did provide me with an atmosphere of Christian values, business, and a spirit of self-reliance and gave me the opportunity to learn ambition and economy. It was there I realized what it means to be a human being rather than a piece of property. By emphasizing industrial training, it furnished a more useful education for my life work than Harvard University or Yale University could have.

At Hampton Institute, I learned to love labor in the service of others as a way of building character. In order to prosper, Negroes have to apply their brains and skills to the common occupations of life, to glorify common labor, and to realize that there is as much dignity in tilling a field as in writing a poem. While "being worked" in slavery meant degradation, "working" means civilization.

One of the most important lessons I learned at Hampton Institute was the value of the Bible for providing guidance in the direction of my life. Every day, I take the time to read a chapter or some verses from the Bible. One cannot have a complete life unless he owns a Bible that he has made a part of his life.

General Samuel Chapman Armstrong, who was worshipped by his students, was a savior of my race. He demonstrated his love for us in his direction of Hampton Institute and by his generous efforts on behalf of Tuskegee Institute and other Negro institutions. I am indebted to his teaching and counsel for whatever, under God, I have done.

I am grateful to the American Missionary Association for

its significant contribution to the progress of the South by its consistent support of Negro education. Hampton Institute is a child of the Association, and Tuskegee Institute, a grandchild.

The whole South will readily appreciate the vital work of hundreds of unselfish teachers who, at the close of the Civil War, came into the South for the improvement of my race.

If I did not have other reasons to cherish the Christian life, the Christlike work that all denominations of the Church have done for the elevation of my race would have caused me to be a Christian. Through its influence, guidance and donations, the Church has been principally responsible for what our race has attained in the past fifty years.

For the near future, the accomplishments of Negroes would depend mainly upon the teaching and influence of the Church. But the Church must do more to confront our social problems and to educate poor whites as well as Negroes. The Church should realize that the problem is to save the soul by saving the body. She must teach practical ideas that will help people better their material condition even before they can improve their moral and religious lives. At Tuskegee Institute, we teach that the best way to have a relationship with Jesus is to have land, crops, and a good bank account. Then, you have a religion you can rely on seven days a week.

One of the main goals of Tuskegee Institute is to educate men and women to become leaders of the masses of Negroes in the Black Belt. The greatest need of our race is for strong and unselfish leaders who have religion, common sense, and training in industry.

At Tuskegee, we provide academic training but also teach an industrial skill, help students realize the civilizing power in intelligent labor, and encourage them to develop Christian character. We also emphasize that they can win the respect of whites if they learn to do something as well as anyone.

The studies in our curriculum have been designed to lead students into an atmosphere of truth, virtue, unselfishness, and love in order that they will develop a spirit of generosity which aims to elevate all persons, regardless of color.

We teach the sciences, mathematics, and literature to the extent our students require them to understand the principles of the industries and to cultivate the habit and love of study. The students also examine the actual needs of the people so that they can help them ennoble the common things of life.

Our students told me that when some of our chickens came out of their shells, they helped other chickens to break out of their shells. It was a joy to know that these chickens, so early in life, had absorbed the Tuskegee spirit of helpfulness.

My policy is to appoint only Negroes as regular full-time resident faculty because I intend Tuskegee Institute to perform as a model of self-help that can provide a stimulus and instill confidence in our people. For the same reason, we have only Negroes in our National Negro Business League.

Education should aim for the formation of character having courage and self-control over every passion and appetite and for the elimination of prejudice, malice, and jealousy. With this self-control, the student can enjoy harmony among all his activities of body, mind, and heart.

Some Negroes should pursue higher education, but a large majority of our people should be educated in industrial skills that will enable them to secure the material necessities of life. While providing mental training, industrial education teaches how to earn a living and how to utilize the forces of nature so that the labor will not become wearisome but dignified and beautiful. This type of education promotes a desire for the ownership of land and makes the Negro a producer and the white man dependent on him to a degree. Consequently, there will be a greater peace and union between the races as well as an improvement in their moral and religious lives.

Tuskegee Institute has provided abundant evidence of the power of industrial education. When I founded it in 1881, we had one building. In 1900, there were forty-eight buildings, all of which, except four, were constructed by our instructors and the students, who also produced the bricks. The students cultivated 700 of the 2,500 acres. In addition to the academic and religious training, there was instruction in twenty-eight industrial skills.

An ounce of application is worth about a ton of abstraction. More Negroes should apply their education to conquering the forces of nature by starting a farm, brickyard, sawmill or coal mine. An educated Negro, by the production of 1,000 bushels of excellent potatoes, can do more toward solving our racial problems than dozens of orations or newspaper articles.

A Negro youth who receives only a literary education often develops an exaggerated estimation of his worth in the world and multiplies his desires for things that his education cannot supply.

In 1892, we began the annual Tuskegee Negro Conferences that had about 800 representatives from the Black Belt. They discussed the industrial, moral, and educational conditions of the masses and did try to determine the most effective ways Tuskegee and other institutions could assist them. Members of the Tuskegee Workers' Conference, who were officers and instructors from Negro schools in the South, attended these conferences.

In addition to industrial education, the majority of Negroes need academic, moral, and religious education. The academic education should include emphasis on the lives of great men and women. Training in gymnastics also would be helpful.

The salvation of the American Negro will depend on his acquisition of education, Christian virtues, an industrial skill, thrift, and prosperity. The possession of property constitutes evidence of certain attributes—mental discipline, will power, capacity for self-sacrifice, and interest in national and local governments.

There is no American more aware of the injustices against my race than I am. But I am aware also that demands will not change these conditions. The Negro has an obligation to be modest in his political claims and to depend for the complete recognition of his political rights upon the gradual but sure influences that derive from his possession of high character, intelligence, and property.

What have been the worst things slavery did to my people? It prevented the development of family life and deprived them of a sense of self-dependence, the habit of economy, and the executive power that distinguishes the Anglo-Saxon race. It will take more than twenty-five years to correct habits that have existed for 250 years but industrial education and object lessons by Christian leaders can facilitate this correction.

In their first years of freedom, due to inexperience and a lack of knowledge, Negroes attempted to begin at the top by seeking a seat in Congress or the state legislature instead of at the bottom by learning a real estate or industrial skill.

Some Negroes, instead of relying upon themselves, look to federal officials to create positions for them. Often, I wished I could transfer them to rural districts so that they might have a real base on the soil.

If Negroes who have spent their time and money attending political conventions had started a truck garden or dairy farm, they could have established a basis for pursuing our political rights.

Educated men and women should develop such a degree of independence that they will not rely upon the government for support, but through their education induce the government to depend on them for support. They must become not mere consumers but producers and pioneers. I consider as a pauper anyone, educated or ignorant, who consumes more than he produces.

My advice to the Negro worker consists of several basic rules. Make certain that your conscience regulates all of your work. Be efficient, skilled, and reliable. Retain your job and acquire property. Establish a reputation for moral virtue and thrift. Do even more than your duty demands. The concrete achievements of Negro workers will do more for our race than all of the abstract eloquence that can plead our cause.

One of my principal objectives at Tuskegee Institute is to

maintain such control over my work—completing the tasks of each day—that it never drives me. The awareness of being master of one's work, in all its details, is a source of spiritual, mental, and physical satisfaction.

Audiences differ from each other, and I engage all of my sympathy, thought, and energy to reach the heart of each of them. Moreover, before every lecture, I ask God's blessing on my effort.

The individual who invests serious study and hard work in his life will generate strength and enjoyment. The individual who is indifferent and reckless only makes himself miserable. In our relationships, if we are willing to love, we will receive love.

A man can experience the highest happiness if he can lose himself in his work for the sake of a noble cause. I thank God I have the privilege of working for the elevation of my race.

Who are the happiest people I have known? Those who do the most for others. Who are the most miserable? Those who do the minimum for others and who continually seek their own happiness. The longer I live, the more convinced I am that the only thing most worth living for, and, if necessary, dying for, is having the opportunity of using all your powers of mind, body, and heart to make someone happier and more useful.

The greatest race is the one that has learned to cultivate the greatest patience and self-control and to live without hatred and acts of cruelty. To hate another because of his race is the worst form of slavery. Race hatred never solved a problem. To become embittered is to lose one's capacity to be useful.

I encouraged Negroes to attend the Pan African Conference in London in 1900 that protested Britain's mistreatment of her African subjects, especially in South Africa and Rhodesia. The Conference examined how the European powers could atone for their plunder of Africa and how Africans could promote their own industrial development.

After conversing with Africans, Negro missionaries, and Negro diplomats who have lived in Africa, I have concluded that American Negroes would not improve their condition by moving to Africa. European nations have divided up most of Africa, and there is little hope for self-government except in Liberia, which has its own undesirable features.

In an address before the National Afro-American Council in 1903, I affirmed that the same laws should apply to whites and blacks. They should receive equal treatment in regard to citizenship, the right to work, and the protection of life and property. Otherwise, our government is weakened and runs the risk of being destroyed.

I oppose the passage of every segregation law. I reject such laws as unnecessary, unjust, unwise, and illegal. Like other forms of discrimination, the administration of segregation has not only embittered the Negro but has harmed the moral fiber of the white man.

In my speeches, I have condemned the conditions that many Negroes endured—mortgage rates on crops ranging between fifteen and forty percent, as many as ten persons living in a one-room cabin, a school session of only three months in the plantation districts, an allocation of ninety cents a year for the education of a Negro child in Alabama compared to $18 for a white child in Massachusetts, and a salary of only $16 a month for some Negro teachers in Alabama compared to $50 or $100 for teachers in New York City.

Negroes should never shield criminals simply because they are members of their race. Nonetheless, in order for Negroes to be willing to be active in discovering criminals, they must believe that every Negro charged with a crime will receive protection and justice before the courts.

In accordance with a universal and unchangeable law, no race can injure another race merely because it has the power to do so without being degraded and spiritually injured. When the white man deprives a Negro of a ballot or imposes a "Jim Crow" law, the white man is permanently injured. When a Negro is lynched, the perpetrators then suffer the death of morals—the death of the soul. "Whatsoever a man soweth, that shall he also reap."

I did not denounce every lynching. If I had, I would have provoked controversy that might have obstructed my work at Tuskegee Institute. Still, I have rebuked lynchers throughout the nation. I have written letters to newspaper editors, stating that I oppose mob violence, that legal methods should be used to establish guilt and punishment, and that a thorough mental, religious, and industrial education of both races is the remedy for lynching.

In my speeches, I advocated a property and educational test for voting which ought to be applied justly to both races. This would eliminate a mass of ignorant voters of both races that is a corrupting factor in Southern politics.

In his final hours, President William McKinley expressed the hope that his assassin would be treated with fairness. In a letter to a newspaper editor, I suggested that the best way we could show our love and reverence for the president would be to decide in every community that the majesty of the law must be upheld at any cost.

Can American colleges train students to open the doors of all industries to all men regardless of color? I cannot decide who is worse: the former slaveholder who forced his slave to work without compensation or the man who, because of his prejudice or cowardice, prevents the Negro from working for compensation.

A man cannot be moral and religious if he lacks adequate food and clothing and even some comforts and conveniences.

In the preparation of an individual to be a citizen, no color line should be drawn. If the Negro is kept in ignorance, how can he be expected to know the law or to have the self-control to obey it?

Educating young Negroes to be law-abiding and productive citizens is far more Christian and economical than punishing them after they have committed a crime.

Justice requires that we Negroes have access to all of our constitutional rights. To achieve them, we have to become the most useful and independent citizens. I am convinced that our usefulness will prove to be our most powerful and permanent protection.

In a letter to President Theodore Roosevelt, I asked him to write to the Interstate Commerce Commission about railroad accommodations for Negroes and emphasized that all Negroes were opposed to the principle of separation. I requested that he express his intention that wherever separation existed, the accommodations for whites and Negroes be rendered equal in convenience and comfort for the same charge. The president wrote a letter containing this intention and asked me to review it before he sent it.

I dispatched my proposed plank for the Republican Party in 1908 to Secretary of War William Howard Taft, a presidential candidate. The plank did include an appeal for justice for all human beings, without regard for race or color, an approval of the efforts of President Roosevelt and the Republican Party to secure equal accommodations on railroads and other public carriers for all citizens, and support for the exact enforcement of those constitutional amendments designed to protect and advance the Negro.

Even though I knew I would be criticized by the Southern press and would even be risking my life, I accepted President Roosevelt's invitation to dine with him and his family at the White House. I believed that it was my obligation to accept the invitation as a recognition of my race.

No president since Lincoln had been more concerned with the elevation of our race than President Roosevelt. Because of his encouragement and assistance to Negroes not only in the North and the West but in the South despite the most severe and irrational criticism, I believe that he had our best interests at heart. A president who had agreed with us on nine out of ten issues deserved our support.

The numerous discriminations against Negroes in regard to public travel and other public conveniences will diminish to the extent Negroes become educated, refined, and prosperous because they have produced something that the white man wants or respects.

When Frederick Douglass was compelled to ride in a cattle car, someone tried to console him by stating how disgraceful it was for him to be so humiliated. He responded that it was impossible for him to be humiliated. Whenever we fight our battles, we should adopt this attitude.

In a letter to Douglass, our greatest hero, I expressed my gratitude for his gift of himself to the cause of our race and asserted that his life was a rebuke to many who live only for self.

I take great pride in the achievements of the Negro in this country. They provide the most effective ammunition for the fight against prejudice. If I had the privilege of reentering the world and the Great Spirit were to ask me to choose the color and race to clothe my spirit, I would ask that He make me an American Negro.

As evidence of what our people can do, I sent an account to a newspaper about John Smith, a Negro, who at an auction acquired an extensive tract of land in Cahaba, Alabama.

Negro newspapers have made significant contributions to the elevation of our race by demonstrating the managerial and editorial skills of the Negro, informing whites about Negro achievements, and motivating our people to educate themselves and their children.

Americans have succeeded in every conflict except one. They still have to win the victory over racial prejudice. Until whites and Negroes conquer this evil, we shall have a cancer gnawing at the heart of the republic that will be as dangerous as any military attack upon us.

We must depend mainly upon educated Negroes for racial peace. During the last four decades, by advocating patience and self-control under difficult circumstances, the educated Negro has averted a war between the races.

After the nation hears many accounts of the heroic exploits of the Negro in the Spanish-American War from Northern and

Southern soldiers, ex-abolitionists, and ex-masters, it can then decide if a race that is willing to die for its country should be given the highest opportunity to live for its country.

My advice to my daughter, Portia, has been not to think too much on American racial prejudice. Continuous thinking and discussion of prejudice eventually renders one incapable of useful activity. Those Negroes, especially in the North, who constantly talk about race prejudice, only render their lives miserable.

We ought to denounce lynching and segregation and other major evils. But it does more harm than good to dedicate so much of our attention to the numerous minor discriminations we experience. We should focus more on our opportunities and less on our difficulties. We are unjust to our children if we constantly tell them about the miseries of the race. One constructive progressive program can do far more to reduce discrimination than whining and resentment.

The plantation songs, the spirituals, provided the members of my race with relief from sorrow and despair, and fostered the faith and hope that their Father would lead them out of bondage into the Promised Land of freedom. This faith and hope enabled them to survive. The pathos and beauty of these songs excite intense religious fervor. They are often sung at Tuskegee Institute, Hampton Institute, and Fisk University.

While many think of the Kingdom of God as remote, above the clouds, the Bible proclaims that the Kingdom of God is within us. This implies that we can cultivate the self-control to find beauty and happiness within ourselves, regardless of our situation. In our presence, others will then feel stronger and happier and believe that they are in an almost holy place.

God has provided us with many goods for our food, shelter, and enjoyment. We are morally responsible to utilize them to strengthen our bodies and enhance our capacity to serve.

Whatever one's success in business, one lives a lower life if he acquires material possessions so that he can cater to his selfish ambition and desires, and lord it over others. One lives a higher life if one utilizes material possessions to achieve a deeper spiritual life for himself and to help others.

Whenever we make a criticism, we should add a suggestion as to how the situation can be corrected. But I have found that rather than oppose the faulty actions of individuals, often it is more beneficial to encourage their productive actions.

When whites in the Southern press condemn me, they are aiming through me to condemn my race. Still, several Negro leaders, like Dr. Du Bois, my most severe critic, seem to be unaware that when they join these whites in condemning me, they, in effect, are condemning their own race.

What has been the most important thing I have learned? There is sufficient opportunity in this country for every man, if he has the courage, to develop materially, educationally, and morally. However, the masses of Negroes should remain in the South. In the Northern cities, the temptations are too great and the competition from foreigners too intense.

In their theological education, some Negro ministers have learned about the soil of the valley of the river Jordan but not about the soil of their future parish. They should be taught to love outdoor work and how to cultivate their own gardens and farms. Their ability to earn a living from the soil would then release them from the idleness which leads to temptation and would give them greater freedom to challenge the sins of their parishioners.

In judging a teacher, minister or leader of our people, we should use a high moral standard. If he has led an immoral life, he does not deserve and should not receive our esteem and confidence. We have to distinguish between the virtuous and the vicious.

Genuine statesmanship does not stifle the aspirations of a people but so inspires them that they are eager to contribute their souls, minds, and bodies in noble service of the state.

It is lamentable that when Negroes attend conventions, we have to spend almost all our time in speaking about ourselves. I look forward to a day when at our conventions we will be able to devote our discussions to the needs of another race.

For our material needs, we Negroes must not depend on the energy and generosity of other races. We should imitate the initiative of those Italian and German immigrants who, unable to speak English, arrive here, work hard, save, and become executives in great industrial enterprises.

To the extent that the stronger race elevates the weak race, it strengthens and ennobles itself. No man can lift up a poor member of another race without being made more Christlike.

Because of all our service to America, we Negroes believe we are entitled to her assistance not with our material needs, which we should fulfill, but with our educational, moral, and religious lives.

At one time, I almost succumbed to the temptation to enter political life but I realized that it would be selfish for me to pursue this type of success since I would have to ignore my mission to help establish a foundation for my race through a generous education of hand, head, and heart. Though I am a Republican, I will never allow my political affiliation to keep me from speaking and acting on behalf of the Negro race and the whole South.

Recognition and reward will come to a man, regardless of his race, color, religion, or previous history, if he continues to contribute to the moral, intellectual, and material well-being of his community.

Fame has never been one of my objectives. I am gratified with whatever fame has come to me only if I can use it as an instrument for doing good.

Which is the strongest nation today? Not the one with the most powerful army or the most destructive power. It is the nation which has the most efficient laborers and the most productive machinery.

While establishing empires, creating heroes, and making history, the carnage of war has ingrained hate and suspicion in nations that can never be reconciled with Christianity and civilization and that centuries may not remove.

Who are making the most meaningful contributions to the life of this nation? The European immigrant and the Negro by teaching the lessons of brotherliness, tolerance, patience, and helpfulness.

While races, like individuals, can assist each other, every race and every individual, as a rule, must work out their own salvation. The major reason for my confidence in the masses of Negroes is their demonstrated willingness to learn how to help themselves and to become independent.

How can I have a strong faith in the future in the face of some discouraging impediments? It is because I believe in a loving Providence that led us out of the wilderness of slavery. We entered slavery as pagans, property, and with chains. But with divine help, we emerged from slavery as Christians and citizens with a ballot. Since the emancipation, we have made immense progress—obtaining education, Christian character, and property. Under God, progress shall continue to be our eternal guiding star.

THE POWER OF THE NEGATIVE

While condemning the horrendous evil and barbarity of slavery, I recognize that the Negroes who went through the school of slavery and their descendants are stronger morally, mentally, religiously, and materially than an equal number of black people elsewhere.

From the experience of slavery, the Negro gained the habit of hard work. We have to motivate the masses to acquire the knowledge and skills for the higher forms of labor.

I do not regret that I was born a slave and raised on a farm. From my work on the farm and that poverty, I learned some things about life I would not have learned had I been born in prosperous conditions.

If I had not lived on a plantation, I would not have had the opportunity to learn about nature and to love animals, birds, trees, flowers, and the soil. Most of my present strength and ability to work is due to my love of the outdoor life.

Had I not been a slave, I would not have had daily contact with the slaves. Although they were ignorant of books, I was pleased to take lessons from them.

I carried the books of my white friends but was not allowed to enter the schoolroom. My mother explained that a Negro child was forbidden to learn from books there. As soon as I became aware that I could not enter a schoolroom and that it was dangerous for me to learn to read, I resolved that I would never be content until I learned this dangerous practice.

Harsh statements in the speeches about my race, that I was forced to hear as a boy, at first made me want to go to some distant place where race prejudice did not exist. Eventually, however, these statements drove me closer to my own people so that I had a deep sympathy with them and related to them as I did to my mother.

In my youth, I heard public speakers claim that the Negro lacked the ability to learn from books and that it would be a waste of time and money to try to teach him subjects in the ordinary school curriculum. My reaction was to resolve that I would make any sacrifice to do my part to demonstrate to the world that the Negro could secure an education and apply it in his community. Had I not heard this false claim, I doubt that I would have had more interest in my studies than the average white student.

If I had a distinguished ancestry with an inherited fortune, and if I had been a member of a popular race, I would have been inclined to depend upon my ancestry, fortune, and color instead of my own effort.

Criticisms of our race have, in effect, given thousands of black people the forms of race pride and race consciousness that are so necessary for them to develop their best potential. Due to these criticisms, they give more thought to their racial problems, develop closer relationships with their own people, and treasure the songs and history of slavery.

The procedure at Hampton Institute was that the institution would arrange for the benefactors to pay the tuition while the students had to provide for their own board, books, clothing, and room by work or by a combination of work and money. The constant effort the students made through the industries to defray their personal expenses helped them form character and develop a spirit of self-reliance.

Tuskegee students are taught that it is a privilege for them to work to pay for some of the cost of their education. This work raises their self-confidence. The Bible says, "Work out your own salvation with fear and trembling." If someone is unwilling to work to pay for his education, he will do nothing worthwhile with it after he gets it.

For our farm at Tuskegee, I deliberately chose land of poor quality because I did want our students to become intelligent farmers by learning how to convert poor land into good land.

In expanding Tuskegee Institute, we had to undergo many

physical discomforts and inconveniences. Nevertheless, upon reflection, I am pleased that we had these experiences and that the students had to dig out the places for the kitchen and dining room. If we had begun in beautiful and convenient rooms, I am afraid we would have lost our heads and become conceited.

My policy at Tuskegee Institute has been not to introduce classical studies or the study of any foreign language. Some Negroes have criticized me for these restrictions. But one of my central concerns has been that our students have the time to become proficient in the use of the English language.

One of my chief aims is to use the local practical activities of each community as a basis for much of the mental training in its schoolroom. The students will thereby manifest greater interest and understanding. I am convinced that this aim can be better implemented with my race rather than with the white race because, for generations, my race has not been educated in the old formal methods, and the white race has much to unlearn.

One way to motivate the Negro to desire an education is to let him know that there are some people in the community who do not want him to have it. The census figures for the years 1900 and 1910 indicated that in four of the Southern states where most public schools are poor—North Carolina, Georgia, Arkansas and Alabama—Negroes did demonstrate more rapid progress in learning to read and write than in any other part of the country.

In advising our students who intend to become teachers, I have stressed that when a teacher does not know the answer to a question, he should clearly state he is unable to answer the question. Students respect such candor.

In 1905, I emphasized that New England had been the main source of money for Negroes for the previous four decades. Out of love and sympathy, the people of New England were able to make their contributions by denying themselves many luxuries and being willing to wear the same clothes year after year.

Our educated young people should emulate the generosity

of those who have sacrificed to contribute to their education. The life of an educated person ought to consist mainly not of spending or hoarding but of giving.

My advice to our students at Tuskegee has been that they should develop a missionary spirit and determine to sacrifice their lives so they can become centers of life-giving power and create institutions for the elevation of their people.

Our real heroes include the graduates of Hampton Institute, Tuskegee Institute, Fisk University, Atlanta University, and Spelman College and other educational centers who, with no certainty of receiving salaries, have lived in wretched districts in order to instruct our people on how to improve their moral and religious lives, obtain land, and construct decent homes and schools.

Two white ladies from Maine, who wanted to devote the rest of their lives to the uplift of my race, asked me to select a location for a school they wished to start. On a rainy day, we arrived at a place I chose in Calhoun, Alabama. As we stood in the mud at the site for the school, I told them that if they could still keep their courage and establish the school despite the poverty-stricken conditions, everything would turn out all right. The prediction was correct. The school did transform the community.

From my own experience and observation, I concluded that those who try to withhold the benefits of civilization from any race or group sometimes, in effect, assist that race or group to obtain these benefits.

When the Negro is the target of racial discrimination, he is motivated to generate more steam. Whenever this steam has been exhausted in agitation, it has produced no good result. But, when he has controlled and rightly directed this steam, it has become a powerful force for the improvement of the race.

I did counsel several Negro activists not to do anything that could obstruct President Roosevelt's efforts or would cause him to assume that we were trying to own him. I wanted him to fulfill his noble objectives. I assisted with his speeches on racial issues and welcomed him at our Institute.

In a letter to President Roosevelt, I included the names of 178 Negro newspapers and indicated that all of them, except five, had supported him. I assured him that the opposition or uncertainty of the five caused the other 173 to intensify their support of his administration.

How can those who have enjoyed success in life understand the many messages of hope and freedom in the Bible as well as members of my oppressed race who are struggling upward? The highest ambition of the older slaves, once they were free, was to learn to read their Bibles.

Negroes can find inspiration in the life of Abraham Lincoln who derived moral strength from his self-denial to transcend his poverty and ignorance and achieve a position of high power and usefulness.

The Mormons were forced to suffer inhuman persecution. Joseph Smith, the founder of the church, and hundreds of his followers were killed. Many were deprived of their property. But the more they were persecuted, the more they developed their unity, strength and will to succeed. Without the injustice they were compelled to face, I question whether the Mormon Church would now be flourishing.

Suffering is necessary for progress. Dedicated whites have suffered for our race. Our race should be willing to undergo even greater suffering than it has. I believe that no one has suffered for the race in recent years more than I have—often confronting danger without complaining.

The physical assault upon me in New York City and its consequences proved to be quite an ordeal but one result of the assault was that it revealed to me how many friends I had in the country, especially in the South. Since the assault, the invitations for me to lecture have nearly doubled.

History testifies that the highest freedom is achieved only gradually and at a tremendous price. The noblest freedom has always been a conquest—never a bequest. Those who are most free physically, mentally, and morally are those who, equipped with patience and persistence, have continued the struggle for more freedom despite severe restrictions.

Some of the most miserable and ineffective people I have encountered are those who, from a distance, appear to have all of the privileges the world can bestow. To enjoy privileges in the highest sense, a person must have had the experience of being denied these privileges. Those who most enjoy wealth are those who have experienced poverty.

Socrates had a wisdom that allowed him to associate with the affluent. Still, he desired to know the common people so that he could help them. It was his poverty that enabled him to relate to the common people, and his philosophy was filled with illustrations from their lives.

Socrates abstained from some physical pleasures and even decided to neglect his family so that he could devote himself to correcting the morals, religion, and politics of Athens. He claimed that he was not wise and sought wisdom about virtue.

When asked how I can derive so much happiness from my work while I am aware of the suffering of my race, my usual reply has been that I can be happy because I judge the present in relation to the past and realize the depths from which we have emerged as well as what we have achieved.

How should we evaluate the progress of the Negro race in the United States? Not by the level of its success alone, but also by the obstacles it has overcome in attaining that success. We can then conclude that few races in history, if any, have attained the kind of progress which the Negro race has in the same amount of time.

In order to attain recognition, the Negro youth usually has to work harder and perform his tasks better than a white youth. This persistent struggle creates in the Negro youth a strength and a type of confidence that are not found in a person whose path in life, by reason of wealth and race, is smooth.

Successful men usually have had to overcome formidable difficulties and to master problems. Consequently, they have gained a mental power and a clarity of vision that only a few persons, who live a life of ease, possess.

Pity should be extended not to a man who faces stubborn problems every day but rather to a man who does not have the problems and hardships that could summon his latent powers and structure his character.

In my life, problems have frequently been the occasions for unusual opportunities. Problems have even turned races into nations and kingdoms.

I thank God that all our problems have not been solved. I rejoice that I am able to live in an age when we have to solve immense problems. I do not care to live where there would be no wrongs to be corrected or persons in need of assistance. I like problems because they require work and I love work—the work of overcoming ignorance, narrowness, and prejudice.

As long as the Negro race is making progress, it is not at a disadvantage when it confronts the basic problems of securing land, constructing houses, and forming businesses, schools, and churches. These experiences help generate a strength of character that can be achieved in no other way.

Prohibition was a real blessing for the Negro. When it was enforced, crime decreased, and he was more willing to work hard, save money, and buy property.

A great deal can be learned from the mistakes of the white race which took 3,000 years to realize that it should not have restricted education to the mind but should also have included industrial education.

Our race must be willing to go without something today so that it may have it tomorrow. We must save and also invest a portion of our earnings but spend nothing on superficialities.

I endorsed a recommendation by the First Tuskegee Negro Conference that poor people should make every sacrifice and practice every form of economy so that they could purchase land and liberate themselves from the onerous habit of living in debt.

Negroes have had many business failures, including the closing of several banks, but we must not become discouraged by these failures. Only through a combination of failures and successes can we ultimately obtain the experience necessary for permanent success.

In a speech before the National Negro Business League, I stressed that we should not regard material possessions as the chief end of life but rather utilize them as means for securing an education that will render us willing and able to serve our fellowman and country.

When I had to dismiss a member of our staff for repeatedly failing to preserve the confidentiality of her work, I advised her that she had an opportunity to profit from her mistakes.

The more difficulties we have to overcome, the greater will be our success.

No race attained its goals without trials and persecutions. We Negroes may have to engage in a struggle for decades and centuries before we achieve our economic and political goals.

Our struggle keeps us humble and causes us to develop our relationship to the Giver of all gifts. "Whom the Lord loveth, He chasteneth." Persons who have not experienced anxiety, poverty, injustice, and struggle will probably fail in genuine living and not develop their full potential.

The Negro minister must possess the courage to challenge public opinion, when it is necessary, and be willing to endure misunderstanding and abuse. Our people should receive moral direction more than flattery.

It is not helpful to a race to be continually condemned for its faults. Neither is it helpful if a race is continually praised for its virtues while its faults are overlooked. Moreover, it is an indication of maturity when a race is willing to measure its weaknesses as well as its strengths.

My advice to our teacher of dressmaking was that if she wished to be successful, she should encourage her colleagues to offer criticisms of her work, express gratitude to them for the criticisms, and not let her personal feelings interfere with her work.

If a man is to be of the highest service to his fellows, he

must be willing to hear from those who disagree with him as well as from those who agree with him. He should welcome adverse criticism in the same spirit as he welcomes praise. I number among my best friends some of those who differ with me on many essential points. I have learned more from frank criticisms than from praise of the work at Tuskegee Institute.

In commenting on a Montgomery race conference in 1900, I asserted that if persons had feelings antithetical to what we regarded as the best interests of the Negro, it was better they express these feelings. The Negro does not have to fear the person who expresses these feelings sincerely but rather the person who represses his antagonistic feelings.

Because I did not have a distinguished ancestry, I resolved to leave a record which would be a source of pride for my children and might inspire them to still higher efforts.

3

Marcus Garvey

As long as one race retains a monopoly of creation, other races cannot be expected to be satisfied. We desire peace and prosperity for the white race in America and Europe and for the yellow race in Asia, but we also desire and demand peace and prosperity for the black race in Africa.

A race can be free only if it has its own strong nation. We Negroes have a moral right to own Africa, and we denounce the greed of those nations who by force, slave labor, fraud, and conspiracy have seized its territories and natural wealth.

In order to achieve our emancipation from oppression and ensure self-preservation, 400 million Negroes throughout the world have to unite to reclaim Africa from European tyranny and build a republic there that will compel the respect of all nations and races.

In January 1918, twelve men and women and I started the Universal Negro Improvement Association (UNIA) in New York City. After one year, partly as a result of my efforts in thirty-eight states, there were one million members, and the next year, two million in 700 chapters and divisions in several countries. Within a few years, we had four million members in the United States and seven million in Africa, South and Central America, the West Indies, and Canada.

The UNIA, believing in God, our Father Who is the Source of our human rights, and in the brotherhood of man, teaches its members to respect the rights of all races and to work for the economic, social, and political liberation of the Negroes of the world. The motto of the UNIA is "One God! One Aim! One Destiny!"

The objectives of the UNIA have been: to unify people of the African race in a universal confraternity; to promote pride and love of the race; to reclaim the fallen of the race; to aid the needy of the race; and to join in civilizing the backward tribes of Africa.

Other objectives of the UNIA that were assigned to our African Communities League (ACL) have been: to contribute to the development of the independent Negro countries and communities; to establish agencies in the chief countries of the world for the protection and representation of all Negroes; to promote Christian worship among the tribes of Africa; to found universities, colleges, and schools for racial education of our people; to create worldwide commercial and industrial enterprises; and to strive for better conditions in all Negro communities.

The UNIA and the ACL had to be incorporated separately because the state laws did separate the functions of fraternal organizations from those of business organizations. But both of these organizations had been designed to be guided by the same principles, and when the UNIA has been involved in business, it has relied upon the ACL or our other business organizations.

The highest purpose in life for successful Negroes should be to assist the poor members of their race. They ought to use whatever influence they can exert on national and local levels with governmental and philanthropic agencies to assist the desperate Negroes improve their condition.

The UNIA has encouraged its members to feed the hungry, clothe the needy, provide work with a decent wage for those who desire it, and assist the illiterate. It has also promoted an active concern for the physical and moral well-being of Negro women. We have taught our members that they become noble through service to their race.

Reflecting the spirit of the UNIA, our Black Star Line aimed to link Negroes in the Western Hemisphere with Africa and to provide them with opportunities to demonstrate their initiative and self-reliance.

My titles have indicated the extent of my involvement in my mission—President-General of the UNIA and the ACL, President of the UNIA of the World, Provisional President of the Republic of Africa, President of the Black Star Steamship Corporation, Negro Factories Corporation, and Black Cross Navigation and Trading Company, Managing Editor of *The Negro World*, Editor of *The New Jamaican*, *Blackman*, and *Black Man*, Principal of the School of African Philosophy, and the Municipal Councilor of the Kingston and St. Andrew Corporation.

In my youth, I read books that inspired me to abandon my desire to be a wharf-man or a cowboy and begin to develop an ambition to become a personality in the world. Some of these biographies and autobiographies indicated that the humblest boys could become the world's greatest men.

The UNIA has upheld the purity of the Negro race and the purity of the white race. Negroes should develop themselves into a healthy whole rather than commit race suicide through squandering their physical and moral identities by engaging in miscegenation. God would not have made us originally separate from other races if He had intended that we lose our identity. When Negroes do not preserve their racial identity, they are in rebellion against God.

It is natural that the white majority will not grant what they want to the Negro or to any other race. As the Negro threatens to compete further with the white man for jobs, a conflict will inevitably occur within a century, and the weaker race will become the target of a plan of economic starvation. In order to prevent such a conflict and their extermination, Negroes should have the opportunity to develop their own civilization in Africa.

At the 1938 UNIA convention, we unanimously approved of a resolution in the United States Senate that became the

Greater Liberia Bill, which sought financial support from the government for the repatriation of the Negroes who wished to return to Africa.

Our African republic should not be socialistic. It should be based mainly on American democracy even though the state, to some extent, should own those things necessary to human existence such as coal and railroads.

In the last 500 years, there has never been a serious attempt to free Negroes. We have been hoodwinked into believing that Abraham Lincoln or Queen Victoria freed us, but we are still industrial, social, and political slaves. Any restricted liberty that arbitrarily deprives a person of the complete rights and prerogatives of full citizenship is a modified form of slavery.

The ideals of freedom and righteousness have prospered in this century only when they have not challenged the cravings of those who control governments for oil, rubber, diamonds, gold, coal, iron, sugar, coffee, and other such minerals and products.

In 1919, I predicted that within thirty years, there would be a world war between the white and yellow peoples. If the white man were to give us our share of democracy, I asserted that we would rescue him when the yellow race would be about to subdue him. Otherwise, we would turn a deaf ear to him.

My advice to the delegates of the 1919 Peace Conference was that if they wished to prevent wars, they should satisfy the claims not only of the white man but of the yellow man and the black man. There could be no lasting peace without justice.

In 1920, the UNIA petitioned the League of Nations that the German colonies be given not to the European nations for further exploitation but to the native peoples and the Negroes of the Western world. In 1936, I warned that these colonies should not be restored to the Nazi regime to the destruction and death of other peoples.

The new Negro desires a freedom without limitations, and we will not stop until we achieve a democratic Africa. While we strive for the redemption of Africa, we continue to stress that our economic expansion and solidarity are necessary to gain our political and social rights.

In responding to questions about my allegiance to America, I have declared my love for America because of its principles, Constitution, and some of its institutions that are democratic. America presents the opportunity to all peoples to come and agitate about the issue of liberty. It has assisted the Irish, the Jews, and people of the Eastern states of Russia to state their grievances before the world.

I am not a Bolshevik or a socialist and have always resisted communists who sought to influence me. I have never been connected with any movement that aims to destroy or impair the American government or the Constitution. Negroes should never associate with communists. Their system deprives the individual of personal initiative. Because there are not many Negroes living in Russia, they have been treated rather well. If millions of them were there, their condition would be no better than Negroes in the South.

The UNIA has encouraged its members to seek changes through voting, to obey the laws of their communities, and to avoid unjustified rebellious movements and riots. They have been advised to assist the police in maintaining order.

Even as we Negroes in the UNIA empathize with others striking out for freedom—"Ireland for the Irish," "Jerusalem for the Jews," "Egypt for the Egyptians," and "India for the Indians"—400 million Negroes, with the vision of liberty, have to work toward the goal of "Africa for the Africans" and build a United States of Africa.

At the 1920 UNIA convention, I read a telegram extending the greetings of our 25,000 delegates to President Eamon De Valera. It expressed the sympathy of all Negroes for his cause and our belief that Ireland should be as free as Africa shall be for Negroes of the world. It urged him to keep up the fight for a free Ireland.

From the 1921 UNIA convention, I sent a message to His Majesty George V which did advocate the emancipation of the people of Ireland, India, and Egypt. I appealed to him to help prevent race wars by being just to all races.

Would an Irish-American who fights for the independence of Ireland or an American Jew who fights for the establishment of a Jewish state in Palestine thus be disloyal to the United States? Why then should an African-American who fights for the redemption and freedom of Africa be seen as disloyal?

Blacks should develop pride in the beauty of their history, tradition, and culture as a people. Upon the banks of the Nile 3,000 years ago, black men excelled in government and were founders and teachers of art, science, and literature while other races were still barbarians, living in caves. Blacks were once great, and when we form an organized nation, we shall be great again.

Because Negroes receive an education that proclaims the superiority of the white race, protects its interests, and seeks their obedience, they must be given additional instruction—using textbooks that glorify the Negro. They must be taught Negro history, racial pride, and self-respect in their homes, schools, meeting halls, and clubs.

Instead of worshiping heroes of other races, we Negroes ought to canonize our own saints, venerate our martyrs, and honor black men and women who made heroic contributions to the history of our race such as Sojourner Truth, the greatest American Negro woman, Crispus Attucks, the first Negro to shed his blood in the war for American independence, and General Toussaint L'Ouverture, who on the plains of Santo Domingo liberated his country.

If it were not for the two million Negroes from Africa, the West Indies, and America who did force the Germans out of France and Belgium, the white men who fought on the side of the Allies would have lost everything they had.

As President of the UNIA, I appealed to the French people, whom we had defended in the war, to support our petition for justice at the Peace Conference. I asked for their intervention in helping to stop the violations of human rights in the United

States—the lynching and burning at the stake of Negro men, women, children.

We Negroes should not only imitate the useful activities of other races but strive to be creative so that we will be ready to withstand threats to our existence.

My principal goal has been to lead the Negro to become an independent person in every walk of life. The best of a race do not rely upon the patronage and philanthropy of others but endeavor to do for themselves. In several cities in the United States, I have seen successful commercial enterprises owned and managed by Negroes. In all activities that contribute to happiness, Negroes must develop self-reliance, and not blame others for their condition or simply hope to receive things that whites have purchased with their lives. Though some liberal whites share their possessions with Negroes, we do not have a guarantee that this generosity will continue.

The UNIA has not promoted hostility toward whites. We believe that all people, whatever their color, are creatures of God. We love all humanity. We are striving to achieve by our labor, skill, and genius what whites have achieved.

During the Great Depression, millions of Negroes had to depend on others, not to employ them but to give them food. What kind of charity is worse than this? Being fed without contributing to that food deprives a person of his manhood, character, and independence.

Negroes in Jamaica should not blame the government for their condition—the Home Authorities or the King—since their constitution has allowed them to organize to better their condition. They have to blame themselves.

The most effective way for Negroes to attain their freedom is to improve their economic condition. Wealth is power, and for them it will mean justice and human rights.

Negroes should not criticize anyone because of his wealth. Rich men have an obligation to fulfill. They provide work for us and thus are the props of our communities. They deserve our admiration, not our envy.

The only protection of a race, nation, or individual against injustice is power, not any petitions. Power has proven to be the supreme regulator of human nature. Mussolini, by his invasion of Abyssinia, which I denounced, provided a further demonstration of the role of power in life. Power controls the expressions of freedom, equality, and righteousness. Negroes must aim to attain power in politics, education, science, and industry. To fail to do this is to share the fate of the American Indian.

To adopt the fatalistic attitude that God has accorded each of us a position and condition, and that we should not attempt to change them is to hurl an insult at God Who has created everyone to be free, equal, and autonomous. We must shape our environment, be architects of our fate, and masters of our destiny.

When I reflect on the love, majesty, and omnipotence of God, I cannot believe that He did intend that 400 million of us be slaves, hewers of wood, and drawers of water. To think that we are inferior to another and to bow down to him is to offend God, Who has made us in His own image to reflect His greatness, be lords of His creation, and achieve what other men achieve. The Bible states, "He created of one blood all nations of man to dwell on the face of the earth" (*Acts* 17:26). I would prefer that all of us die rather than believe that God created us inferior to the white man.

We have been given life for a purpose—not to be slaves or serfs, but to be men. If, as a race, we are to be free, we have to live without any pleading, cringing, bowing, and scraping. We must continue to organize and utilize constitutional means to secure our rights.

Every person should have a specific purpose in life, work toward an achievement, and not waste his life on nonessential activities. A person without a definite purpose in life is better off dead.

In a 1921 editorial in the *Gleaner*, I did maintain that the people of Jamaica needed a religion that would prepare them for heaven not only by providing spiritual food but also by promoting the value of living clean, healthy, and prosperous lives. No person who is without adequate food, shelter, and clothing can think and act like a good Christian.

Because I advise Negroes on how to improve their physical condition, I serve as an effective example by living in decent conditions with access to culture rather than by living with a vow of poverty in a hut.

If I did not continue to proclaim racial righteousness, racial truth, racial honor, and racial self-respect, I would be untrue to my God, the faith of my fathers, and my conscience.

Religion has proven to be the most powerful civilizing and socializing force. Even though it has been abused, were it not for religion, the world would be populated with barbarians.

Only through belief in God can an individual live a rational life. Without faith and confidence in God, mankind would be reduced to savagery and be destroyed.

It is absurd for man to try to analyze why God does or does not do something. Limited human intelligence cannot grasp the intentions of the Universal Intelligence. Because of the finite nature of man's mind, there will always be mysteries he cannot explain.

Christian teachers caused the enslaved people of Jamaica to begin to realize that they were similar to their masters and to claim affinity with God. In the face of opposition from the planters, their mission was to liberate people—their bodies as well as their souls.

When we Negroes pray, what should we ask God for? Not for material benefits but for the wisdom, moral courage, and strength that empower us to care for ourselves.

We are all created as human beings, and therefore, external accidental differences are not important. Since all of us share a common human destiny, there should be no estrangement between any races or groups.

Just because a white man declares that he wishes to be my brother, I do not automatically accept him. He has to manifest to me how much of a brother he really is before I accept his brotherhood. In heaven, we can all be brothers in Christ.

I have no grudge against whites. I love them but I love my own people more. The white race does not need to fear us. We will be as charitable and merciful toward whites as we have been for more than 500 years. Through our accomplishments, we want to demonstrate the emptiness of their claim to racial superiority.

With all of their peace conferences, do the statesmen of the world truly understand the meaning of peace? Real peace is motivated by a love that Jesus came to give us—love for all, the high and the mighty as well as the meek and the lowly.

Much racial discrimination has been due to the failure of the majority of Christians to comprehend and practice Jesus' message of universal love.

Many educated Negroes have withdrawn from the masses of their people who are backward and require conscientious leadership. This prejudice has been partly responsible for an indifference to the Negro race from other races that preserve their ties to their own people, whatever their position.

Negroes should add to their good qualities through loving themselves and all other Negroes. They ought to be mindful that they are all members of one family and be more loyal and respectful to each other. Together, they should strive to reach the highest standard of civilized culture.

Because government is so sacred, it should be entrusted only to those who are morally clean and righteous.

I did praise President Franklin Delano Roosevelt in several editorials in the *Black Man* for his honesty, his New Deal policies and programs, his appointments of Negroes to high administrative positions, and his support of benefits to war veterans, but I challenged his refusal to extend civil rights to Negroes. I did endorse him for a second term.

If the Negro is allowed to have fifty years of freedom, he will demonstrate to the world that he is the most liberal and charitable of God's creatures and will teach the white man the way to justice and mercy.

My enemies, particularly those within my own race who have resented my success, distorted my positions on several issues for the press. The UNIA does not disseminate hatred or foster racial antagonism.

While I am a Christian and the UNIA accepts Christ as its spiritual leader, I do believe in "an eye for an eye and a tooth for a tooth." I will dispense mercy to the other fellow who has injured me only after I get even with him. I want him to feel what I felt.

Because my main concern is the freedom of the Negro, no person or thing has the power to intimidate me. I fear neither jail nor death. God is the only one I fear. I identify with the noble advice of Theodore Roosevelt, "Fear God, and you have no need for fear."

The UNIA has rendered more service to the Negro than the combination of the efforts of all other Negro organizations in the last hundred years. It has endowed the Negro with new courage, self-assertion, self-determination, independence, a consciousness of race pride, a program of racial nationalism, the motivation to resist discrimination, an improvement of his economic status, and training in the use of political power. The UNIA has planted the seed of black nationalism and has awakened Negroes in all of Africa with its slogan, "Africa for the Africans, at home and abroad." Under pressure from the UNIA, some European governments with colonies did grant more privileges to Negroes—including employment in the civil service.

I have been incarcerated not because I have committed any crime against society or defrauded anyone but because I have led the Movement to redeem Africa. Before God, I can match my character against the character of any person in the world. I have chosen to retain the honor and cleanliness of my soul rather than seek approbation from the agents of injustice and corruption. May the Lord have mercy on their souls!

THE POWER OF THE NEGATIVE

In Jamaica's western parishes in 1831, the Negro slaves revolted and damaged the properties of their masters. The militia ended the revolt, maiming and executing many of the slaves. Yet, the revolt did inspire prominent members of the British Parliament and the British press to champion the cause of the slaves. On August 1, 1838, the slaves in Jamaica were declared free.

Having been annoyed at being the object of prejudice from my early youth and having witnessed injustices to Negroes in Jamaica, the West Indies, South and Central America, and Europe, I decided in London in 1914 to become a race leader. When I returned to Jamaica, I organized the UNIA and the ACL within a week. To end the injustices, I believed that our race had to unify itself through a world organization and create a great nation.

Reading Booker T. Washington's *Up From Slavery* helped me decide to become a race leader. Although my aims were more comprehensive than his, I admired him because he could triumph over many obstacles, never forgot the less fortunate of the Negro race, and did his best to assist them. Without the contributions of such a man—race leader, scholar, educator, orator, and philanthropist—American Negroes would have shared the fate of American Indians.

When we began the UNIA, some of our friends suggested that we were trying to do the impossible—unifying Negroes throughout the world and obtaining the necessary financial support. But such advice only motivated us to generate more determination to succeed.

Why should "Universal" be in the title of our organization? Reports I received about the pitiable conditions of native life in Africa were so horrifying that I concluded the name of the organization should refer to all blacks. The oppression of the Negro is universal. I want freedom for Negroes everywhere.

We are not going to be granted our rights just because we ask for them. Human nature is overly selfish. We must expect to experience all kinds of opposition. If we are to attain our rights, it will require our toil and struggle. This is the reason why we initated the Black Star Line and the Negro Factories Corporation.

A genuine leader belongs to the shock battalion. He has a personality that enables him to capture the attention of men by his shocking words and actions.

Leadership means the willingness to give up everything for the cause. Those who aspire to be leaders must become poor so that they can interpret the desires of the poor. They must prepare themselves to endure the ingratitude of those whom they will serve.

Whenever a Negro is harmed, I feel as if I am harmed. I have suffered for my race and will continue to suffer. When I recall the sacrifices Eugene Debs and Robert Emmett made, there is no sacrifice I will not make for 400 million Negroes. No matter what tactics my opponents use, I will not stop until we secure our rights.

The United States Constitution does allow us to participate in political agitation. It affirms the right of public assembly and the right to protest.

When an African anywhere is deprived of his land or the privileges of citizenship by a law, he should disobey any such unjust and immoral law. Neither should he respect any other immoral law that discriminates against him because of color. Such disrespect is a condition of our emancipation.

Jesus died to make men free. I am ready to die in defense of our rights and to inspire courage in my race. Even if I am crushed by the system, the cause will remain to challenge the conscience of the corrupt.

At the beginning of our Movement, a man from my town in Jamaica was extremely critical of me. Because the consensus of public opinion approved of my work, his outrageous and wicked attack caused the UNIA to be even more prominent and helped me to distinguish the friends of the cause from its enemies.

My objective has not been the acquisition of money. My many financial sacrifices for the cause indicate my priorities. My legacy to my sons will not be material possessions. I will leave them only my joyful service of our race that can ensure the quality of their future.

Should our race be blocked from reaching the heights those above us have achieved, then we will pull them down and let them sit where we are. If, however, they do what is right and not allow us to remain in disease and hunger, then we will push them up as we climb.

In order to make the UNIA more effective, I left Jamaica in 1916 for the United States. I had inferred that Negroes in Jamaica continued to think in terms of the customs and ideas of their former slave masters and hence were not sufficiently racially conscious. In contrast, American Negroes, because they had been subjected to organized racial prejudice, were compelled to develop a rare racial consciousness.

It has been painful to me to witness the "Jim Crow" system and to hear about the lynchings but if it were not for these evils, the Negro would still be unaware of his real situation. The Southern white man made the Negro aware of the malice of racial prejudice. When the blacks in Africa and the West Indies learned of the lynching of Negroes in America, they became conscious of race and class.

Who is doing the most to organize Negroes for the UNIA? It is not I. It is those who oppress Negroes. The best means to weaken my Movement and me is to strive to establish justice for Negroes everywhere.

Because England granted freedom to Negroes in Jamaica and she was fighting to conquer the tyrants of Europe and to restore the peace, I declared that Negroes should support her in the World War and regard it as an honor to die for such a noble cause.

In the World War, when the British rejected a large number of the West Indian Negroes who wanted to be officers in the army, they, in effect, helped many Negroes become aware of the reasonableness of our program. The propaganda developed by these West Indians supplemented our program.

Because we Negroes have been deprived of the privileges of democracy we have fought for so nobly in the war, we will organize our 400 million to create our democracy in Africa. If the white man, our fellow-citizen, claims that the United States is his country by force of numbers, and therefore, that we are not entitled to opportunities he enjoys, then we have to form our own country.

The war helped to transform the consciousness of Negroes by making them determined that, after the sacrifice of their sons and brothers in France, they would no longer tolerate the unsafe conditions in the South or be satisfied with the poor economic conditions in the West Indies.

In 1919, I maintained that millions of Negroes could have died in the war for the salvation of the white race and that the next time we fight and die, it should be for our emancipation. How glorious it will be to be martyrs for the liberation of the race!

The suffering of my persecuted ancestors over 300 years in the Western Hemisphere shall continue to be my inspiration in the struggle for freedom in Africa. The more I remember the lynchings and burnings in the South, the more I will fight on, despite the obstacles.

In my office in 1919, George Tyler shot me four times. One bullet grazed my forehead and the other three hit my legs. Tyler was sent by enemies of the UNIA because I had been responsible for some politicians losing their jobs. The shooting enhanced my motivation to continue my work and even increased the sales of stock in the Black Star Line 2,000 percent.

In January 1919, the legislature of British Honduras voted to ban the circulation of our newspaper, the *Negro World*, in the colony, where 500 copies had been distributed weekly. In their response to this suppression of information about Negro progress, the Negroes in Belize, British Honduras, organized a branch of the UNIA. In April 1920, the branch had more than 8,000 members.

The death of Terence MacSwinney, the lord mayor of Cork, in 1920 as a result of a hunger strike, did more to promote the freedom of Ireland than probably anything they did for 500 years. Death is the price of liberty. Even as the Irish have their thousands of martyrs, so too Negroes must be prepared to give their lives for the freedom of their race.

If my radicalism can free Africa, I am content to be called a "radical." Jesus Christ was the greatest radical in history. His message challenged a world of sin.

The National Association for the Advancement of Colored People (NAACP) received additional financial support from whites because of my presence in the United States. It was able to warn whites that if they did not support the moderate NAACP, they would have to deal with the extreme UNIA and its radical leader.

Some preachers recommend that we go easy on those who control twelve million square miles of our land. Because the Allies believed that their cause was righteous, they decided not to go easy on Kaiser Wilhelm II. If they had, he would be in Buckingham Palace.

At a UNIA convention, we decided that our flag would be red, black, and green. Red represents the blood that has to be shed for our redemption and freedom. Black is the color of our noble race. Green is the color of the luxuriant vegetation of our Motherland.

In 1920, even when the leaders of the European nations, encouraged by their deliberations in the League of Nations, predicted peace, I did warn that an even bloodier war would erupt between the forces of Europe, led by England or France, and the peoples of Asia, led by Japan. We Negroes will use that conflict to strengthen our republic in Africa by assisting the side that supports our cause.

The exigencies of war and the devotion of Negroes to the cause of the redemption of Africa might make it possible in my grandchildren's day to observe the formation of the United States of Africa.

At our 1920 UNIA convention, I indicated that, after three centuries of separation, it was our common suffering which brought together our delegates from the Western Hemisphere, Africa, and every other country. We had to unite morally and financially so that we could work to eliminate the injustices still holding us in slavery.

At that convention, I explained that we would develop the language for our Bill of Rights by focusing on the centuries of our sufferings. My judgment was that we had to use very forceful language when we formulated the declaration of our freedom.

The UNIA rejected the Pan-African Congress because it fostered race suicide with its campaign of miscegenation. We are convinced that the black race and the white race should each maintain its purity.

We did not allow whites to share in the leadership of the UNIA, be members or attend any of our business meetings. Neither would we cooperate with any white organization nor with any Negro organization where whites were represented. The Negro must not become obligated to any race.

In 1921, the native leaders of Jamaica did not possess the courage to challenge those harming the country. Real leaders, in the service of their country and the cause of humanity, are not concerned about whom they might offend by their words and deeds. Jesus spoke the truth no matter who was offended.

At our 1921 convention, I cautioned our executive officers that if any of them were dishonest, I would expose them, and I did. My primary obligation has been to fulfill my duty to God, the UNIA, and the people—not to protect friends or relatives. After they were jailed, I would try to assist them.

Dr. W.E.B. Du Bois's criticisms of my business procedures

and my rhetoric reached Chicago before my visit in 1921 and actually helped our Movement. I believe that it was because of these criticisms that the Chicago division of the UNIA did receive 500 new members.

The million dollars we lost when our enterprises failed was but a small fraction of the value of the lessons we derived from these failures. Our past mistakes can make us and other race leaders more efficient in new ventures.

My opponents thought that they had disposed of me when I was sent to prison. Still, my imprisonment did increase the momentum of our Movement 1,000 percent and publicized it throughout the world.

Prior to my imprisonment, my work in the Movement did not allow me time to use my library of 18,000 books. But in prison for nearly two years and ten months, I had access to 2,000 books and ample time to read, reflect, and prepare myself.

Because my enemies were fearful lest I would appeal to the American conscience, I was deported in 1927 from the United States to Jamaica. But the deportation inspired me to be more willing to present our cause to the bar of international justice.

For more than ten years, I had been away from Jamaica, but all that time, my painful memories of the prevalence of poverty and disease there caused me to work hard for blacks not only in the West Indies but in America and Africa.

In Jamaica, I explained that I had not changed my beliefs. They had been rooted in a horrible experience—a racial, not a personal experience. The world had made being black a crime but I hoped to make the world regard being black as a virtue.

As I stated in Royal Albert Hall in London in 1928, because the Britons had been slaves to the Romans, they had become a sturdy race and had developed the determination never to be slaves again. Like the Britons, Negroes wish to possess their own country, Africa.

The disloyalty of my associates blocked me from executing the aims of the UNIA, and therefore, I retired so that another could better manage it. When my successor demonstrated his inability to implement these aims, the members requested that I once more become the leader. I then resumed my duties with a Bismarkian determination.

In 1932, why did we start *The New Jamaican* in Kingston? Jamaica was so very deficient economically, politically, and socially. We launched the paper to help establish a standard of decency in the country and to promote a spirit of cooperation and comradeship among all classes.

The French did not make adequate preparations to confront their enemy. This weakness caused them to be courteous and hospitable toward blacks since they depended principally on their colonial empire, mainly in Africa, for assistance in times of trouble.

Forced by the Allies, the Kaiser had to abandon his vision of a central colonial empire in Africa. His defeat in the war allowed the renewed Negro to develop a vision not only of a central Africa for Africans but of a united Africa for Africans of the world.

Because we in the UNIA have believed that, at any time, hostile forces can destroy any advancement by Negroes in this Western alien civilization, we seek to build a nation in Africa powerful enough to protect Negroes wherever we are.

The Pilgrim Fathers and the early settlers suffered, bled, and died in order to realize their vision of liberty. They began the transformation of a vast wilderness into a great country. What they did and what we helped their descendants do, we can do for ourselves by transforming the wilderness of Africa into a great country.

As Negroes display their increasing ambition, whites will clash with them within a century unless Negroes have their own nation. There are some well-intentioned whites who will want to prevent this clash by helping us form our nation.

In 1936, I contended that the experience of the Jews had provided a good object lesson for the Negro. To secure the power to protect themselves, the Jews were very efficient in acquiring wealth, but their wealth provoked envy and caused their victimization. Recently, they have concentrated also on establishing a nation that could protect them. The Negroes of the world should work to acquire wealth but they should use a part of it to establish a nation in Africa to protect them.

In explaining the new spirit of the UNIA, I asserted that if the Negro is to progress, he must learn to compromise and not be too aggressive. The Negro does not administer his economic existence, and therefore, he has to make concessions to those who do.

Like other nations, we Negroes will have to struggle for our freedom. We must be prepared to die, if necessary, in a war against whites on the African plains so that we can prevent our extermination and achieve complete independence. War is the only means to secure salvation. We have to recall the words of Patrick Henry in the Virginia legislature, "I care not what others may say; but as for me, give me liberty or give me death."

The Japanese earned new respect as a result of their war with the Russians. When Negroes can teach some nation on the battlefields of Africa as the Japanese taught the Russians, there will be an end to the burning and lynching of Negroes in all parts of the world.

The Fathers of the Church, in pursuing their mission, had to endure sufferings, and there were many martyrs. We also are involved in saving souls, and our race must be willing to make sacrifices.

When more Negroes comprehend that every attack on me has been an attack on them as well, then these attacks will compel them to realize that the time has come for racial pride, cooperation, and emancipation. To the extent that the attacks have this effect, I am grateful for them.

If there were no propaganda opposing the UNIA, I would be embarrassed and judge my work as not significant enough to provoke opposing views. I would infer that I was fighting an unnecessary battle. The opposition is one more indication of our progress.

My enemies have attacked me because I have labored to

liberate the black race. Through their condemnations of me and actions against me, they have tried to discourage Negroes from seeking to help themselves. But we should understand that our trials and difficulties are only tests of our worthiness to fulfill our destiny.

I find it annoying when I am defeated. In one defeat I find a reason to wage a persistent struggle to reach the top.

What is the cause of my success? Opposition. Oppose me and I will intensify my efforts.

Our Movement has had its numerous opponents—officials of the United States, foreign governments, local politicians, members of the press, and even some Negroes because they have not been able to profit from it personally. Given all this opposition, shouldn't we devote ourselves completely to the noble cause of the UNIA?

Because Negroes have been forced to experience so many severe hardships, they are among those who possess the best understanding of human nature. Their suffering has equipped them for human sympathy that will make them better rulers than those who have had lives devoid of misfortune.

Jesus triumphed through His sufferings and resurrection, and we Negroes hope that we also will triumph through our sufferings and the resurrection of our race—embracing higher ideals, a nobler purpose, and a truer conception of life.

4

W.E.B. DU BOIS

I regard as sacred the obligation to seek the truth, whatever it might be, and no person will prevent me from fulfilling this obligation.

As creatures of God, all men are brothers. We all possess a soul, do not differ in any essential feature, and are capable of infinite development. Religion and science affirm the basic equality of the Negro race with other races and hence its right to just treatment.

Jesus, the Prince of Peace, preached the ideals of justice, love, peace, and poverty whereas the white power structure in our nation, even though it professes to be Christian, engages in exploitation, racial hatred, war, and imperialism.

The devil and his evil spirits do exist and loathe the image of God in human beings. These demons believe the worst and work to produce it by limiting the opportunities of those who strive and by striking those who cannot strike back.

What kind of independence were white Americans seeking in 1776? Even though they were proclaiming the equality of all men, they held 500,000 slaves, whom they classified as real estate. After using 5,000 blacks to win the war, they then continued their exploitation of them.

John Brown, immersed in Biblical religion with its stress on personal responsibility to God and in the social doctrines of the French Revolution, could not endure the oppression of Negroes. He proved that he loved his neighbor as himself.

The real cause of the Civil War was slavery, and we should not evade this fact by referring to the "Union" and "States." There can be no doubt about the cause of the war if one reads the *Congressional Globe* from 1850 to 1860, the biographies of Northern and Southern statesmen and other public figures, the discourses in the newspapers and the accounts of meetings and speeches.

I did admire President Abraham Lincoln, but in a letter to Horace Greeley in 1862 he explained that his main goal in the war was to save the Union and that if he could save it without freeing any slaves, he would do it, that if he could save it by freeing all the slaves, he would do it, and that if he could save it by freeing only some of the slaves, he would do it.

The decisive actions which ended the Civil War were the emancipation and arming of black slaves. This became evident from the debates in Congress. Lincoln acknowledged that the war could not have been won without the military help of the black freedmen. They provided 200,000 soldiers, who fought in about 200 battles and skirmishes, and also at least 300,000 laborers and helpers.

The Freedmen's Bureau, created in 1865 to assist former slaves, had failures and successes. It was unable to promote good relations between the freedmen and their ex-masters, to use efficient methods, free from paternalism, and to fulfill many of its promises to provide the freedmen with land. But the Bureau created a system of free labor, initiated peasant proprietorship, obtained recognition for the black freedmen in courts, and established the free common school in the South.

White historians have attributed the faults and failures of Reconstruction to Negro ignorance and corruption. But what restored the South to the Union and formed a new democracy for whites and blacks? It was the loyalty of Negroes and their vote.

If the social conditions of the majority of Negroes were not inferior, it would be a miracle. Sickness and crime are the inevitable consequences of a heritage of 240 years of chattel slavery, present poverty, unjust wages, and ignorance.

What is the problem of the twentieth century? At the first Pan-African Conference in 1900, I maintained that it would be the problem of the color line. To what extent would racial differences be used to deprive the majority of human beings of the right to develop their abilities and to participate in the opportunities and privileges of modern civilization?

To those who complain that Negroes ought to perform their duties before clamoring for rights, we respond that the rights we seek are necessary to enable us to perform our duties.

Our Niagara Movement was founded in 1905 to advocate freedom of speech and the press, manhood suffrage, and the abolition of all caste distinctions based on race and color. It affirmed the principle of human brotherhood and the dignity of labor.

Our National Association for the Advancement of Colored People (NAACP) was established in 1909 with whites on the board of directors. Designed to fight for political, economic, civil, and social Negro rights, it campaigned against lynching and mob law and achieved a series of victories in the courts, especially against residential segregation.

At the 1909 National Negro Conference in New York City, I affirmed that the Fifteenth Amendment was a demonstration of foresight because the black voters of the South created the public schools, gave the ballot to poor whites, modernized the penal code, and helped produce many of our current laws.

After Booker T. Washington died, I referred to him as the greatest Negro leader since Frederick Douglass. He motivated Negroes to accumulate property, established Tuskegee Institute and encouraged the spread of industrial education.

Booker T. Washington made a noble effort to turn Negro artisans into businessmen and property owners. Still, in the face of competition, they could not defend their rights if they did not have the right to vote. He emphasized self-respect and thrift but did propose a silent submission to civic inferiority that could only emasculate the Negro. He defended the value of common school and industrial training but depreciated the institutions of higher learning. However, the former, including Tuskegee Institute, could not function if the teachers were not trained in Negro colleges or trained by their graduates.

His program had significant undesirable consequences. It served to promote the Negro's disfranchisement, the creation of a distinct legal status of civic inferiority for the Negro, and the steady withdrawal of aid from institutions for the higher education of the Negro.

Methods for generating, managing, and distributing wealth serve the oligarchy in control rather than the common good. The industries should and will be reorganized in order that the people will own and control the means of production as well as benefit from the equality of adequate income. The Negro in America will achieve freedom through socialism.

To improve the relations between the races, Negroes must work to overcome the evils of immorality, crime, and laziness in their communities—a heritage of slavery—and whites must become impartial in their judgments of ability and have a greater respect for the liberty and dignity of every individual.

Negroes do have the principal responsibility for their own social regeneration. Nevertheless, if this responsibility is not to be a mockery, whites must encourage this regeneration and remove the obstacles to it, especially in education, work, and political activity.

How can our nation discourage lawlessness when it has so often disregarded the Thirteenth, Fourteenth, and Fifteenth Amendments, and the legal system has been used mainly not to protect the rights of the Negro but to oppress and humiliate him?

Real education aims not only to produce breadwinners but, more importantly, to develop persons with integrity who are committed to eminent ethical ideals and possess a capacity to appreciate the higher spiritual life. Training a man only to earn a living is not educating him. Industrial schools require broadly educated teachers who can teach manual dexterity but can also foster mental discipline and moral habits.

The "Talented Tenth" among Negroes must receive special training so that, through prolonged study and reflection, they could cultivate their potential for the intellectual leadership, inspiration, and salvation of the rest of the race. We should also aim to arrange that all other children assimilate as much education as their abilities and conditions allow.

As we struggle to obtain laws against segregation, we have to invest even more energy and resources into improving the Negro elementary school so that it truly educates students and does not prepare them to be only laborers and servants. To the extent we are not willing to do this, our high schools will be ineffectual and our university endowments will be wasted.

The Negro college must preserve the standards of popular education, promote the social regeneration of students, foster interracial contact and cooperation, and develop men who are able to share the treasures of their inner life and contribute new perspectives to the world.

An educated Negro who chooses not to communicate with whites becomes provincial in his judgments and attributes to whites a conscious racial prejudice and hatred many of them do not have.

The government must lead in the battle against illiteracy. Education must become a compulsory discipline for everyone at public expense. Unless the government conquers ignorance through its support and transformation of schools, ignorance will destroy the United States.

The choice is evident. Pay for good schools and teachers or pay ten times this amount for police, jails, and courts to deal with the young people who are neglected as children, left in ignorance, imprisoned, and hung before they are thirty.

America is facing decadence unless it succeeds in teaching our children how to behave as human beings. In order to send them a moral message, America has to stop lying and calling it "advertising," stealing and attempting to justify it as "free enterprise," and killing in the name of "national defense."

Who have emerged as the worst opponents of Negroes? Our compromising "friends" who are satisfied if we receive less than half a loaf. When the South objects to the desire of these "friends" for Negro education, they no longer call for Negro colleges, but for high schools. Under pressure, they do not call for the literary training of Negroes but for industrial training that is so limited as to allow for the training of most Negroes as servants and field hands. These "friends" permit the South to claim that it will protect the civil rights of the Negro even as it denies him the vote.

I was convinced that ignorance and deliberate ill-will were the causes of the race prejudice of whites and that when the truth would be presented to them, their prejudice would melt away. However, I have come to realize that their race prejudice has been consciously and subconsciously developed mainly to protect their wealth and power.

My study of psychology occurred before the Freudian era but it prepared me for Freud's interpretations. In the light of his theory, I was able to view race prejudice not simply as a rational conscious determination by whites but as involving also irrational and unconscious drives and habits. I concluded that we would need patience to wait as well as power in order to sustain ourselves in a long siege.

The chief cause of World War I was an avaricious struggle among the imperial powers over how they would distribute among themselves territories, raw materials, and the cheap labor of millions in Africa and Asia. Permanent peace could have been possible only if the principle of government by the consent of the governed had been extended to the natives of Africa, Asia, and the West Indies, and to American Negroes.

I take pride in the black blood that flows in my veins and regard myself as an African by race. I treasure the beauty of the genius of my race, its spirituality, and the strength of its meekness that shall inherit the earth. My racial sentiment has played a prominent role in my life and in the formation of my character.

American Negroes can discern some of the causes of their predicament if they compare their struggle against oppression with the struggles in Africa, Asia, Central America, South America, and the Union of South Africa against the forces of imperialism, capitalism, and colonialism.

Our Pan-African Movement emphasizes several principles: Negroes everywhere have the right to participate in their own governments; their native rights to the land and the natural resources should be recognized; all civilized persons must be treated as civilized; and children deserve a modern education. The Movement also maintains that Africa must be developed for Africans, and that industries there and elsewhere have to be restructured to serve the welfare of the many rather than to enrich the few.

I helped to organize Pan-African Congresses in 1919, 1921, 1923, and 1927 to encourage concerted action among colored groups on an international basis. The effective development of this Movement was diminished whenever it was confused with Garvey's Movement and its shortcomings.

Marcus Garvey, an extraordinary leader of one of the most interesting spiritual movements, was idealistic, determined, sincere, and unselfish. Unfortunately, he did not possess the knowledge needed for success in his business ventures.

In a 1930 commencement address at Howard University, I extolled certain ideals that should be directing the progress of the nation: the ideal of a simple healthy life with an income that corresponds to one's real needs, the ideal of hard work in a worthwhile endeavor, the ideal of the vigorous pursuit of knowledge, and the ideal of sacrifice of personal comfort for a noble cause. I have derived inspiration from the thought that the work I have done well will justify my life.

In 1934, I resigned from the NAACP board of directors and was no longer the editor of its official journal, *The Crisis*. I had become impatient with the lengthy procedure of attacking discrimination through the courts and became convinced that Negroes should strive to accumulate economic and political power through self-segregation and socialism.

A craving for colonies was the main cause of World War II. The determination of Italy to embark upon an imperial career in Africa precipitated the conflict. Germany wanted the return of her colonies as well as new ones.

Living with the consequences of slavery and the pressures of economic competition and native prejudice, we Negroes have to trust in our abilities, believe in our great destiny, and rely on ourselves.

To increase our power and self-confidence, we Negroes must train ourselves to cooperate more effectively with each other as producers, consumers, teachers, and voters.

Among all the instruments that are indispensable to human progress, the ballot might be the greatest. In our competitive society, the workers and property owners cannot defend their rights without the ballot. We ought to try to use the power of the ballot to equalize wealth through taxation and to place the power of the state in the hands of the workers.

The government must increase substantially the number of citizens who can vote. It ought not view these possible voters as the sharers of a limited treasure but as sources of wisdom and strength.

Because of an illegal and a systematic disfranchisement, a minority can outvote a majority of voters. Senator Eastland of Mississippi, who represented less than 150,000 voters, was even more powerful in the Senate than Senator Lehman of New York, who represented five million voters.

Popular education and universal suffrage are important for emancipation, but even more crucial than these rights is the way in which the labor of human beings is organized to meet their needs. All other questions of political power, education, and happiness depend on how we respond to this economic issue.

The government should function not for the benefit of an aristocracy but for the people. Industries should enhance not the wealth of the owners but the welfare of the workers.

Negroes must not succumb to a temptation to abandon the quest for truth, beauty, goodness and freedom in favor of the acquisition of wealth. What a spiritual tragedy when a person seeks and thinks that he or she finds the ultimate meaning of life in the deification of the means of living!

In determining the prosperity of any country, one should not consider the number of its millionaires, but whether it has eliminated poverty, attained a prevalence of health, produced effective public schools, and has a significant number of its citizens who read worthwhile books.

In order to fulfill his vocation in a civilized nation, a man must not only know the technique of his work but understand his essential duties as a father, citizen, voter, maker of public opinion, conserver of public health, and one who subscribes to moral customs and can value some of the higher spiritual life of the world.

The United Nations, established to eliminate wars, is also the greatest source of our hope for abolishing colonialism and poverty. American Negroes should persist in petitioning the United Nations to challenge the denials of our human rights.

Because of the techniques of production and transportation and the earth's abundance, every human being in the world could have sufficient food, clothing, shelter, education, and health care if many would not still demand excessive profits or high wages while others starve.

Every man in a civilized society participates in the colonial system. The conveniences and luxuries that he enjoys depend upon the degradation of the majority of men—colonial and quasi-colonial workers who are kept in ignorance so that they will not revolt.

In 1946, I affirmed that the South should be regarded as the firing line of a great crusade for the emancipation not only of the American Negro but also of the Negroes of Africa and the West Indies, and the colored races as well as the white slaves of capitalistic monopolies. Workers, blacks and whites, had to come to realize that their cooperation was necessary for their emancipation.

During the Montgomery Bus Boycott, I sent a message of my support to Dr. King. In a 1958 symposium on socialism, I asserted that after stopping discrimination against bus riders, the next objective of the Negro Church should be that they be allowed to earn a decent living.

I reject violence, except for self-defense. War is worse than hell and seldom leads to any real progress. Violence is not the only means to produce an economic revolution. It would be nonsensical for Negroes to attempt to use violence to achieve a reform of the state.

While I was chairman of the Peace Information Center, the government could not confirm in court its allegation that the Center was an unregistered agent of a foreign organization, the Committee of the World Congress of the Defenders of Peace and its successor, the World Peace Council.

Friends and strangers who stood for principle helped me in my defense. Nevertheless, my trial demonstrated that freedom of speech could be assaulted. Leaders of religions, presidents of the great universities, and most of the prominent scientists did not say a word to protest this assault. There is no greater threat to our civilization than such a silence.

Our greatest cause, next to the peace movement and the struggle against racism, is the emancipation of women. Given all their accomplishments despite the prejudices they face, it is inconceivable that any reasonable person could refer to the "weaker sex." Women require the ballot to correct the world that brutally neglects their rights and the rights of children.

I can forgive the white South for its slavery and fighting a war to perpetuate this evil as well as for its racial pride and strutting. Nevertheless, in this world and the next, I will never forgive its persistent degradation of black womanhood. Negro women fulfill a significant role in determining the destiny of their race.

Americans should have the right to vote on crucial matters such as education, racial bias, unfair taxation, flood control, universal military service, the expenditure of more than half of our income on war, the war in Korea, and the maintenance of 100 military bases all over the world.

In national elections, we do not have a real choice because the two parties are not different from each other. All of the candidates—whether it is Eisenhower or Taft, Kefauver or Stassen or Warren, Dulles or Dewey—follow the commands of their masters, the powerful corporations which govern the media and oppress the worker.

My travel was crucial to my intellectual development. My journeys to Europe, Africa, China, and Russia provided me with a depth of knowledge which proved to be invaluable for judging modern conditions, especially the problem of race in America.

Although I have not believed in Karl Marx's dogma of the necessity of revolution to transform the economic order, I have accepted his thesis that economic forces determine the development of religion, literature, and the basic patterns of culture. In my ninety-third year, before moving to Ghana, I joined the Communist Party of the United States.

The history of America refutes the assumption that only a small group of exceptional men can be responsible for the significant changes in the world. This history indicates that contributions to civilization can be made by educated persons from the ranks of peasants, laborers, and servants.

Negroes must strive for a society that extols equality of opportunity. Even though their means is race solidarity, their ultimate goal should be a united humanity that respects the liberty and dignity of every person, regardless of race.

Would America be America without the gifts of her Negro people—their spirit, songs, military service, contributions of labor to her economic empire, and warnings about the need for justice? By their genius and spiritual strength, Negroes enhance humanity as no other race can.

THE POWER OF THE NEGATIVE

In my birthplace, Great Barrington, Massachusetts, the people were quite restrained in their speech and expressions of their emotions. This type of conditioning and my numerous perceptions of real or imagined discriminations caused me to withdraw into myself. These withdrawals, however, probably allowed for the expansion of my inner life.

Because my mother's income was inadequate, I was eager to supplement this income by a series of jobs as I entered high school. I came to believe that all who were prepared to work could earn a living and that poverty indicated sloth and a lack of thrift.

My African racial feeling, a critical influence on my life and character, derived from the culture of my mother's people and developed through my studies, my experiences at Fisk University, and my evaluations of the assumptions of whites.

I studied philosophy at Fisk University and also in my first year at Harvard University. Dr. William James, a professor of psychology, advised me that if I had to study philosophy, I would, but if I could turn to something else, I should because it would be difficult to earn a living with philosophy. Due to his advice, I turned to the study of history, economics, and social problems.

As a college student, I learned about the recurrent horror of lynching. From 1885 to 1894, 1700 Negroes were lynched in the United States. Each death scarred my soul and did cause me to consider the plight of other minority groups, such as the Italians, lynched in New Orleans; the Chinese, targets of riots in the West; and the Jews, victims of pogroms in Russia.

During my years at Fisk University, Harvard University, and the University of Berlin, I would have conformed to the prevailing ideas of the social trends and would have regarded all protests and upheavals as but the frictions necessary for all advances were it not for the problems of racial and cultural contacts. I would have readily worshiped at the shrines of the social order and economic expansion if the race problem had not early enveloped me.

When I was a member of the faculty of the University of Pennsylvania, I concluded that the world had made incorrect judgments about race because of ignorance but that scientific study could remedy this ignorance. Knowing that the Negro problem could be the object of a systematic investigation, I initiated a thorough study of the Philadelphia Negro. After the completion of that study, I announced my plan to explore the entire Negro problem in the United States.

In my New Year's resolutions, published in *The Crisis* in 1912, I referred to my intention to defend the divine right of the Negro race to equal and just treatment and to utilize my writings, money, and actions to oppose the crime of lynching, the "Jim Crow" legislation, all forms of racial discrimination, the disfranchisement for race or sex, the evil of war, and the inequitable distribution of work and wealth. I resolved to defend the poor of every race, and I continue to be willing to wage this struggle even if it costs me pain, poverty, slander, and my life.

President Wilson's first Congress introduced twenty bills proposing discriminatory legislation against Negroes such as advocating "Jim Crow" cars in the District of Columbia, racially segregating federal employees, barring Negroes from commissions in the army and navy, prohibiting intermarriage of Negroes and whites, and excluding all immigrants of Negro descent. Until that time, the NAACP did not have a definite program, but these congressional acts caused it to create an intense program of opposition to discrimination, segregation, and this proposed legislation.

Booker T. Washington demonstrated a singleness of vision and oneness with his age by the implementation of a program of industrial education, conciliation of the South and silence, submission, and adjustment on civil and political rights. But the program became a "Gospel of Work and Money" which almost ignored the higher aims of life. It seems as if Nature, to make men forceful, must make them narrow.

Oppression tends to generate a craving in the oppressed to oppress others. In 1914, I did argue that when Southern white women, who had been oppressed, obtained the franchise, they would zealously act to disfranchise the Negro. But I believed that Negroes, in the long run, could successfully secure their support because women would have experienced the injustice of disfranchisement.

The 1916 Amenia Conference in New York involved many Negroes of distinction who represented almost all phases of Negro thought. Because of the pressure of race hate, none of us could afford to be entirely uncompromising. Although we emphasized different methods, all of us wanted the Negro to vote, the laws enforced, and lynching abolished.

By the summer of 1916, because of the death of Booker T. Washington and the pressure of external forces, Negroes were forming a unity of thought and action. The increases in racial segregation, discrimination, and mob murder compelled us to realize that we had to stand together.

In a 1918 editorial in *The Crisis*, I appealed to Negroes to forget their special grievances about disfranchisement, "Jim Crow" cars, and other injustices and to fight for their country against the German power that meant the death of all their aspirations for equality, freedom, and democracy. But later I doubted the merits of this appeal. The passive resistance of twelve million Negroes to any war activity might have spared the world for blacks and whites.

In World War I, the United States Army did discriminate against Negro troops in a variety of ways. After receiving no instruction in artillery and engineering, Negroes were judged to be unsuited for them. They were not supplied with proper equipment and decent clothing. Court-martials were ordered for some trivial offenses. There were "Jim Crow" places of accommodation and amusement. A systematic effort to poison the French against them was unsuccessful. Instead of breaking their spirit, all these discriminations caused the Negro troops to develop a greater hatred for prejudice and filled them with a determination to fight for equality in America.

During World War I, the NAACP retreated from pursuing its major objectives so that it could attend to more immediate needs. It aimed to ensure that Negro draftees receive decent treatment in the encampments, that a reasonable proportion of them be sent to the front not as laborers but as armed soldiers, and that some become commissioned officers.

Before Marcus Garvey tried to organize the black peasants of the West Indies, they did not have an effective leader to express their spirit of protest. They had only the rudiments of education and few economic opportunities. Their grievances caused Garvey to develop his tremendous vision.

Garvey's plan for the redemption of Africa required that Negroes accumulate and minister substantial capital, organize industries, and interconnect all their centers by commercial enterprises. I regarded this plan as feasible but thought that its execution would take long years of self-sacrificing effort as well as all of the ability, knowledge, experience, and devotion in the Negro race.

The music of the Negro religion originated in the African forests and was adapted and enriched by the spiritual life of the slave. Subject to the law and whip, it became an authentic expression of a people's sorrow, despair, and hope.

The Negro Sorrow Songs—the message of the slave to the world—portrayed strife, fear, suffering, and death. Still, in addition to all their references to sorrow, they did express a faith and hope in the ultimate triumph of justice which would evaluate men by their souls and not by their skins.

Many forces are struggling for domination in the South. To praise the evils is just as wrong as to condemn the good. The South needs objective criticisms for the improvement of its white sons and daughters and for its healthy intellectual and moral development.

Attempts to suppress criticisms by honest opponents can be dangerous. Such attempts silence some of the best critics and even provoke others to engage in speech so intemperate as to lose listeners. The earnest criticisms of government officials by citizens and of other leaders by their followers constitute the soul and safeguard of democracy.

Humanity progresses with the help of those who shout ugly things to an ugly world about the disinherited and are willing to be immersed in the blood and dust of battle. With a perfect hatred, they hate oppression and will be heard. They make the world feel so much discomfort with the weight of its own evil that it attempts to reform and does improve.

A nation will not ascend and a social class will not advance without a bitter struggle, a soul-sickening battle with severe impediments—internal and external—such as only a few in the privileged classes can comprehend.

Negroes have a duty to seek every single political, social, and economic right that belongs to a freeborn American and to oppose the barbarism of segregation by voting where they may, and by being involved in ceaseless agitation, sacrifice, and work. Without this involvement, a Negro can fear that he is losing his soul.

Some of the friends of our cause advise us not to engage in agitation because they judge it to be negative and destructive. They do not see that even as pain alerts us to the presence of disease, so too agitation is necessary to inform citizens about the evil effects of race prejudice in order that remedies might be found.

In order to challenge race prejudice successfully, Negroes have to develop economic stability as well as a campaign of propaganda that is carefully planned, persistent, and patient since it has to contend not only with conscious racist attitudes and customs but with conditioned reflexes and subconscious reasoning which influence so many activities.

A more extensive and systematic use of the boycott could

arouse our fellow citizens from a false sense of security and appeal to their sense of justice.

In order to alert the world to race prejudice, we also have to publicize complaints of those Negroes who have suffered most from white attitudes and habits and from the wrongs they perpetrate.

Sam Hose, a Negro in central Georgia, killed his landlord in a wage dispute. To arouse the passions of the mob, he was charged also with the rape of the man's wife. I wrote a report for the newspaper, stating the facts in the case. When I heard that he had been lynched and his knuckles were on display at the grocery store, I suddenly realized that it was not possible for me to maintain a completely scientific detachment in such a South.

Relying on reason and truth, we should complain about evil conditions. This illustrates our optimism because we believe conditions can be improved. A crushing pessimism prevails when people refuse to complain because they do not see any possibility of improvement.

From 1918 to 1928, I was involved in a series of lectures, conferences, and expositions throughout the country. While the directors of the NAACP and my friends preferred that I concentrate on a few activities, I felt I had to participate in the worldwide revolution and to feel its scars in my soul.

In 1940, I acknowledged that Africa was very deficient in communication in terms of human contact, the movement of goods, and the dissemination of knowledge. But in the United States, we are smothered by goods from the rest of the world and overwhelmed by facts from the newspapers. I decided that one of the joys of the African bush was that it did provide an escape from the "news."

Though Africans, without access to scientific knowledge, were compelled to suffer from preventable diseases, hunger, and capricious weather, the isolation of their village life did allow them a deep knowledge of each other. While they knew fewer souls, they knew their neighbors far better than we in the

West know each other.

Why do I feel such an intense kinship with those of African descent? It is not so much because of the physical bond. The badge of color has an importance only as a badge. Rather, I feel this kinship since we share the social heritage of slavery and discrimination.

We Negroes can find sources of strength not only in shared ambitions and ideals and in our determination to demonstrate ability but in common recollections of past sufferings and in present experiences of degradation and threats of extinction.

Negroes possess a powerful hereditary cultural unity which derives from slavery and the restrictions and denials of rights. Their cultural gifts to America have arisen from this unity.

Who knows the suffering of a soul? Only the person who suffers. Despotisms and aristocracies have displayed immense ignorance about the needs of their citizens. The best judges of their own real needs have been the citizens. Only when the masses possess political and economic power, may that power be applied to seek to achieve the greatest good for the greatest number.

The increase in the number of Negro college graduates from 215 between 1876 and 1880 to 10,000 between 1931 and 1935 has been evidence of the superior degree of their moral strength to preserve their souls while being subjected to an almost universal disparagement and discrimination and to be eager to sacrifice for an ideal that might not be actualized by their generation.

Before my *Dusk of Dawn* was published in 1940, there had been almost no scientific study of the consequences of race intermixture. Given this willful neglect, I decided to describe in that book the manner in which Africa and Europe had been united in my own racial history by including an account of my white great-grandfather, Dr. James Du Bois.

In a 1927 *Crisis* editorial, though I affirmed the morality of interracial marriage, I warned it was not socially expedient.

The imperfections of individuals who have had a positive

impact on history and the obstacles they have had to confront do not diminish but increase the significance of all of their achievements. I especially revere Abraham Lincoln because he had to struggle through poverty and transcend an unethical political environment to be the noblest friend of the slave and perhaps the greatest figure of the nineteenth century.

Some Negroes believe that a protest is useless if it does not appear to have a reasonable chance for success. They do not understand that even an unsuccessful protest can proclaim the objectives of the protest to political opponents and also can have a positive effect upon the self-esteem of the protesters.

In 1934, I asserted that while we Negroes had to live with much segregation, it was necessary, at times, for us to decide to increase our separation from our fellowmen to secure our survival and to progress toward breaking down the barriers. The purpose of this self-segregation would be the eventual elimination of segregation.

In reacting to the unjust, stupid, wasteful, and dangerous system of segregation forced upon them, millions of Negroes have correctly chosen to segregate themselves by developing their own churches, colleges, and businesses. Through these institutions, they have demonstrated their efficiency, ability, and discipline and have thus provided a powerful argument for the abolition of the color line.

Whenever an expansion in self-segregation would benefit Negroes and could assist the struggle against oppression, I supported it. Therefore, I advocated group action by Negroes in elections, better teachers and additional funds for Negro schools as well as a segregated camp for the training of Negro officers in World War I.

Even while subject to segregation, we Negroes should use our reason to take advantage of it to organize our power as producers and consumers by establishing our own centers of cooperative effort—our own industrial system in conjunction with the national industrial system. With economic power, we could be spiritually free to become creative in other fields and ultimately, to end all segregation based on color.

In a 1946 conference sponsored by the Southern Negro Youth Congress, I told the black and white delegates that they were participating in a holy crusade to emancipate mankind, abolish race prejudice, and elevate democracy—a crusade involving great sacrifices and dangers.

My 1949 journey to the devastation of the Warsaw ghetto, where resistance to oppression did involve the sacrifice of so many lives, provoked me to revise my conception of the race problem. I then realized that prejudice influenced all sorts of people and that our struggle had to be expanded and directed against religious discrimination and plutocratic oppression as well as racial segregation.

With the sweat of the brow and sorrow of the soul, three laws form the foundation of the necessity of earning a living. The law of work requires that one must toil continuously in order to live. The law of sacrifice necessitates that one refrain from today's self-indulgence for greater satisfaction in the long run. The law of service demands that we do assist each other and thus make our lives worth living. To be a recipient of public charity involves not only the depth of misfortune but a certain guilt.

When one understands how one's work should be done, is willing to sacrifice constantly for it, and derives satisfaction from it, and if the world does need that work, one's life can approximate heaven. Otherwise, life can be hell—even with a high income. I have attained success and a reasonable degree of happiness mostly because I have enjoyed the work I have done for a living and have been able to serve humanity though my work.

A modern attitude judges hard labor as degrading and evil instead of regarding it as contributing to the development of civilization. The more difficult the labor is, the greater the contribution of those who do it. Labor has been the Negro's greatest gift to America.

In order to provide for an increase in the happiness of our

people and of those yet unborn, some of us have to be willing to sacrifice some of our own happiness. We must be prepared even to be crucified.

In my 1958 lecture for the Accra Conference of African States, I emphasized that the bond between Africans and the colored people of China, India, the rest of Asia, the Middle East, and the sea isles was not only the color of skin but the deeper experiences of wage-slavery and contempt. I appealed to them to regain their continent as well as their freedom and dignity.

At the Accra Conference, I reminded the Africans that they faced a critical decision. Would they squander their income on luxuries from the West or would they abstain from some pleasures and utilize their savings to educate their children and to expand their industries so that they could develop their abilities, self-reliance, and self-defense?

If our nation is to be regarded throughout the world as free and democratic, it has to abandon all alliances with colonial imperialism and purge itself of other human rights violations.

Instead of training more of its youth to teach and to heal, our nation has been training them to build weapons and to kill. We who believe that a third world war can and must be avoided should demand that atomic weapons be outlawed and work for universal disarmament.

An African child soon understands that to be a member of the tribe, he has to give over some of his freedom to the tribe. When the tribe unites with other tribes, it has to surrender some of its freedom to the paramount tribe. For Africa to be united and become Pan-Africa, each part, each tribe, and each nation must relinquish some of their freedom for the good of the totality.

If American Negroes are to achieve complete liberty, they must eventually move from emphasis on race solidarity and the idea of an American Negro culture to a concept of a world humanity that transcends race and nation.

5

Malcolm X

Mr. Elijah Muhammad teaches a man how to recover from his spiritual, mental, economic, and political disorders. His doctrines endow a man with a racial pride and racial identity, encourage him to develop his potential, and motivate him to identify with his brothers in Islam.

I was a numbers runner, procurer, bootlegger, drug dealer, addict, and armed robber. My antireligious attitude caused my fellow prisoners to name me "Satan." But Mr. Muhammad's teachings transformed me from a criminal to a believer in the Nation of Islam (NOI). He taught me how to dedicate my life to Allah and to respect and love myself as a black man.

As a representative for Mr. Muhammad, I appealed to the white man to atone for his crimes against blacks by giving us several states on American soil where those of us who wanted could establish our own government, economic system, and civilization with financial support from whites for twenty-five years. But I now think that we blacks, for the present, should stay where we are and fight for our rights.

Why was I suspended from the Nation of Islam? It was not because I made a comment on the assassination of President Kennedy. It was that certain officials in the NOI in Chicago did envy me and I had objected publicly to Mr. Muhammad's immorality.

The Nation of Islam shuns political activity and refuses to participate in the black struggle for human rights. But a true

Muslim must be not only a believer but a social activist. He cannot live in a political vacuum. I thought that disciplined Muslims should have been at Little Rock and Birmingham as well as other protests for all the world to see.

After leaving the NOI, I founded the Muslim Mosque, Inc. to teach the meaning of Islam. I also intended to construct a black nationalism that would focus on our cultural roots and empower our people to obtain control of their communities. Whites have controlled even the minds of our people.

Having witnessed how the nations in the Organization of African Unity (OAU) could convene to discuss their common problems, I formed the Organization of Afro-American Unity (OAAU), a non-religious group for persons of African origin. It seeks to utilize any means necessary to achieve freedom, equality, and respect as human beings for African-Americans, the independence of all the people of African descent in the Western Hemisphere, and their unification with their African brothers.

The motto of the OAAU is "By Any Means Necessary." When I contend that blacks are justified in using any political, economic, social, and physical means in order to eliminate injustice, I mean taking any action that is just, intelligent, and legal.

The OAAU aims to re-educate blacks to realize that the way to obtain their freedom is to do the same things the white man has done for himself in politics, education, business, and housing. It has, therefore, been involved in voter registration, voter education drives, and a housing improvement program. It will organize political clubs to run independent candidates for office and will support African-Americans in office who are responsible to the African-American community.

The OAAU is willing to cooperate with any individual or group, whatever their color or political, economic, and social philosophy is, as long as they are prepared to take the steps necessary to end the injustices to black people in this country. We will work with them on rent strikes, school boycotts, and voter registration drives. We will cooperate in local struggles for human rights in the South and elsewhere to elevate the political consciousness of blacks.

What is my first responsibility? To my twenty-two million fellow blacks in this country. Because of our color, we have been indicted even before we were born and have suffered the same indignities. My personal problem will be solved when the problem is solved for all of our people.

Before blacks can be organized in order to pursue specific goals, someone whom they trust has to wake them up to their human worth and heritage. They must be made aware of what has been done to them. Then, they will develop an abundance of energy that can be channeled constructively.

American racists have long known that they could more easily rule African-Americans if we had a negative image of ourselves. To produce such an effect, they instilled in us a negative image of Africa as devoid of civilization. The result has been that our people, even without realizing it, have hated their African identity and have felt inadequate to do things for themselves.

But as Africans have achieved their independence and have projected a positive image, blacks in the West subconsciously have begun to identify with that positive African image and to become more united, militant, and self-reliant. The African revolution inspired the Black Muslim Movement that, in turn, has pushed the civil rights movement.

Like a person, a race of people cannot achieve fulfillment unless it is proud of its history, uses its abilities, develops its culture, and asserts its selfhood.

We have to educate our people about their cultural roots. When the ancestors of Europeans lived in caves, there were palaces on the African continent. Learning about the histories of African civilizations will empower our people to recapture their glorious heritage and rediscover themselves.

If the American people were properly educated about the history and contributions of blacks, whites would not feel so superior while blacks would not feel inferior and would be able to have a balanced knowledge of themselves.

While the federal government has pretended to be solving problems of blacks, it has produced tokenism which benefits only a few. The masses of our people have to suffer from the problems of inferior housing, inefficient schools, and menial jobs. Instead of the American dream, they are compelled to live with a nightmare, modern slavery.

Hypocrisy abounds when so many whites pretend that they want blacks to be free, and blacks pretend that they do believe these whites want them to be free.

Consider the way the white liberal fights for the freedom of blacks and the way he fights for his own freedom. For blacks, he participates in the nonviolent protests and sings "We Shall Overcome." However, whenever his freedom or property is endangered, he is not nonviolent.

When white liberals join a "Negro" organization, they want to dominate it and tell us how to solve the race problem. It is as if Jesse James were to advise the marshal on how he should come after him.

During my pilgrimage to Mecca, Muslims of all colors, moved by the power of God, displayed a spirit of unity, and white Muslims demonstrated their brotherly love for me. I also witnessed white students working with blacks in several parts of Africa. As a consequence of these experiences and my spiritual rebirth, I no longer make general indictments of whites, denouncing them as devils. I now realize that some American whites have a brotherly love for blacks and want to end the racism destroying this country.

Racism is the most explosive and pernicious evil in the world—the inability of God's creatures to live as one. I am not a racist in any form whatever and am absolutely opposed to any form of segregation or discrimination. The religion of Islam teaches that one cannot judge a man by the color of his skin. In evaluating a person, my primary concern is about his attitude and actions. I wish nothing but freedom, equality, and happiness for all people.

What do non-white peoples around the world think of the United States when, in the nonviolent demonstrations, its law officers set dogs on black citizens, turn fire hoses on them, beat and jail them—including the blacks who have served the country so well in war and peace? Is this an effective way to win non-white peoples to democracy?

The collective white man distorts Jesus' message of love by teaching blacks to turn the other cheek while he does not turn it. Even as he uses the Bible to teach blacks humility, he exhibits his arrogance. He has brainwashed them to think they will get shoes and honey in heaven while he makes certain he enjoys his heaven on earth.

My struggle is against only those whites who are racists. Nonetheless, despite their activities, I do not consider these racists as inherently evil. They are the products of a political, economic, and social atmosphere in America that persuaded them to act in evil ways and to think that they are superior to blacks.

What is condemned as black racism is usually a reaction to white racism. All white racists have to do to get our good will is to stop doing evil things to us and to show their good will.

Those who preach nonviolence advise us to love the racist and to be willing to suffer. But why should we blacks waste brotherhood on a white man if he hates us and tries to put us in the grave? I do not have hate in me but I do have sense. I am not going to love someone who intends to lynch me. We should be practicing much more brotherhood among ourselves rather than seeking goodheartedness in an oppressor who does not know what nonviolence is?

As long as others are willing to practice brotherhood with me, I am willing to practice brotherhood with them. But I am not going to waste brotherhood on those who persist in being responsible for the condition of my people.

We blacks are often accused of introducing "separation" and "isolation." Yet, it is the racist system that has separated and isolated us in this country.

We have to generate black unity before we can achieve the black-white brotherhood which is my ultimate objective. We need black solidarity before we can attain worker solidarity. We do not have whites in our organizations but they are free to support them financially. They could also try to change the consciousness of other whites, teaching them not to be racist and violent toward us. But they should not attempt to tell us what to do or to change our attitude.

The law of retaliation is divine. We possess the God-given right to defend ourselves against racists. The *Koran* teaches us to fight against those who attack us. The Bill of Rights upholds our right to bear arms. The government taught some of us how to utilize violence to defend its interests overseas. When the government is not willing or unable to protect our lives and property and to bring racist oppressors to justice, our people are justified in defending themselves with whatever means that are necessary. Nevertheless, we should not initiate attacks against whites.

Our struggle has been named "the Negro Revolution" but real revolutions have involved bloodshed and no compromise. How nonviolent were the American, French, Chinese, Cuban, and Algerian revolutions or the rebellion of the Mau Mau in Kenya? Revolutionaries did not aim to be an essential part of a system. They wanted to replace it with another system. This country, nonetheless, can prevent a bloody revolution if gives blacks the full use of the ballot in every one of its states.

I am quite proud of the contributions our women have been making to the freedom struggle. Women should be accorded ample opportunity for self-development since they have made more significant contributions than many of us men.

African diplomats at the United Nations have advised me that we blacks should refer to the violations of our "human rights," which are more basic than "civil rights." Because our problem with racism would thereby be viewed as a problem for all humanity and as a threat to world peace and not be restricted only to the jurisdiction of this government, then our African, Asian, Latin American, and Chinese brothers would feel free to place our problem on the agenda of the General Assembly of the United Nations.

By internationalizing the problem—including it within the global struggle for human rights—blacks would no longer have to beg for their civil rights from those in Washington, D.C. who have made us victims.

The violations of our "human rights" constitute violations of the United Nations' "Declaration of Human Rights" and the United Nations Charter. I have appealed to the heads of African states, who have condemned Portugal's colonialism and South Africa's racism, to help us bring our problem to the attention of the General Assembly of the United Nations.

I have asked several African leaders to recommend that the United Nations Commission on Human Rights commence an investigation of our problem. In the United Nations' debate over the Congo in December 1964, some African delegations criticized American racial policy at home and abroad.

We African-Americans have to develop solidarity with the world's Pan-Africanists. Even though we, as a people, would not return to Africa physically, we ought to be involved in a spiritual, psychological, philosophical, and cultural migration to Africa that would generate substantial support for us there.

As a spokesman for the Nation of Islam and in reaction to a discriminatory society, I did consider interracial marriage to be evil and harmful to the freedom struggle. Because of my later belief that humanity is a family, I regard interracial marriage as basically a human being marrying another human being.

My purpose has been not to condemn America but to tell the truth and to seek whatever benefits humanity as a whole. I dare to believe that my voice has helped to save America from a catastrophe—possibly even a fatal one.

THE POWER OF THE NEGATIVE

While my mother would deny the occasional requests of my older brothers and sister for snacks after school, I would cry out in protest until she gave me what I wanted. She asked why I couldn't be nice and quiet like my brother Wilfred. But I saw that Wilfred did not get the snack. I learned early that if you want something, you better make some noise.

In my youth, I learned that tests, trials, and tribulations are necessary to make one grow into manhood.

Though I was one of the school's best students, my eighth grade teacher advised me to become a carpenter because he thought it would not be quite realistic for a black boy to think about becoming a lawyer. He did me a service by this advice. Had he encouraged me to become a lawyer, I would probably be a member of some city's black bourgeoisie, pretending to be a leader of the suffering black masses but really concerned to grab a few more crumbs from whites for myself.

In a boxing match when I was thirteen, I was knocked out after only a few seconds in the first round. Since I became a Muslim, I have believed that if Allah had not used that fight to end my boxing career, I might have become punchy.

The best thing that ever happened to me was that I had to spend seventy-seven months in prison because it was there I heard the message of Mr. Muhammad that did transform my life. His doctrines brought me from behind the prison walls to become a speaker at prominent colleges and universities. In 1946, I had been sentenced in Cambridge, Massachusetts, and in 1961, I returned there to be a guest speaker at the Harvard Law School Forum—though I had only eight years of formal education.

Prison did prove to be a blessing also because I was able to study there more intensively, at times, even as much as fifteen hours a day with the help of a night hall light, than if I had attended some college with its many distractions. My studies included especially history, philosophy, anthropology and the dictionary. This opportunity to read aroused my long dormant craving to be mentally alive.

My reading in prison did confirm Mr. Muhammad's main contention that the collective white man had acted as a devil in nearly every one of his contacts with the world's collective non-whites. My extensive studies of the horrors of slavery—the systematic obliteration of our people's family structure, personal identity, language, religion, and culture by means of rapes, whips, clubs, chains, and auction blocks—so affected me that later as a minister many of my lectures described the atrocities of slavery.

My participation in the debating program in prison gave me as much pleasure as my reading. I would study everything I could find to support my side but I would also determine what arguments I would employ if I were on the other side. I would then decide how to negate those arguments.

I found it very painful to accept Mr. Muhammad's message and to make the necessary radical changes in my life but it did save me from spiritual death. I am convinced also that if I had not converted, I would have remained a criminal and then been killed or sent back to prison or committed to an asylum. The great strength of the Nation of Islam is its capacity to reform people whom society has made criminals.

It would be almost impossible to discover a black man in America who was more ignorant than myself or who suffered more anguish than I had. But only after the deepest darkness can one feel the greatest joy, and only after slavery and prison can one best appreciate freedom.

My own history indicates that a man who has been at the bottom of society, such as a junkie, can change completely. Mr. Muhammad told us to go after those in the mud of society because, if they converted, they could become even exemplary Muslims.

Who can receive the truth about God and himself? Only the person who admits that he or she is guilty of having sinned. Jesus could not help the Pharisees since they did not feel that they needed any help.

Convicts who converted to the NOI were able, while still in prison, to condition themselves to live in accordance with the moral laws of the NOI so that they were fully qualified after prison to become registered Muslims. Often, they were better prepared than other prospective Muslims who were never in prison.

The Muslims gave me my "X" that symbolizes my African family name I could not know. I viewed my "X" as replacing the name of "Little" that a white slave-master had imposed on my ancestors.

Before the advent of the Black Muslims, the white power structure was suspicious of the National Association for the Advancement of Colored People and the Congress of Racial Equality as radical and wanted to investigate them. After the Black Muslims had arrived, the white power structure was grateful to God for the NAACP.

In our Boston Temple, when I ended an address by asking for new followers for Mr. Muhammad, I was amazed to see Ella, my sister, stand up. She had taken five years to convert. We learned that those who are the most difficult to convince make the best Muslims.

Although the NOI cooperated with the government insofar as it improved the lives of its members, I refused to disclose the number or the names of our members. I thought that we ought to keep concealed some of what we were. Roots are the most important part of the tree, and they must remain beneath the ground if the tree is to live.

The Black Muslim Movement received its first important publicity in New York City because of its disciplined protest against a police assault upon our Muslim brother. A sizable organization, like the NOI, can remain almost unknown until some incident brings it to the attention of the public.

Some law enforcement agencies utilized threats to frighten blacks from becoming Muslims. Evidently, these agencies failed to recognize that a new black man had emerged. The more these agencies harassed blacks, the faster the NOI grew.

The questions, challenges, and criticisms I received at my lectures and debates before college audiences never failed to assist me in furthering my education and improving upon my presentation and defense of the teachings of the NOI.

Envious comments within the NOI that I was taking credit for Mr. Muhammad's doctrines as well as attempting to assume control of the organization and to build an empire for myself did not anger me. Instead, they helped to reinforce my inner resolve that such comments would never in truth apply to me.

My suspension from the NOI by Mr. Muhammad did cause me to examine my loyalty to him and the organization. After realizing that the rules of the NOI applied to everyone and that I was responsible for the suspension, I was more devoted to him than ever. The subsequent extension of the suspension, however, compelled me to reassess my relationship to him and the NOI.

Mr. Muhammad had a powerful impact on me as a symbol of moral, mental, and spiritual reform. I had worshiped him as a divine leader who was sent to our people by Allah. Under his influence, I was celibate for twelve years and fulfilled an oath of poverty, not acquiring anything in my own name. But I no longer consider him to be a divine leader, free of human weakness. His immoral acts have convinced me that he is not God's prophet.

When Mr. Muhammad failed to acknowledge some of his actions as human weakness or the fulfillment of prophecy and tried to cover up what he had done, I began to understand that I had believed in him more than he had believed in himself. I was shocked to discover that he did not believe that God had taught him the doctrines we preached. For the first time in twelve years, I summoned the strength to face the facts and to think for myself.

Our Organization of Afro-American Unity essentially is a peaceful organization based on brotherhood. Still, I contend that if you are to have peace, you must be ready to protect it. Even as whites die protecting their peace, I will die protecting mine.

In the OAAU, we are seeking students, particularly those in political science, to launch independent studies of the race problem in this country and then to share the results of their research and their recommendations with us so that we can design an action program that will alter the political structure. Our emphasis will be on youth, who can be objective in their analysis, since they have less of a stake in this corrupt system than adults usually have.

Representatives from twenty-nine countries in Africa and Asia at a 1955 conference in Bandung, Indonesia did agree to submerge their religious, cultural, economic, educational, and political differences and to emphasize the exploitation they suffered in common. They could thereby work on problems of racism, colonialism, and imperialism. Using this conference as a model, we black leaders should submerge our differences about integration and tactics and consent to work in unity for freedom, equality, and justice. If President Kennedy could sit down with Khrushchev and construct agreements on nuclear weapons, we can and should cooperate in the struggle against racism.

Blacks in America benefit whenever some African or Asian country acts in an independent way. When the white power structure here has to worry about some other power, it tends to grant a little more leeway to those inside its borders.

White nations have established the rules that favored them. But dark nations which have become truly independent do not necessarily conform to these rules.

In Algiers, I saw the conditions colonialism had imposed upon the people. To free themselves, they first had to realize that oppression, degradation, discrimination, and segregation made them brothers.

Whatever our class, all blacks suffer oppression. Everyone who has been subjected to the same kind of hell as I have is my blood brother. This racist system makes all blacks one.

We blacks have to stop thinking of ourselves as a minority. We should act as if we were part of the dark majority engaged in a global rebellion against the oppressor. Adopting this new approach, we can proceed with an eleven-to-one advantage in the world rather than a six-to-one disadvantage in America, and we will no longer be begging but demanding.

Most of the independent African states adopted a policy of non-alignment, and thus they can receive assistance from the East and West. This policy of neutrality empowers them to be primarily concerned with their own development.

We blacks have to practice our own form of non-alignment. When we align ourselves to a political party, we just squander our bargaining power. We should register as independents in order that we will be in a neutral position—prepared to take the political action that will be beneficial to us.

When we consider the sacrifices that blacks in Mississippi are making in order to become registered voters, we blacks in the North should conclude that it would be a sin if we were not registered and did not vote.

The colonial powers had to leave Africa not because they had become benevolent but because the black man refused to be exploited any longer and was willing to risk his life and take the lives of those who tried to take his. To be a man, one must be willing to fight and die for what is one's right.

The day when we black men in this country indicate that we are willing to risk death just as quickly to protect our lives and property as white men have shown—including the Founding Fathers—many whites will have more respect for us. If we give evidence of this willingness, even the bigoted whites will have to change their attitude and strategy toward us.

Blacks who proved their bravery in Korea and Vietnam should demonstrate that bravery here by being willing to die for their freedom. If it was moral for these blacks to defend

America's interests abroad, then it is certainly moral for them to defend their own interests here.

Anyone who wants to follow me and my Movement has to be ready to go to jail, the hospital, and the cemetery.

Robert Williams made some mistakes in implementing his program of advocating guns for blacks that caused him to be vilified as a criminal and brought about his exile to Cuba. We can and should learn from his mistakes.

I sent a telegram to George Lincoln Rockwell, the leader of the American Nazi Party, warning that if his racist agitation in Alabama caused physical harm to Dr. King or any other black persons seeking to exercise their rights, we would use maximum physical retaliation against him and his associates. Like everyone, he fears power, and I have not heard about him since.

One of my roles has been to lend support to the nonviolent groups by presenting to whites a violent alternative. If whites know that violence is a real alternative, they may be willing to accept the demands of the nonviolent organizations for the ballot and other rights.

The only time power takes a step back is when it is forced to do so by even more power. It does not retreat because of a smile, a threat or a nonviolent action. Power recognizes only power, and those who have realized this have made progress in Southeast Asia, the Congo, Cuba, and other parts of the world.

Only when this country suffered a manpower shortage in World War II, were blacks allowed to serve in the army and to work in factories. It was the pressure from its enemies, not a moral consciousness in the country, which enabled these Americans to take these few strides forward.

Blacks should not revere the Emancipation Proclamation as a document of liberation because it has not been effective, and "emancipation" in its root meaning refers to the transfer of property. We should, instead, demand a "Declaration of Condemnation" for slavery and continued acts of oppression as well as endorse legislation in the form of a "Proclamation of

Restitution."

By reflecting upon our situation, we can learn just how authentic any new civil rights laws will be. If the Thirteenth, Fourteenth, and Fifteenth Amendments were intended to ensure our rights, why do we still have to struggle for these rights? If the Supreme Court by its 1954 decision wanted to desegregate the schools, then why would the decision allow for loopholes so that ten years later, only eight percent of the schools are desegregated. The 1964 Civil Rights Act banned discrimination in voting but the federal government will not protect blacks in Selma who attempt to register without being murdered.

Why have I warned about the increase in black rage? Not to advocate violence but so that the power structure might heed my warnings and the country might avoid a disaster. The best thing a person can do for you is to reveal to you how fed up with frustration the man in your house has become. Instead of being grateful for my warnings, Americans are so filled with fear and guilt that they pretend the powder-keg situation does not exist.

I have been denounced as an "extremist." It is true that I am extreme in my love for my race. Extremism is justifiable when it is directed intelligently in the defense of liberty. To be moderate in the pursuit of justice is sinful. Extremism did define the American struggle for independence. Was Patrick Henry moderate when he demanded "liberty or death"?

In the white man's press, I have been accused of being a demagogue and of inciting blacks to violence. No one has to incite black people. The white man has already incited them. These attempts to make my name poison have succeeded only in causing millions of blacks in America to regard me like Joe Louis.

Portraying me as a monster all over the world was the best thing the white man ever did for me. I can visit any African country, and our brothers there know where I stand.

I would rather have to face the white supremacists, who are criminals but practice what they preach, than the hypocritical white so-called liberals, who deceive the blacks into believing that they aim to achieve integration. Blacks have made some progress in the struggle for civil rights in the South because they could see that the system was so opposed to them.

There should be a debate between a white supremacist and a black race leader. It would be a bitter confrontation but it would help get some of the real issues out into the open. This country needs this kind of exchange of truth that would help clear the air of racial mirages, clichés, and falsehoods that conceal the real conditions of our people.

The belief of most whites that they are superior to blacks is deeply rooted in their subconscious. Many of them are not even conscious of their racism until they encounter a test that causes it to emerge in one form or another.

All intelligent and informed blacks in America repudiate the term "Negro" as a badge of slavery and as helping only to perpetuate oppression and discrimination. Its usage should be considered as unenlightened, objectionable, and deliberately offensive.

In Ghana, the white Algerian ambassador objected to my designation of my philosophy as "Black Nationalism" because he thought that such a designation would alienate the white revolutionaries in several countries dedicated to overthrowing the systems of exploitation. Consequently, I have not used this designation in several months although I still aim for the political and economic control by blacks over their lives and communities.

I have had some impact on this country because I studied its weaknesses and because the more the white man groans, the more I know I have struck a nerve.

When railway officials in Maritzburg, South Africa ordered an Indian lawyer, Mohandas Gandhi, to leave the first-class compartment of a train and to move to the baggage car, he showed his first-class ticket and refused to move. A policeman was summoned, and he was thrown from the train onto the station platform. Incensed by the injustice, Gandhi launched his Movement and eventually twisted a knot in the tail of the British Lion.

The more the white racist resisted me and attacked me as a leader, the more certain I was that I was acting in the black man's best interests.

I continue to condemn what whites collectively have done to the non-whites—the English in India, apartheid in South Africa, and slavery and segregation in this country. I have also denounced American neo-colonialism in Vietnam and the Congo.

Being away from this country on my trips to Africa, the Middle East, England, and France has been beneficial. This separation has allowed me to be detached from the emotional issues in the OAAU and the Muslim Mosque and to examine our whole situation with more objectivity. From a distance, I developed a better understanding of the problems within our organizations.

Dick Gregory is indeed one of our most prominent freedom fighters. Any time you see someone like him jeopardize his income to be in the frontlines of the battle, then you and I have a moral obligation to our race to stand with that person.

Many blacks reject as a stereotype the charge that we are not ready for political involvement. But before we can win any political struggle through the ballot, we have to analyze ourselves and discover our liabilities as well as our assets.

Because I have wanted to run militant black candidates for political office, I have been asked if I would be a candidate. My response has been that I am certain I am more effective in attacking the establishment by not being a part of it.

Black leaders should not fear criticism. If we cannot stand criticism, we can never grow. No one should be immune to criticism. The moderate civil-rights organizations avoid me as too militant while the militants avoid me as too moderate.

When I did not do well in a poll that asked blacks in New York City to name the black leader who was doing the best work for them, I did assert that some of the greatest leaders in history were recognized only after they were safely in the ground.

My father was murdered for preaching Marcus Garvey's message. I know that I have to pay the price for challenging the white power structure and the leadership of the Black Muslims. I have been prepared to be a martyr for the cause of brotherhood to save this country. Whatever happens to me is the will of Allah.

6

Martin Luther King, Jr.

The main influence in my life has been my Christian faith that developed in the Black Church. I am the son, grandson, and great-grandson of Baptist preachers. After my junior year in college, I had a strong urge to serve God and humanity and devote my life to the absolute and eternal. Therefore, I decided to become a minister.

I can readily conceive of a God of love primarily because I grew up in a family where love was ever present. The family atmosphere contributed to my optimism.

Without the support of my courageous wife Coretta, I could not have done what I did. During the Montgomery Boycott, she was a source of strength for me as she remained serene in the midst of death threats and the bombing of our parsonage. Coretta's many significant contributions to the struggle—her participation in several of our campaigns and her work with the peace movement—provided me with continual inspiration.

While I do not subscribe to fundamentalism, I believe that God's self-revelation in Scripture should be the foundation of Christian theology. I do revere the necessary contributions of tradition, Christian experience, and reason, which includes certain insights from Biblical criticism.

My philosophy is Personalism, that has provided me with evidences to enhance my faith in the existence and attributes of a personal, provident God and with a metaphysical basis for the dignity of human personality.

Life at its best must be complete and have length, width, and height—a rational love of self, a love of neighbor that matches our love of self, and a love of God involving all of our heart, soul, and mind. The length and the width together are inadequate for self-fulfillment. As St. Augustine affirmed, "We were made for God, and we will be restless until we find our rest in Him." Our continuous effort is necessary for the development of all three dimensions.

An all-powerful and supremely good God is in control of history and wills our cooperation with His loving purpose in the establishment of His kingdom. Those who participate in the nonviolent movement can believe that He is with them in the struggle and that their sacrifices will help to further the expansion of freedom and justice. Good Friday must succumb to the triumph of Easter.

Scripture describes two types of faith. With the faith of the mind, the intellect affirms a belief that God exists. With the faith of the heart, the whole person surrenders self to God in an act of trust. The faith of the heart enables a person to open his whole life to God's grace. This faith gives us the inner equilibrium to face our inevitable fears and burdens.

Our main purpose in life should be not to avoid pain, enjoy pleasure, and be happy, but to do the will of God. We must be prepared to stand up for His truth.

In this life, virtue is not always rewarded with happiness. We can find the solution to this problem in the doctrine of the immortality of the soul. In another existence, the love and justice of God will provide that all virtue will be rewarded.

Central to the Judeo-Christian tradition is the belief that every human being is a child of God, made in His image. We ought to respect the sacredness of human personality and its power of freedom.

What is greater than freedom? It constitutes a part of the essence of a person. To withhold freedom from a person is to deny his humanity.

Freedom is one reality. It cannot, therefore, be distributed in installments. We are not free if we are not completely free. The goal of our Movement is total freedom.

The Negro wants and clearly deserves all of his rights now. Institutionalized tokenism and court decisions that sanction it are hypocritical and unacceptable. Procrastination that aims to curtail the freedom of Negro citizens is immoral.

Racism contends that one race is the source of progress and the center of value and that other races, which it views with contempt, must kneel in submission. Eventually, racism aims to commit spiritual or physical homicide upon the out-groups. The National Advisory Commission on Civil Disorders stated that white racism is the principal cause of the division of the nation into two hostile societies. Our nation must not continue to underestimate the scope and depth of its racism. It can solve this moral problem only if it admits its guilt.

The ways we deal with racial discrimination will affect our moral health as individuals, a nation, and the leader of the free world. The United States cannot be a first-class nation if it has a second-class citizenship.

As a boy, I abhorred segregation because the very notion of separation challenged my sense of dignity and self-respect. Segregation, fueled by racism, engenders total estrangement because it separates not only bodies, but minds and spirits. It does scar the souls and degrade the personalities of both the segregator and the segregated. It confirms the former in his false estimate of his superiority and compels the latter to feel inferior. Segregation is not only politically, economically, and sociologically unsound but it is morally wrong and sinful. It is opposed to the sublime principles of our Judeo-Christian tradition and our democratic ideals.

The United States Supreme Court in some major decisions has supported the recalcitrance of the segregationist forces. In 1896, the Court through the *Plessy v. Ferguson* decision created a new type of slavery by establishing the doctrine of "separate but equal" as the law of the land. In 1954, the Court raised our hopes when through *Brown v. Board of Education of Topeka,* it did declare that separate facilities are inherently unequal and that to segregate a child on the basis of his race is to deny him equal protection of the law. About a year later, the Court gave its approval to the Pupil Placement Law, and thus, in effect, returned to the states the power to determine the rate of integration. Judging from the rate of integration that has occurred within the schools in the first seven years, it will require ninety-three years more for the integration to be completed.

Many of the segregationists who employed the legislative maneuvers of nullification and interposition, and economic reprisals against us were not evil but were misguided. They were children of their culture, practicing what they had been taught, and were the victims of their intellectual and spiritual blindness.

The most troublesome adversaries to our Movement have not been the bigots but those white liberals who, unaware of their unconscious prejudices, have preferred the order of a negative peace and some improvement rather than justice and equality. We need more white liberals who will protest when a Negro is denied the right to become their neighbor or obtain a top position in their company or become a member of their professional association.

President Eisenhower sincerely conveyed to me his belief in racial justice. Still, as president, he had no inclination to define racial justice as a supreme domestic issue because his colleagues and advisers did not share his belief on this issue, and their rigid conservatism would not allow for a sudden structural change in American society.

President Kennedy, partly because of his very thin margin of victory, did vacillate in his first two years with regard to racial justice. In his third year, however, as he understood the moral necessity for social change, he began to give evidence of his commitment. A few months before his death, he gave a speech which was an earnest and profound appeal for racial justice.

Jesus' love involving universal altruism provided the spirit, motivation, and regulating ideal for our nonviolent movement from its very inception while Gandhi furnished the methods. Gandhi proved that the love ethic could be a powerful force among groups and nations. In my judgment, he was one of the half-dozen greatest men in world-history.

The participants in a nonviolent movement should strive to practice *agape*, an unconditional, understanding, redemptive goodwill that can enable them to love all persons not because they are so likeable but because God loves all persons. *Agape* transcends aesthetic or romantic love and friendship, in which there is a mutual affection, and seeks the good of the other. Those who are dedicated to the life of *agape* can elevate their own souls, exalt the personalities of their opponents, appeal to their consciences, and achieve a transformation of society. *Agape* is the love of God operating in the human heart.

Agape involves an awareness of the fact that all men are brothers and that we are our brother's keeper. Because we all participate in humanity, whatever directly affects one of us affects all of us indirectly. The agony of anyone lessens me, and his salvation expands my spirit.

Self-centeredness can cripple a personality. When a person with this condition does not receive the attention he craves, he may experience frustration, bewilderment, disillusionment, and anger. One of the ways to overcome self-absorption is to dedicate one's life to serving a noble cause that can provide meaning and make one happy.

The highest expression of power is love implementing the demands of justice. Love that lacks the power to change what is opposed to it is sentimental and anemic, while power that is not rooted in love can be reckless and abusive.

Essential to nonviolence as a way of life that is regulated by *agape* is the willingness to forgive "not seven times, but seventy times seven" to establish and preserve community. *Agape* requires that we understand that the evil deeds of the oppressor, caused by pride, ignorance, prejudice, fear, and hate, do not fully constitute him as a person. Only forgiving love of our enemies can conquer racial injustice and cast out their fear of integration.

We have the potentiality to relate to God and become His sons. Through our love for our enemies, we can actualize this potentiality, participate in the life of God, and experience the beauty of His holiness.

If we were to respond to hate with hate, we would distort our personalities, destroy our objectivity, provoke more hate, intensify the existence of evil, and obstruct the creation of community. How many countries and individuals have been destroyed by pursuing the path of hate? We must confront the forces of hate with the power of love. Only love can break the chain of hate and turn an enemy into a friend.

Love enhances, unifies, and illumines life whereas hatred diminishes, disrupts, and darkens life.

Several constructive methods must be used in the struggle for civil rights. Petitions, litigation, nonviolent direct actions, and voter registration are necessary to produce and implement legislation and court orders in order to regulate behavior and to remove the physical barriers to integration. But education as well as religion are necessary to transform the prejudiced attitudes of the opponent and overcome the spiritual obstacles to integration.

Nonviolence, directed by *agape*, seeks reconciliation and redemption by striving to establish the beloved community, a community where all men live as brothers according to the law of love—the supreme unifying principle of our life. The beloved community is the Kingdom of God, the expression of His will for humanity. Motivated mainly by a commitment to brotherhood and not by laws against segregation, its members would repudiate every kind of discrimination and practice full integration that is genuine intergroup and interpersonal living with a real sharing of political power and responsibility.

During the Montgomery Boycott, a white citizen asked me why did my associates and I attempt to destroy a tradition of peaceful race relations. I stated that we never had a real peace but only a negative peace in which the Negro was forced to submit to insults and exploitation. Our struggle was therefore necessary to obtain a positive peace involving the presence of justice, brotherhood, and the power of the Kingdom of God.

As the boycott developed, I experienced more and more the spiritual power of nonviolence. I accepted nonviolence as the most practical method to achieve freedom but also chose it as a way of life.

As Gandhi indicated, nonviolent resistance is not a method for cowards. If one adopts this method due to fear or because he does not possess the weapons of violence, he is not really nonviolent.

Our nonviolent resistance has attempted to appeal to the majority who, victimized by either blindness, fear, pride or irrationality, have allowed their consciences to sleep. I am convinced that there is, at least, a potential good in everyone, that God's grace can alter a prejudiced mind, and therefore, that the worst segregationist can become an integrationist.

The nonviolent resister is passive in the sense that he is not physically aggressive toward his opponent. But he is active spiritually because he uses his mind and emotions to convince his opponent that he is wrong. Our nonviolent demonstrations aim to arouse a sense of moral shame in the opponent.

Booker T. Washington, born a slave, was one of our great leaders. He lit a torch that dispelled darkness in Alabama. I have often quoted his warning, "Let no man pull you so low as to make you hate him." Yet, his counsel to Negroes that they be content to do well what society permitted them to do provided for too little opportunity. Because of his belief in a patient and pressureless persuasion, he did underestimate the forces of evil. His social philosophy enabled these forces to intensify their oppression.

The aim of our nonviolent demonstrations has been not to defeat or humiliate our opponents but to help them as well as ourselves. We have attempted to secure their friendship and understanding. Our ultimate purpose is to achieve integration based on mutual respect.

The principal international influence on American Negro students has been the liberation struggle in Africa. They have often told me that if their brothers in Africa could break the bonds of colonialism, surely the American Negro can defeat segregation.

The freedom songs that we sing at our mass meetings and demonstrations constitute the soul of our Movement. They are adaptations of the songs of faith and inspiration the slaves sang—the sorrow songs, shouts for joy, battle hymns, and anthems. Like the slaves, we are in bondage, and the freedom songs help to unite us, endow us with courage, and increase our hope that "Black and white together, we shall overcome someday."

Nonviolent direct action produced a number of significant achievements. The 1956 Montgomery Boycott helped to end segregation on the buses in that city and almost every other city in the South. The 1960 Sit-ins, guided by the philosophy of nonviolence, desegregated lunch counters in more than 150 cities. The 1961 Freedom Rides led to the end of segregation in interstate travel. The 1963 Birmingham Movement secured the passage of the 1964 Civil Rights Bill. The 1965 Selma Movement facilitated the passage of the Voting Rights Bill.

Nonetheless, there is a tragic chasm between the passage of civil rights laws and their implementation. In 1967, I asserted that Congress had failed to enforce the 1964 Civil Rights Act in all of its dimensions and had tolerated several limitations on the implementation of the 1965 Voting Rights Act. The 1964 "War on Poverty" had such a restricted budget that it could not conduct even a good skirmish against poverty.

Although the nonviolent movement has made substantial progress in the South through undermining the foundations of segregation, the situation of the Negro masses, particularly in the northern ghettos, has remained about the same or become worse.

In 1965, the five aims of our Southern Christian Leadership

Conference (SCLC) were: to teach the philosophy, strategies, and tactics of nonviolence through workshops; to encourage massive nonviolent demonstrations to expose and remove all the barriers of discrimination and segregation; to obtain the right and exercise of the ballot for every citizen; to achieve for the Negro all citizenship rights and complete integration into American life; and to confront the problem of the cultural discrepancy by our citizenship training program.

In our Movement, we emphasize that the means must be as pure as the end. The end does not justify the means. In a real sense, the end potentially exists in the means. The means are the end as it develops in the process. The means represent the seed and the end represents the tree. Consequently, destructive means, such as violence, injustice, and deception, cannot bring about moral and constructive ends.

As long as a Negro is denied the right to vote, he does not possess himself and cannot live as a citizen in a democracy who obeys the laws he has helped enact. His sense of personal dignity has been wounded. He could be even more indignant about this denial when he sees people of color in Africa and Asia governing their own nations and black statesmen at the United Nations voting on vital issues.

Segregation may have caused many Negroes to believe that whites should be more actively concerned than they about racial justice. If Negroes are to achieve first-class citizenship, they have to assume the primary responsibility for making it happen.

One of the greatest problems of the Negro is his lack of power. Economic power and political power are necessary for the implementation of the demands of love and justice and are the keys to his liberation. The civil rights movement will have to be far more involved in organizing people into groups to protect their interests and produce beneficial changes. It must help unionize the businesses in the ghetto, bring tenants into collective bargaining units, and form cooperatives so Negroes can build their own financial institutions. We urge Negroes to learn investment techniques, cultivate habits of thrift, and form credit unions and savings and loan associations.

Blacks cannot acquire substantial political and economic power independently of whites, and whites will not be able to enjoy power and fulfillment until they share that power by acknowledging black aspirations for freedom and dignity. A program would be immoral and politically counterproductive if it elected all black candidates only because they are black and rejected all white candidates only because they are white.

Blacks must recognize that millions of whites have rejected prevailing prejudices and have been willing to sacrifice some of their traditional privileges and to share power with blacks. There has been a minority of whites committed to promoting absolute equality with blacks. More than a few of these have died for our cause.

Whites who were aware that their freedom was connected to our freedom had a primary role and were spokesmen in our movement. The time has come when they must be willing to assume a secondary and supportive role in our biracial army.

Marcus Garvey established a mass movement emphasizing race pride and rejecting concepts that fostered a feeling of inferiority. His plan for a return to Africa, however, could not appeal to a people who had been in America for three and a half centuries.

Though I admire the achievements of Elijah Muhammad's Black Muslim Movement in rehabilitating ex-convicts, drug addicts, and others who are victims of despair and self-hate, I am unable to endorse the movement for several reasons. Its members reject Christianity, lack faith in the United States, contend that the white man is an incorrigible devil, and call for the permanent separation of the races in this country.

The Black Power Movement rightly extols black identity, group unity, and the acquisition of power, but it erroneously holds that Negroes can achieve political or economic power in isolation from whites. This philosophy of separatism ignores the fact that only federal programs involving many billions of dollars can resolve the massive economic problems of the Negro community. I have had to reject also the frequent call for retaliatory violence by some proponents of Black Power. Moreover, the slogan "Black Power" conveys the notion of black domination rather than black equality.

Violence as a method for social change is immoral because it thrives on hatred, aims to humiliate the opponent, leads to more violence, deepens the brutality of the oppressor, creates more bitterness in the oppressed, opposes wholeness, and aims to destroy community. Jesus did warn us, "He who lives by the sword will perish by the sword." We selected "Justice without violence" as the official slogan of our Montgomery Improvement Association.

Those who do not accept moral arguments against violence and who advocate riots should consider the futility of Negro insurrections in this country, the destructive consequences of riots on ghetto residents and the stores they use, and the fact that a riot cannot make an appeal to the conscience of the white majority but can intensify its fears, relieve its guilt, and lead to more repression.

An examination of the causes of Negro rage and riots must encompass the white backlash that opposes true equality, the discriminatory practices hounding the Negro at every level, the high rate of unemployment for Negro youth in the midst of historic prosperity, their conscription in double measure to fight for democracy in Vietnam as they are denied democracy at home, and the degrading conditions of urban life.

In order to overcome the evils of racism, materialism, and militarism, our nation must undergo a revolution of values. The rights of every person—rather than profit motives and property rights—should be the center of the economy. The government must depend more on its moral power than on its military power.

Our nation must confront the contradictions between its proclamations of lofty principles of freedom and its actions, the contrast between its scientific development and its moral condition, and the chasm between the plight of the multitude deprived of necessities and the situation of the few who enjoy luxuries—at times, as a consequence of this deprivation.

In 1958, I challenged the hypocrisy of American officials who called for free elections in Europe when large sections of our nation did not have them. How many American Negroes have suffered from taxation without representation!

The nations involved in a colossal struggle for supremacy exemplify a distortion of the drum major instinct—a desire to be great and to lead the parade. The Bible and history provide abundant evidence that whenever a nation pursues dominance, God breaks the backbone of its power.

A nation should not only seek peace but use only peaceful means to attain this goal. We in the Movement must preach, teach, and demonstrate to shake the very foundations of our nation so that we can elevate it to a nobler destiny and a new plateau of compassion.

In India, I was depressed when I saw the living conditions of the poor. In Bombay, more than a million people and in Calcutta, more than 600,000 sleep on sidewalks at night. In India, 480,000 make an annual income of less than $90. In our own nation, there are 40 million poverty-stricken people. While examining the conditions in several regions—Northern ghettos, Southern rural districts, and Appalachia—I found myself crying. The affluent must ask themselves the question, "How responsible am I for the well-being of the poor?"

To be great, a nation must have a concern for "the least of these." We spend millions of dollars every day to store our food surplus. Why not store that food in the stomachs of the millions who have to go to bed hungry—in Asia, Africa, Latin America, and in our own nation?

I was severely disappointed whenever certain leaders of the white Church became opponents of our struggle. While some white priests, ministers, and rabbis joined our struggle, and a few of them did shed their blood, most remained silent. In general, the white Church has been a defender of segregation.

The Christian Church should reflect the revolutionary spirit of Jesus and the prophets. It has a moral obligation to take the lead in social reform. It must serve as the conscience of the state and be prepared to challenge it on issues of social and economic justice and peace. It ought to support meaningful legislation, as did a number of clergymen who promoted the passage of the Civil Rights Bill in 1964. The Church is also obliged to keep open the channels of communication between the races.

Reading the works of Walter Rauschenbusch helped me to be more aware that the Gospel deals with the whole person—body as well as soul. Since religion seeks to change the soul of the individual so that he can be at one with God, himself, and other persons, it must also seek to change the social and economic conditions so that the soul can persevere in spiritual freedom once it is changed. Religion must relate to the whole of life and be actively concerned about ghettos that cripple men's souls. The preacher must say with Jesus, "The Spirit of the Lord is upon me because he has anointed me to deal with the problems of the poor."

Because of the inspiration from the Negro Church, faith and nonviolence directed our struggle. It prepared its members for a commitment to nonviolence by its emphasis on the dignity of the self, the value of sacrificial love, the merit of unearned suffering as exemplified in the life of Jesus, and the reality of a personal God Who demands righteousness and seeks justice for His children.

It was at the Negro churches that the meetings were held that initiated and sustained the bus boycott. These churches raised most of the funds needed for the car pool that proved to be so essential to the success of the boycott.

I have insisted that we prevent communists from joining our Movement. Communism is morally unacceptable because in its theory and methods it denies the reality of spirit, rejects the existence of eternal and unchangeable moral principles, utilizes any means to achieve its ends, and reduces persons to mere means for the ends of the state. Its materialism, ethical relativism, and totalitarianism are diametrically opposed to Christianity.

What is the most effective way to contend with the spread of communism? It is not to discourage the movements toward self-determination in the Third World but to work with a zeal, which matches in intensity that of the communists, to remove the conditions of economic exploitation, racial discrimination, and poverty which furnish the productive soil for communism. Could communism ever be successful if Christians lived in accordance with Christian principles?

Capitalism may lead to a practical materialism that is just as pernicious as the theoretical materialism of communism. Driven by their selfish ambition and the profit motive, men can engage in a cutthroat competition. They then measure their success mainly by their salary and possessions and not by their service to humanity.

The federal government has a moral obligation to lead the efforts to help forge a community in which all persons might be able to preserve their dignity, express their creativity, and fulfill their destiny. But only an alliance of liberal, labor, and civil rights forces can persuade the government to devise the necessary programs in education, employment, and housing.

In rejecting discrimination, I did describe my dream that my four children would one day be judged not by the color of their skin but by the content of their character. Nevertheless, since our society has been doing something against the Negro for centuries, including robbing him of any wages, wouldn't justice demand that society do something for him at this time so that he could be equipped to compete on an equal basis and become a part of the mainstream of American life?

Frederick Douglass rightly protested that the Emancipation Proclamation offered the Negro abstract freedom but did not provide him with food, land, and shelter. This was in sharp contrast to the way in which the government, after the Civil War, gave white immigrants free land and credit. Douglass thought that it was a marvel that Negroes were still alive.

In 1964, I proposed that even as the government produced a GI Bill of Rights for war veterans, it should launch a Bill of Rights for the Disadvantaged for veterans of a long siege of denial. This bill could adapt nearly all concessions made to the war veterans and would thus provide the equal opportunity as well as the training to empower the disadvantaged of all races to profit from this opportunity.

In order to promote integration of the schools and provide quality education for everyone, the federal government should provide grants to local school districts for the construction of educational parks that would make available a multiplicity of teaching specialists and superior facilities.

Education aims to transmit information and to train us to think objectively, logically, and critically. Still, if education aims only for efficiency, it can be the most dangerous social force. It must also teach the love of truth and extol ideals and worthy objectives in order to foster the development of moral character.

I recommend to young students that, whatever career they choose, they also become dedicated fighters for civil rights. This form of service to the nation and the world will enrich their spirit and allow them to pursue their careers with a rare sense of nobility.

In everyone there is a drum major instinct. A desire to be great is beneficial if it refers to true greatness. Jesus offered us a new definition of greatness, "Whosoever will be great among you shall be your servant." If you want to be first, then be first in love, service, generosity, and moral excellence.

W.E.B. Du Bois, through his many scholarly books, helped to rescue the Negro heritage and to demolish the myth of the inferiority of the Negro. Dr. Du Bois emphasized the need for special educational opportunities for the Talented Tenth of the black race so they would be able to elevate the rest of the race. However, his plan had no role for the masses and would have had the effect of benefiting an aristocratic elite while leaving behind the untalented ninety percent.

Unless we learn how to live together as brothers, we are going to perish together as fools—community or chaos. Love for one's enemy is the key to the main problems of the world and absolutely necessary for our survival. We are compelled to choose between nonviolence and nonexistence.

If mankind is to survive, all of us have to develop a world perspective. While our scientific genius has made the world geographically one, we are challenged to make it spiritually one—a brotherhood. We must develop a neighborly concern that is not restricted to our tribe, race, class, and nation—an unconditional love for all persons and an overriding loyalty to mankind as a totality.

Preservation of the other, not self-preservation, is the first law of life. Unless we are concerned about preserving other persons, we cannot preserve ourselves. To achieve fulfillment, we need other persons.

Prayer must not be used as a substitute for our efforts. We should pray intensely for peace, racial justice, and economic justice. But we should work for disarmament and suspension of weapon testing, for development of nonviolent programs to end racism, and for an equitable distribution of wealth in our nation and the undeveloped nations.

The philosophies, strategies, and tactics of nonviolence should be studied for their application to every field of human conflict. If only two countries, the United States and Britain, could be persuaded by nonviolent actions to end all economic interaction with the South African government, they could change the racial policies of that regime. National nonviolent movements in the West could persuade governments to repent of their imperialism by providing massive aid to developing countries.

The greatest contribution of nonviolence may still be to world peace. Nonviolence, which responds to the need of the Negro for justice, may yet fulfill the need of humanity for its survival.

Oppressed peoples desire total freedom. We have to work urgently with them so that all their anger at injustice may be channeled into a revolution of love and creativity. Our task is no less than to form a new world.

In the nonviolent movement, we believe that we are serving as the conscience of America and that all of our demands for justice express both God's will and the sacred heritage of the nation. I am confident that we will win our freedom and achieve a totally integrated society.

Among the factors that contribute to the ongoing process of desegregation are the determination of the Negro, the aroused conscience of so many whites, the direction of world opinion, the growing industrialization of the South, and the increasing realization by religious institutions of their duty to promote interracial cooperation.

The nonviolent movement motivated the Negro to summon the courage to dedicate himself to a noble cause. It inspired him to forge other priceless qualities of character and develop new self-respect and a sense of destiny. He has emerged from the struggle with a powerfully integrated personality. This has been his most important victory.

I constantly examine my conscience to determine whether I am preserving my sense of purpose, adhering to my ideals, and directing my people to the proper goals. I welcome the opportunity to work to help improve the nation and the world.

Governor George Wallace has called me an "extremist." Jesus was an extremist for love, truth, and goodness, and we, as Christians, should follow His example. Like St. Paul, I regard myself as an extremist for the brotherhood of man.

At my funeral, let it be stated that I tried to give my life serving others, to love humanity, to feed the hungry, to visit those in prison, and to be right on the war question. Refer to me as a drum major for justice, peace, and righteousness. What do I want my legacy to be? Luxurious possessions or money? No, I intend my legacy to be a life of commitment.

THE POWER OF THE NEGATIVE

After reading the works of Reinhold Niebuhr emphasizing the reality of collective evil and the pervasiveness of sin, I could not accept the excessive optimism of liberal theology about human nature. Neither could I accept the pessimism of neo-orthodoxy which maintained that human nature has been corrupted by original sin. My interpretation of human nature includes a synthesis that reconciles the partial truths in the thesis, liberalism, with other partial truths in the antithesis, neo-orthodoxy. Not only has man a noble power of reason and a potential for goodness which can be developed but he has inclinations to evil and a tendency to use his reason to create rationalizations for his sins.

Having studied Nietzsche's doctrine of "the will to power" and his critique of Christian love, I had almost concluded that Jesus' message of "Love your enemies" is effective only in conflicts among individuals and not among racial groups and nations. But this critique made me receptive to the magnitude of Gandhi's achievement in using the love ethic as a powerful force for social transformation.

One way to know that you are practicing disinterested love within the life of *agape*—seeking only the good of the other person—is to have love for the enemy-neighbor who offers you only hostility and persecution. You then know that you are loving him not for any benefits from him but only because God loves him.

Biology and history testify that birth and growth involve birth and growing pains. Whenever a new order emerges, we witness the recalcitrance of the old order. The tensions that we see in the world are evidence of the birth of a new world order.

Hegel helped me realize that growth in freedom comes only

through struggle. Unless we have massive upheavals, we can no longer assume that the nation, even after it re-examines its conscience, will make systemic changes.

Every advance toward universal justice is the consequence of the passionate concern, sacrifice, and unearned suffering of dedicated individuals. If it were not for the vigorous action of these co-workers with God, the forces for social stagnation would prevail.

Our nonviolent movement appealed to the Negro masses because it extolled the dignity of struggle, moral conviction, and self-sacrifice. The "Commitment Card" which we asked demonstrators in the Birmingham Movement to sign included the pledge that they sacrifice personal wishes so that all men might be free.

In general, it is desirable to be well-adjusted but we ought to be maladjusted whenever we confront the evils of racism, religious bigotry, economic injustice, militarism, mob rule, and physical violence. The salvation of the world will come not through a complacent conforming majority but through a nonconforming minority that is sufficiently courageous to risk criticism and abuse to engage in creative maladjustment.

Because of our ultimate allegiance to the laws of God, we must disobey laws that conflict with the moral laws and not submit to unjust practices. As Thoreau and Gandhi affirmed, we have a moral obligation not only to cooperate with good but not to cooperate with evil. To accept an unjust system is to participate in its evil. Such an acquiescence increases the arrogance of the oppressor but noncooperation may arouse his sense of shame.

A collective evil, such as segregation, is not a privation of being but a colossal, aggressive, and recalcitrant reality that does not voluntarily relinquish its hold unless it is challenged by a persistent resistance.

We must refuse to cooperate with the system of segregation that deprives persons of freedom, treats them as things, and thus denies the sacredness of their personality.

Those who disobey evil segregation laws ought to do so in a spirit of love, in a public way, and with a willingness to accept the legal penalty in order to persuade the community. Such a willingness reveals the highest respect for the notion of law.

The Boston Tea Party, a massive act of civil disobedience, contributed to the formation of the country. Essential to the greatness of America is the First Amendment right to protest.

Some critics ask, "Why can't Negroes wait for the courts to act?" Because Negroes have already waited for more than 340 years for their God-given rights. They have witnessed mobs lynch their mothers and fathers and drown their sisters and brothers. They can see a vast majority of their Negro brothers smothering in the cage of poverty in the midst of an affluent society.

Those in privileged positions very seldom relinquish their privileges without offering strong resistance. To move white America to grant him any civil rights, the Negro has had to resort to coercion in the form of legal or extralegal pressure. I concur with Reinhold Niebuhr's judgment that groups tend to be more immoral and more intransigent than individuals. Ethical appeals for justice should be made but supplemented with some form of constructive coercive power.

Even before spiritual integration can begin, desegregation must remove the legal and social inequities of segregation. While desegregation involves compliance with enforceable obligations regulated by society and law, integration requires obedience to unenforceable obligations that relate to our inner attitudes and personal relationships. A complete integration includes the positive acceptance of desegregation as well as the recognition of the sacredness of every human personality. With a loving spirit, integration welcomes the participation of the Negro in every area of life.

In the evolution of the Montgomery Bus Boycott, the city authorities did not understand the revolutionary change in the Negro's self-evaluation and his new determination, and thus each of their attempts to disrupt our unity only contributed to the strength of our unity.

Years of indignities and injustices caused the boycott. But the arrest of Mrs. Rosa Parks, a former secretary of the local branch of the NAACP, became the precipitating factor for the inception of the boycott.

Just before the boycott began, a white employer received our leaflet about the boycott from her maid and sent it to the *Montgomery Advertiser*. The newspaper printed the contents of the leaflet on its front page to notify the white community regarding our intentions. This report, however, brought news of the proposed boycott also to hundreds of Negroes who had not heard about our plans.

Because Mrs. Parks was found guilty and fined for refusing to give her bus seat to a white man, more Negroes joined the boycott.

Other mistakes by the authorities strengthened the boycott. The police arrested a Negro college student and charged him with intimidating passengers. Since he was only assisting an elderly woman to cross the street, his arrest helped to solidify the college students' support of the boycott.

With orders from the city commissioners, two policemen on motorcycles trailed every bus through the Negro section to prevent Negro squads from keeping Negroes off the buses—squads which existed only in the active imaginations of these commissioners. This attempt at psychological coercion only caused more Negroes to participate in the protest.

Although I did not have adequate time to prepare my first speech in the boycott, it evoked a greater response than any speech or sermon I had ever delivered. The older preachers were right when they assured us that God will speak through us. This experience helped me remember that God's power can transform a man's weakness into his glorious opportunity.

In the first week of the protest, the mayor asserted that the Negroes would be riding the buses on the next rainy day. This prediction only increased the resolve to continue the boycott.

When the police commissioner referred to a law requiring

a minimum taxi fare that could be used to prevent Negro taxi drivers from continuing to assist the protesters, we decided to establish a car pool and to extend indefinitely the boycott that originally had been called for only one day. Members of the White Citizens Council had to acknowledge that the car pool moved with military precision.

The harassment of Negro motorists by the police provoked the Negro middle class to join the protest.

The lawyer for the bus company maintained that it had no intention of hiring Negro drivers in the foreseeable future. In reaction, we developed the slogan, "Stay off the buses until we win."

With two motorcycle policemen following me for several blocks, I was deliberately driving slowly. Nevertheless, I was arrested and charged with driving thirty miles an hour in a twenty-five mile zone. That night, we had to hold seven mass meetings to accommodate those who heard about the arrest.

In the second month of the boycott, my home was bombed while I was attending a meeting. My wife and daughter were not injured. Two days later, the home of E. D. Nixon, one of the leaders of the boycott and former state president of the NAACP, was bombed. These bombings made us even more resolute and produced more moral and financial support for the boycott throughout the nation.

Even after the bombing of our home, Coretta and I decided to dispense with the gun we owned. How could I serve as one of the leaders in a nonviolent movement and use a gun for protection?

After a handbill stating that Negroes should be "abolished" by guns, bows and arrows, sling-shots and knives had been distributed at a meeting of the White Citizens Council, the participants in the boycott intensified their determination.

The indictment of eighty-nine persons, including twenty-six ministers, for violating the Alabama law against boycotts had the effect of providing more momentum for the protest.

Every effort by the opposition to use intimidation, force

or violence to terminate the boycott further united the Negro community and generated even more international sympathy for our nonviolent methods.

The Reverend Uriah J. Fields, the recording secretary of the Montgomery Improvement Association, was displeased since he had not been reelected by the executive board and accused members of the Association of misusing the donations to the boycott. When he recanted at a mass meeting, I requested that the people forgive him, and then they did accept his apology. This situation, that so many had confidently predicted would destroy the Association, served only to unify it more than ever in the spirit of tolerance.

At our prayer meetings during the boycott, we assured the participants that it was an honor to go to jail for a just cause. As the boycott developed, those who had been fearful of jail became proud to be arrested for the cause of freedom.

The principle of nonviolent resistance is an illustration of the Hegelian synthesis. Nonviolent resistance does reject the opposites—acquiescence and violence—as false and extreme total solutions by including truths from both of them. Like the person who adopts acquiescence, the nonviolent resister does reject the destruction of life or property but like the person who resorts to violence, does affirm that evil must be resisted.

While nonviolent resistance, with courageous self-control, does not resort to physical violence, it also rejects the internal violence of the spirit. Nonviolent demonstrators cannot allow themselves to become bitter or engage in hate campaigns.

Were it not for the discipline of nonviolence that restrained the Negro, I am convinced that numerous streets in the South would have been flowing with the blood of both races.

Nonviolent resistance has been directed against the forces of evil and not against persons who have been misguided by evil. We have opposed an unjust system of segregation while we have attempted to demonstrate compassion and love for the perpetrators of that system. We have sought a victory for justice and not a victory over the white man. Our goal has not been to substitute one tyranny for another.

Regulated by love, nonviolent resistance is the most potent weapon an oppressed people can utilize in their struggle for freedom. Its disciplined repudiation of external and internal violence can disarm the opponent and weaken his morale. By working on his conscience and shame, it could then move him toward reconciliation. Nonviolent resistance is the sword that can heal.

Nonviolent direct action seeks to precipitate such a crisis that a community becomes willing to negotiate. Nonviolent gadflies bring tensions and latent hostilities to the surface so that they can compel their fellow citizens to acknowledge the virulent disease of their racism.

Even as a boil is opened with all its ugliness so that it may be cured, injustice must be exposed to the light of conscience and public opinion before it can be corrected.

Our demonstrators must be willing to accept violence from opponents without retaliation in order to stir the conscience of the nation. This does achieve structural changes that remove a significant amount of the massive violence of discrimination which plagues millions of persons on a daily basis.

No tactical theory in a revolutionary struggle for a share of power will ensure consistent success. Mistakes will be made and we must learn from them.

In the Albany Movement, our main mistake was to wage a general attack on segregation rather than focusing on specific, symbolic objectives. In planning the Birmingham Movement, we studied the errors of the Albany Movement and were able to launch a successful practical and symbolic lunch-counter campaign.

In the Birmingham Movement, the city government secured a court injunction ordering us to stop our protests until our right to demonstrate had been established in court. About 300 demonstrators were in jail. Ralph Abernathy and I decided to disobey the injunction. We led a march on Good Friday and were arrested.

Why did we allow elementary and high school students to march in the demonstrations, to freeze and suffer in jails, and to be exposed to bullets and dynamite? Their parents and we determined the risks to be acceptable if, by a single climactic confrontation, we could then terminate the incessant torture of discrimination that maimed our families every day. It was logically, morally, and psychologically constructive for us, united as families, to resist oppression and make this a better nation. The involvement of the children, who were trained in nonviolence, lent impact to the Movement. This was one of our wisest decisions. They had a sense of moral mission, were willing to go to jail for a righteous cause, and added stature to their lives.

Our nonviolent strategies and tactics revealed the temper of their steel within the fires of turmoil. The power of Southern segregation was the hammer, and Birmingham was the anvil.

Clumsy and arrogant responses by segregationists helped to enkindle the righteous wrath of the Negro. After the signing of the 1963 Birmingham agreement, President Kennedy said that we should not be too harsh on Commissioner of Public Safety "Bull" Connor because he, in his way, had done a good deal for civil rights legislation that year.

From one perspective, our Movement did suffer defeats in Cambridge, Maryland and Rome, Georgia. Yet, from another perspective, the blows from these communities enhanced our courage, resistance, and unity.

In discussing our demonstrations in Selma, I stressed that they would be effective in dramatizing injustice and bringing about justice if racists did unleash violence on the marchers. Americans of conscience would react by demanding federal intervention and legislation, and the Johnson Administration would move to implement their demands.

Sheriff Jim Clark of Selma ordered his men to tear-gas and assault our nonviolent demonstrators. In an address before the Congress, President Johnson did respond to this violence by maintaining that the government had to insure by law every

Negro all of his rights as a citizen. He gave his pledge, "We shall overcome" and on August 6, 1965, signed the Voting Rights Bill.

Some of our demonstrators had very violent tendencies but their participation in our disciplined marches enabled them to sublimate their anger. In Chicago, spectators threw bottles at the gang members who marched with us. They bled but never retaliated.

It is preferable for our nonviolent demonstrators to be hit by rocks and to shed some blood in a march to end the evil of school segregation than to have generations of Negro children graduate from high schools without adequate reading skills.

When James Meredith was shot during his Freedom March, Floyd McKissick, the national director of the Congress of Racial Equality (CORE), Stokely Carmichael, the leader of the Student Non-violent Coordinating Committee (SNCC), and I decided to continue the march in order to expose the racism in Mississippi and to demonstrate that Negroes would not be intimidated by violence.

The South will eventually have to acknowledge the James Merediths as the actual heroes whose noble sense of purpose inspired them to endure the jeers and attacks of hostile mobs with the painful loneliness that marks the life of the pioneer.

If I needed an additional reason not to engage in hatred, I would recall the expressions of hatred on the faces of many Mississippi and Alabama sheriffs, many members of White Citizens Councils and many Klansmen, and I would have to conclude that hate is too much of a burden to bear.

The Negro subdued the environment in Africa but he has not been able to subdue the social and psychological jungle in the United States. However, the Negroes who have survived have developed a formidable capacity to cope with hardships. The nation must build on this capacity.

I have been the victim of a near-fatal stabbing, imprisoned several times in Alabama and Georgia, and hit by a rock in a march. Almost every day, my family and I have experienced death threats, and my home has been bombed twice. I have attempted to understand my personal ordeals as opportunities for self-transformation as well as the promotion of a spirit of healing and reconciliation.

In our struggle, we will experience agonizing setbacks and creative advances. We must understand that one cannot truly appreciate a victory without having suffered a defeat.

Whenever we experience failure, we should attempt to see how we could change this liability into an asset. Our shattered dreams and disappointments may break our selfish pride and may enhance our capacity for sympathy.

While abnormal fears distort our lives, fear does warn us of impending dangers and is necessary for survival. Fear is also a powerful creative force. How many significant inventions and intellectual advances derived from a desire to be liberated from some fearful condition!

We are experiencing a national crisis. Yet, a crisis has its opportunities as well as its dangers. The opportunities within this crisis can be utilized for our salvation. My hope, based on faith, is that our nation will yet make the American dream a reality.

The ballot can become one of our most effective weapons. It will empower the Negro to remove politicians who have blocked legislation for decent housing, public safety, jobs, and decent integrated education. By means of the ballot, the Negro can compel the executive and legislative branches of the government to follow the recent courageous examples of the judicial branch.

In our "Operation Breadbasket" program, clergymen have negotiated with executives of chain stores and have been able to pressure them to provide a significant number of jobs to Negroes and use Negro banks.

War has been used as a negative good to stop the spread of evil forces such as Nazism or Fascism. But the destructive power of nuclear weapons now rules out the possibility that war—even a limited war—can any longer serve as a negative good. We must find an alternative to war. President Kennedy warned, "Mankind must put an end to war or war will put an end to mankind."

Justice cannot be divided. If justice is negated anywhere, it is threatened everywhere. Wherever I witness injustice, I am going to oppose it whether it is in Mississippi or in Vietnam.

I have denounced the immorality of the Vietnam War for reasons which are consistent with my nonviolent philosophy, viz., the violence to human life—even burning children with napalm—the dangers it presents of a war with China and a world war, the disproportionate number of young blacks in combat, the war's absorption of funds needed for domestic programs, its rejection of the principle of the brotherhood of man, and its violation of the right of our Vietnamese brothers to self-determination.

In protesting the Vietnam War, I am executing the mission of the Southern Christian Leadership Conference with its motto, "To save the soul of America." I am also responding to the commission imposed on me by the Nobel Peace Prize to work even more for the brotherhood of man and to transcend national allegiances. But even without such a commission, my Christian ministry would have compelled me to speak on behalf of peace.

The nonviolent approach allows us to listen to the enemy's questions and to comprehend his evaluation of us. From his perspective, we may perceive the weaknesses of our position. Thus, the nation may begin to see that it applauds Negroes for adhering to nonviolent tactics here and for using violence in Vietnam. But I am not implying that North Vietnam and the National Liberation Front are moral exemplars.

We who counsel young men about military service should explain to them the immoral nature of this war and challenge them to consider conscientious objection. I urge all ministers of draft age to give up their exemptions and to apply for the status of conscientious objector.

A newsman inquired whether I considered that I should stop

opposing the war since my protest had reduced the financial support for SCLC and had diminished the respect for me. My response was that I did not examine our budget or take a poll of the majority opinion to decide what was right. A genuine leader acts on conscience and does not follow a consensus. He creates a consensus.

The character of a man can be determined not by where he stands in moments of comfort and convenience, but by where he stands when confronted with challenge and controversy. Is he willing to risk his position, his prestige, and even his life for his bruised brothers so that they can live noble lives?

Negroes should be aware that the Jewish people made great personal sacrifices and substantial financial contributions for our Movement. We must remember Andrew Goodman and Michael Schwerner who gave their lives in Mississippi and the rabbis who offered moral witness and marched with us. Moreover, Negroes would do well to emulate the Jewish mass involvement in political action and education.

I lectured before some hostile whites, but the only time I have been booed was at a Chicago mass meeting by several members of the Black Power Movement. My initial reaction was to think of my sufferings and sacrifices over twelve years but I came to realize that they booed me because the dream I had preached had been turned into a nightmare.

Though certain criticisms of us by white men are prompted by malice and contain some distortions, we have to examine them for the elements of truth which can be used as the basis of creative reconstruction.

A militant movement should preserve its vigilance against betrayal by a white colleague. Suspicion does have its place. But occasional betrayals should not be used to rationalize the rejection of Negro-white alliances.

Our nonviolent protests shed light on some of the flaws in our political and economic systems, aroused the conscience of white America, forced a re-examination of the nature of our democracy, and led an insensitive Congress to respond to some of our demands for basic civil rights.

While our Movement challenges America to confront the interrelated systemic evils of racism, economic exploitation, militarism, and materialism—each of which can destroy its spiritual life—we seek a revolution of values and a radical reorganization of society. This includes a reformation of the economy so that it could become person-centered rather than profit-centered. Our nation must not continue to emphasize the value of possessions at the expense of the life of the spirit.

Massive civil disobedience can be effective in our struggle because it can be used to dislocate the functioning of a city without destroying it and to transform the rage of the ghetto into a creative force. It is not wantonly destructive and would be more expensive for the larger society and more resistant to governmental control.

In the Poor People's Campaign, our corps of 3,000 cadre members, trained in nonviolent resistance for three months, initially will direct protests and sit-ins in Washington at the legislative and executive branches of the government in order to secure the creation of a national program for poor people in the Negro, Puerto Rican, Mexican American, Indian, Appalachian white, and other communities.

The massive demonstrations in this campaign will seek not constitutional rights but human rights. They will aim to obtain an Economic Bill of Rights for the Disadvantaged that would guarantee a job for all who are able to work and an annual income for those not able to work, substantially increase the construction of housing for the poor, and provide ample aid to ghetto schools.

Knowing the bitterness of my adversaries and some of the history of my frustrations, people are surprised to learn that I am still an optimist. They do not realize that, by embracing struggle and surmounting obstacles, one can develop a sense of affirmation. My abiding faith in God's love for us provides me with strength and the foundation for this affirmation.

Because of some agonizing situations I have had to endure,

God has become profoundly real to me. I have been aware of His presence and power dispelling my fear and transforming the fatigue of my despair into the buoyancy of hope. In the midst of danger, I have experienced an inner calm. Only God could be the source of the strength I have known.

When we experience disappointments, sorrow, and intense pain, our Christian faith empowers us to preserve our inner peace and hope because we believe, with St. Paul, "All things work together for good to them who love God."

The Cross demonstrates how far God will go to restore the broken community. It reminds me of the beauty of sacrificial love and the redemptive power of Jesus.

The Cross signifies to me the infinite power of God for individual and social salvation and also the sordid weakness of man. It manifests not only the radiance of the divine but man at his worst.

In order to be a Christian, one must carry one's cross with all of its difficulties, agony, and tragedy. Our faith assures us that our willingness to bear our cross with dignity and without bitterness leads to our redemption.

Enduring unearned suffering is, as Gandhi proclaimed, far more powerful than the law of the jungle for converting the opponent. We will wear the opponent down by our capacity to suffer. Unearned suffering can prove to be redemptive for the oppressed and the oppressor.

To understand that we have to suffer in a righteous cause may help us achieve self-fulfillment. We must use our trials for the renewal of ourselves and our nation.

If, in protesting racial injustice, some may have to pay even the price of physical death to free their children and our white brethren from a permanent death of the spirit, then nothing could be more honorable and Christian. Once again, the blood of the martyr may become the seed of freedom.

A man cannot be free if he is afraid of death. If I lived in fear because of all the death threats I have received, I could not function. With God's help, I have conquered the fear of death.

The ultimate evil is not death but to be in opposition to God's will and to be outside of His love.

I choose to identify with the poor—to suffer, sacrifice and when it is necessary, die for them. Philosophically, as a leader, I accept the possibility of my death at any time. I believe my cause is so just that if I should lose my life, in some way it would help the cause. During the Birmingham Movement, the Reverend Fred Shuttlesworth, head of the Alabama Christian Movement for Human Rights, did warn our demonstrators, "You have to be prepared to die before you can begin to live." I would add that if a man has not discovered something for which he is willing to die, he is not fit to live.

7

NELSON MANDELA

In my books, articles, and speeches, I frequently cited the legislation of South Africa that was used for the systematic destruction of the lives of our people. When whites of four territories decided to form the Union of South Africa, the Act of Union (1910) did not recognize the African as a citizen and established the legal right of the white man to dominate him. The Land Acts (1913 and 1936) set the legal limit on the land owned by Africans at 13.7 percent of the country. The Urban Areas Act (1923) created "Native Locations," African slums, to supply cheap labor to white industries.

The Industrial Conciliation Act (1924) did not recognize African men as employees and deprived them of the right to engage in collective bargaining. The Colour Bar Act (1926) banned Africans from the skilled trades.

The Native Administration Act (1927) gave jurisdiction to the Governor-General, representing the British Crown, as the Supreme Chief over all African areas. The Representation of Natives Act (1936) removed Africans in the Cape from the common voters' roll and gave us three whites to represent all of the eight million Africans in a house of 150 representing two million whites. The Native Laws Amendment Act (1937) aimed to eliminate any ways Africans might use to attain full citizenship.

The Asiatic Land Tenure Act (1946), also called the Ghetto Act, specified the areas where the Indians could live and trade and restricted their right to purchase property. They would be represented by token white surrogates in Parliament. This Act provoked a two-year campaign of nonviolent resistance by the Indian community.

The National Party, victorious in the 1948 election with its platform of apartheid ("apartness"), sought to preserve white supremacy by the codification of the laws and regulations that degraded Africans for 300 years. The Dutch Reformed Church supported apartheid for decades, contending that Afrikaners were God's chosen people and that the blacks were an inferior species.

There were laws to preserve racial purity. The Prohibition of Mixed Marriages Act (1949) declared interracial marriages "illegal." The Population Registration Act (1950) granted the government the authority to establish racial classifications for all South Africans—White, Black, Coloured, and Asian. A racial classification determined where one lived or worked and whether one had to carry a pass. The Immorality Act (1950) prohibited sex between whites and non-whites.

Besides being segregated in so many ways and denied the most basic human rights, blacks could be stopped at any time by the police to show their pass. If they did not have a pass, they would be arrested. Under the pass laws, thousands were thrown into jail each year.

The Suppression of Communism Act (1950) declared it a crime, punishable by up to ten years of imprisonment, to be a member of the South African Communist Party (SACP) or to promote its objectives. The Act also allowed the Nationalist government to suppress the opposition to its policies by making it a crime to engage in most forms of political protest. The Act was used to silence and persecute the leaders of our struggle and to attempt to crush the African National Congress (ANC) in addition to the other political organizations representing the legitimate demands of our people.

The Group Areas Act (1950) designated several separate urban areas for each racial group where it could possess land, reside, and trade. Whites, however, could declare any land a white area and take it. This Act empowered the government to force the relocation of the masses.

The Prevention of Illegal Squatting Act (1951) enabled the government to remove unauthorized African settlements from the land reserved for whites. Several million Africans had to give up the land that they owned.

The Bantu Authorities Act (1951) separated Africans into tribal units in the Bantu areas. The government appointed the Commissioners-General who would, in effect, rule the "Bantu National Units," and the Bantu Affairs Department officials under his supervision would administer these "bantustans" or "homelands." The government indicated that the appointed councils of chiefs would gradually be given more power. But the Bantu system had no provision for elections.

Although the government claimed that it wanted to use the system to perpetuate ethnic traditions, it really aimed to foster narrow tribal perspectives and thus impede the development of a national consciousness. The government promoted ethnic rivalries and used this system to establish an African middle class to weaken the ANC.

The Abolition of Passes and Coordination of Documents Act (1952) required all Africans over the age of sixteen to carry a detailed "reference book" of their personal data instead of a pass.

The Native Laws Amendment Act (1952) imposed further restrictions on the right of Africans to live in urban areas.

The Reservation of Separate Amenities Act (1953) allowed that the segregated facilities could be inherently unequal. The State-Aided Institutions Act (1957) enabled the government to enforce segregation in libraries, theaters, and other public cultural facilities.

The Criminal Laws Amendment Act (1953) provided harsh penalties for the demonstrators convicted of offenses during the 1952 Campaign for the Defiance of Unjust Laws. The Act authorized the corporal punishment of those demonstrators

—including even the whipping of women. The Public Safety Act (1953) empowered the government to declare martial law and to depend upon the most ruthless methods to suppress our Movement.

The Bantu Education Act (1953) transferred the control of the African education to the Department of Native Affairs and offered African primary and secondary schools that had been operated by church and mission bodies the options of having the government administer them or get diminished subsidies. Minister of Native Affairs Dr. Hendrik Verwoerd maintained that education had to train students in accordance with their opportunities in life and not arouse expectations in them that could not be fulfilled. Bantu education would aim to train the majority of Africans to be menial workers and to teach them to believe that they were inferior to Europeans. The children of Africans who had collaborated with ruling settlers would be allowed an education in tribal colleges that would teach the doctrine of perpetual white supremacy.

The apartheid education was a crime against our people. Deprived of the vote, they could not compel the government to be responsive to the needs of their children. Our aim in the liberation movement is a unitary nonracial education system.

The Natives Resettlement Act (1954) furnished the basis for preventing Africans from living in the central cities and for situating them in remote and isolated townships.

The Promotion of Bantu Self-Government Act (1959) set up eight separate ethnic bantustans on thirteen percent of the land. Africans were considered as citizens only in their "tribal homelands." According to De Wet Nel, the minister of Bantu Administration and Development, each individual could best develop in his national community, and Africans could never be integrated into the white community.

The Extension of University Education Act (1959) barred non-whites from universities that had been racially "open" and thus established apartheid in higher education.

The Unlawful Organizations Act (1960) did authorize the

proscription of the African National Congress (ANC), the Pan Africanist Congress (PAC), and other similar organizations.

The General Law Amendment Act (Ninety-Day Detention Law) (1963) empowered police to detain, without a warrant, any person suspected of a political crime. A person could be detained without a trial, a charge, any access to a lawyer, and protection against self-incrimination. The police, emboldened by this law, subjected prisoners to electric shock, suffocation, and other forms of torture. They even imprisoned the wives and children of freedom fighters.

The Nationalist government often rejected the charge that it was a Fascist government based on the theories of Hitler's Nazi Party. It was evident, nevertheless, that its proclamations, laws, and policies constituted ample evidence to substantiate this charge.

Racist apartheid denied that any human being is a person of equal value with any other and treated an entire people as subhuman. By imposing hunger and other deprivations on our people, it tried to dehumanize us.

The plight of millions of people was made more intolerable by the opulence of many whites and the cruel manipulation of the economy to contribute to that opulence.

The brutal system of apartheid incorporated the racialism, oppression, and inhumanity of the previous white supremacist regimes. The world condemned it for its repression, political persecution, and terrorization of non-whites.

Some individuals are inclined to be criminals because of either their genes or an abusive upbringing. But the system of apartheid made many otherwise law-abiding citizens become criminals. An immoral and unjust system which enslaves its citizens fosters contempt for its laws and regulations.

In my youth, I lived with the regent of Thembuland. At the beginning of each meeting that he called for the discussion of national matters, he thanked the participants, explained the purpose of the meeting, and then listened to all the men from chiefs to laborers—even to their criticisms of him without defending himself. Only at the conclusion of the meeting, that might last several hours, would he speak and attempt to form a consensus from the views expressed. He believed that a ruler should resemble a shepherd who directs his flock from behind. Listening to how he conducted his court helped me to understand what it means to be a leader.

The organization of early African societies in this country contributed to the development of my political consciousness. The whole tribe—not any individual—owned the land that was the principal means of production. The societies had no classes and were free of economic exploitation and poverty. Each government was based upon the freedom and equality of all of the members of the tribe. They participated in all of the significant decisions of the ruling council.

In 1944, I joined the African National Congress. As the leader of the liberation movement, it has denounced apartheid and raised the political consciousness of the masses. Its main goals have been to organize Africans and to achieve their full political rights. President-General of the ANC Albert Luthuli believed that we could form a society which would provide the world with a new paradigm for democracy. The ANC has always been non-aligned and has welcomed support from both capitalist and socialist countries.

In 1947, in the ANC Youth League, I voted for a resolution demanding the expulsion of the members of the Communist Party from the ANC but the resolution was defeated. I thought that the communists would dominate the ANC due to their superior education, experience, and training, and that they would dilute the concept of African Nationalism.

In a 1948 ANC Youth League policy statement, we defined the objectives of African Nationalism to include 100 percent literacy, free compulsory education for all children and mass adult education with emphasis on moral values. Our aim was to prepare students for responsible citizenship in a democratic society.

The nonviolence in the 1952 Defiance Campaign was not

an absolute, inviolable principle but a tactic required by the situation. Had we used violence, the government would have crushed us.

In Kliptown, near Johannesburg, on June 25 and 26, 1955, more than 3,000 delegates, including more than 300 Indians, 200 Coloured, and 100 whites, assembled for the Congress of the People and approved the Freedom Charter, a revolutionary document that contained the essential requirements for a free and democratic state. The ANC branches had contributed to the framing of the Charter and in 1956 they adopted it as their program. In my speeches in 1993, I continued to affirm that the Charter expressed the economic policy of the ANC.

According to its Preamble, only when a government is based upon the will of the people can it justly claim authority. Only then can it experience internal peace and stability.

The Preamble stated that South Africa should belong to its inhabitants who ought to have equal rights and opportunities. It affirmed that only a democratic state could secure for all the people their birthright to land, liberty, and peace without distinction of color, race, sex or belief.

The Charter maintained that every man and woman would have the right to vote and the right to become a candidate for legislative bodies. People would have the same rights in the state, courts, and schools irrespective of their race, color, sex, or group. They would possess the right to promote their own culture and customs. The law would protect national groups from insults to their race and national pride.

Several provisions in the Charter affirmed the right of the people to share in the wealth of the country. The people as a whole would become owners of the unmined mineral wealth, banks, and monopoly industries. All the land would be given to those who work it.

The legal system would be revised. Everyone would have the right to a fair trial before imprisonment, deportation or restriction. Imprisonment would be imposed only for serious crimes and its purpose would be re-education, not vengeance.

The courts would represent all the people. The police and the army would protect them and respect the privacy of homes. The law would guarantee to every individual the freedoms of speech, the press, assembly, worship, education, and travel.

The Charter did specify the rights of workers. They could join trade unions and, through their elected officers, negotiate wage contracts. All would have the right to work and, if it were necessary, to receive unemployment benefits. Men and women would receive equal pay for equal work. There would be a forty-hour work week, a national minimum wage, paid annual leave, sick leave, and maternity leave on full pay for all working mothers.

The Charter required that the government encourage the development of culture. Education would promote the love of one's people, and the values of human brotherhood, freedom, and peace. Subsidized by the government, education would be compulsory and equal for all the children. All students would have access to higher education or technical training.

The Charter upheld the right of all people to live in decent housing wherever they chose. The state would make unused housing space available and would lower rents. The price of food would be reduced. The state would provide free medical care for all and assume responsibility for the care of the aged, orphans, the disabled, and the sick. All would have the right to recreation.

The conclusion of the Charter expressed our desire in the ANC that South Africa become a state that would respect the rights and the sovereignty of all nations, work toward world peace, and endorse negotiation, not war, for the resolution of international disputes. South Africa would recognize the right of all African peoples to self-government. The Charter ended with an appeal to all who loved their people to state that they would fight until they achieved their liberty.

The ANC adopted the principles of education in the United Nations' "Universal Declaration of Human Rights." Everyone has a right to an education that fosters the development of the personality and promotes respect for human rights and basic freedoms. Parents should have the right to choose the type of education given to their children.

Our educational program would use the valid elements of the African's own culture and civilization as a foundation and assimilate the best elements from European and other sources. Africa could thereby make a distinctive contribution to human progress and happiness.

Ever since its founding on April 6, 1959, the Pan Africanist Congress (PAC) rejected the multiracialism of the ANC. Its leaders thought that the white communists and Indians were dominating the ANC. Robert Sobukwe, the president of PAC, did demand a government of Africans, by Africans, and for Africans, and viewed whites and Indians as foreign minority groups or aliens who did not have any right to be in Africa. In May 1961, PAC tried unsuccessfully to sabotage our strike by issuing pamphlets that urged people to go to work and not to protest.

Our 1956 Treason Trial, concluding in 1962, charged 156 political leaders with taking part in a conspiracy, inspired by international communism, to use violence to overthrow the South African state. When the judge asked me if the idea of a classless society appealed to me, I asserted that it did since the existence of classes causes many evils. One class exploits another.

The ANC has never been a communist organization. In our Treason Trial, the judge declared that the prosecution had not proven that the ANC was a communist organization or that our Freedom Charter contained a plan for a communist state. The ANC and the South African Communist Party have been distinct organizations that have been cooperating on certain short-term objectives like the overthrow of racist oppression and the building of a nonracial society but with quite different ultimate goals. The ANC has been willing to work with any group against racist oppression.

On March 21, 1960, unarmed and controlled demonstrators

outside police headquarters in Sharpeville were protesting the laws requiring them to carry passes. The police shot into the crowd of men, women, and children, killing 69 and wounding 186. A state of emergency was declared, and nearly 20,000 people were detained.

How did the government respond to our "stay-at-home" peaceful and disciplined protest in May 1961? By mobilizing its armed forces, arresting our activists and passing laws so that it could detain them without trial for twelve days.

What impact did our nonviolence have on the government leaders? Nonviolence did not curb the violence and could not change hearts. They interpreted our nonviolence as weakness and as an invitation to use violence without fear of reprisals.

Several barbarous methods were used to support apartheid. Unarmed demonstrators were arrested, prosecuted, and jailed, and many of them were then tortured and murdered, including children. Millions were evicted from their homes and lands without recompense and then relocated so that they would be available to work for miserable wages to satisfy the appetites of the land barons and industrialists. African laborers were whipped and murdered by European farmers for participating in a strike and even for verbal insubordination. Families were disrupted, and the children were separated from their mothers, and given an inferior education.

The government promoted hatred between non-whites and whites and among non-white groups. Under apartheid, lives of non-whites, individually and collectively, were regarded as insignificant.

In my address at the Pan-African Freedom Conference in Addis Ababa in January 1962, I indicated that since 1952, the government had used its legal powers to impede the activities of the leaders of the ANC. Many were forced to resign. Other leaders were prohibited from attending ANC meetings for up to five years or restricted to certain districts or banished from their homes or deported from the country.

In my Rivonia trial in April 1964, I revealed that when, as

a youth, I listened to the elders of my tribe describe the wars in defense of the fatherland, I began to hope that I might have the opportunity, like our glorious heroes, to contribute to the freedom struggle.

While I was in prison at Robben Island, I taught a course in political economy for several years. I attempted to present the economic evolution from communal societies to feudalism, capitalism, and socialism. I consider socialism as the highest stage in this evolution.

I have always believed in the value of physical exercise for dispelling tension and producing health, clarity of thought, and peace of mind. In my Robben Island cell, from Monday to Thursday, I followed my boxing routine of exercise, including stationary running for 45 minutes, 200 sit-ups, 100 fingertip push-ups, 50 deep knee-bends, and other calisthenics. Later, in the communal cell at Poolsmoor Prison, I would wake up an hour and a half early to do my exercises—which did not please my colleagues.

We had to determine whether the ANC should reach out to government-sponsored institutions or boycott them. Although several of my colleagues thought that we should disavow the chiefs of these organizations, I believed that the ANC could become stronger by cooperating with them. Therefore, I met with a group of Thembu chiefs who visited the prison.

Chief Albert Luthuli has affirmed that a chief is a servant and voice of his people. Our country has had some dedicated chiefs who served the interests of their people, but there have been those chiefs who increased the suffering of their people by collaborating with the system of apartheid. Several of the latter have altered their ways, and we commend them for their transformation.

The Congress of Democrats (COD), a party for left-wing, anti-apartheid whites, worked for full equality between blacks and whites, and supported the ANC. Whites made substantial contributions to the labor struggles in the 1970s as members of the Trade Unions Advisory and Coordinating Council and the Wages Commission. The white European students at the University of Rhodes and Witwatersran University took part in ANC demonstrations.

Since 1976, the ANC was indebted to Angola for allowing us to establish military camps to train our young people in our values and discipline, to intensify our armed struggle, and to receive weapons from other friendly countries.

In my Rivonia trial, I maintained that, like Gandhi, Nehru, Nkrumah, and Nasser, I did recognize the need for some form of socialism so that our people could overcome their extreme poverty. In July 1989, I reiterated this position in a letter to President P. W. Botha.

In his inaugural address on September 20, 1989, President F. W. de Klerk asserted that the only way to peace and justice for all was the way of reconciliation and that his government would negotiate with any group committed to peace. He then dismantled some of the structure of apartheid, released some of my comrades from prison, and allowed a march to protest police brutality.

The South African Communist Party (SACP) made several sterling contributions to our struggle. General Secretary Joe Slovo was able to persuade me that the ANC ought to suspend the armed struggle to generate an atmosphere for negotiation. Moreover, in a published paper, he proposed that our new government include power sharing with the National Party for a definite time, an amnesty for the security officers, and the honoring of contracts of civil servants.

The officials of the ANC understood that the majority of whites feared that the principle "one person–one vote" might result in black domination. We knew that we had to persuade these whites by our conduct that a new South Africa would be nonracial in its policies and would provide peace and security for all its citizens.

In 1990, I did not anticipate much difficulty in making the transition from a racial to a nonracial society. We did have the example of Namibia, that was able to create an effective government of national reconciliation with the support of all population groups.

In a speech upon my release from Victor Verster Prison on February 11, 1990, I expressed my gratitude to those who had contributed to our struggle: the millions of people in South Africa and throughout the world who had campaigned for my release, Oliver Tambo for his fine leadership of the ANC, the members of the ANC, the combatants of our military wing, Umkhonto we Sizwe, who sacrificed their lives, the women of the nation—the foundation of the struggle—the Black Sash, the South African Communist Party and Joe Slovo, the United Democratic Front, the National Education Crisis Committee, the South African Youth Congress, the Transvaal and the Natal Indian Congresses, the Mass Democratic Movement, the Congress of South African Trade Unions, the working class, the National Union of South African Students, the young activists, the Frontline States, religious communities who were the voice for the Movement when organizations were silenced, and especially my wife and family.

In a 1973 interview in prison, I revealed that I had never experienced a moment of depression because I knew that our struggle would be victorious. In a 1990 speech at Wembley Stadium in London, I affirmed that in all my many years in apartheid dungeons I had always remained confident that I would be released. In my 1994 autobiography, I indicated that I had never seriously considered the possibility that I might not be released.

Oliver Tambo was my best friend for fifty years. He was able to keep the ANC united and strong under very difficult circumstances and place it on the political center stage. He served as a splendid ambassador for the ANC to other nations. In *The Republic*, Plato used "the allegory of the metals" to classify persons in the best possible state as gold, silver or lead. Oliver Tambo was pure gold because of his intelligence, warmth, tolerance, generosity, capacity for self-sacrifice, and loyalty.

Students provided vitality for our political movement. The emergence of a national consciousness among them involved defeat for those who had resisted the demands and legitimate aspirations of the African people.

Under Prime Minister Margaret Thatcher, who did differ with us about our methods, Britain provided support for our Movement by its condemnation of apartheid. Emperor Haile Selassie, though he was a feudal ruler, also contributed to our struggle. Despite its internal policies, the Soviet Union, with a lengthy history of condemning racism, supported us.

The policies of the ANC have appealed to my convictions. Because I have been a loyal and disciplined member, I agree with its objectives, strategies, and tactics. I have not been a member of any other organization. After being released from prison, I was asked by the press about what role I would play in the ANC. My response was that it would be what the ANC ordered.

In the ANC, we held that those who would negotiate with the government and establish the foundations for a new South Africa, including framing a nonracial constitution, should be democratically selected in nonracial elections. Their decisions could then be supported by the majority of the people.

At a 1990 town meeting in New York City sponsored by the Council on Foreign Relations, I asserted that the ANC would not restrict the right of women to participate in the political activities of the country. Women were members of the ANC delegation to Cape Town.

In response to a question in 1990, I stated that it was not for me to declare who would be the first president of the new South Africa. That was for the people to decide.

Freedom is indivisible. To deny the rights of one person is to diminish the freedom of others.

The ANC's attitude toward a country has been determined by that country's attitude toward our liberation struggle. Yasir Arafat, Muammar el-Qaddafi, and Fidel Castro supported our Movement with their rhetoric but also with their resources.

We did identify with the Palestinian Liberation Organization (PLO) since it struggled for the right of self-determination.

Several countries in the West approached our struggle only from the point of view of their own interests and expected us to join with them in their vendettas and to reject our comrades in Cuba, Libya, and the PLO who remained so loyal to us. We refused to do that.

We in the ANC have supported the right of Israel to exist as a state within secure borders. We have sympathized with the Jewish people because of the persecutions they endured. We have been impressed with the absence of racialism in their communities. When we were prosecuted, Jewish lawyers did decide to defend us. Although many Jews have contributed to our struggle—some in prominent positions—we have not been willing to regard the enemies of Israel as our enemies.

At a 1990 rally in Durban, I warned that we should not rely too much on our political leaders to negotiate a settlement. Only the ordinary men and women of the country—the real makers of history—through their participation in political decisions and their united action could attain true democracy and freedom.

In the struggle, we had to remain on the moral high ground. While we could be flexible with regard to our tactics, we had to adhere consistently to our principles. One who changes his principles depending on the situation cannot be the leader of a nation.

In my June 1990 address at the United Nations, I asserted that the only victory all South Africans ought to be seeking was not the victory of one party over another but the victory of the people as a whole.

Chief Mangosuthu Gatsha Buthelezi, head of the Inkatha Freedom Party (IFP) and chief minister of KwaZulu, called for the unbanning of the ANC and would not negotiate with the government until it released all of the political prisoners. Nevertheless, he opposed our armed struggle, criticized the 1976 Soweto uprising, opposed international sanctions, and rejected the idea of a unitary state of South Africa.

I wanted the ANC to meet with the IFP so that we could solve the problems between us and end the violence in Natal. At several rallies in 1990, I insisted that no solution could be achieved without the participation of Chief Buthelezi.

Although President de Klerk did recognize the necessity of change, he adopted a gradualist approach toward emancipation and aimed to ensure that ultimately the white minority would share political power. Before negotiations could commence, we required that he take several steps, including ending the state of emergency and freeing all political prisoners.

In a 1990 speech to business executives in South Africa, I asserted that blacks should be allowed to participate in the expansion of national wealth in the form of higher incomes. I did emphasize that our proposed democratic state would have a responsibility to increase the public spending in education, housing, health, unemployment benefits, pensions and other areas in order to protect the most disadvantaged.

The leaders of the ANC were practical men and women who focused on the conditions in our country. As we planned for a new South Africa, our concern was not with economic models or labels—Marxist, socialist or capitalist—but rather with generating a vigorous economy that would ensure full employment and maximum production as well as stimulate development of social justice by providing whatever makes a life human and joyful.

In a 1990 address to the Congress of the United States, I referred to our plan to design a relationship with the Western nations whereby our people would profit from their capital, technology, expertise, and markets. Moreover, it would be a mutually beneficial relationship, free from the subservience that marked the era of white domination.

Before our nonracial constitution was written, I indicated that we would examine the Constitution of the United States and other constitutions in addition to the legal provisions in the United States against discrimination to determine what we could adopt.

In a 1990 address before the United Nations, I warned that some South African whites were forming paramilitary groups whose stated purpose was the assassination of the leaders and members of the ANC.

In response to a question in 1990, I explained that usually I did not think about death threats and that the ANC gave me enough assignments to require my attention from morning to sunset.

In 1990, I did assure the Congress of the United States that in our new government the rights of every individual would be guaranteed and protected by a democratic constitution, the rule of law, and a bill of rights that would be enforced by an independent judiciary and a multi-party system.

How could we have read the United States' Declaration of Independence and not have chosen to join in the struggle to guarantee the people's right to life, liberty, and the pursuit of happiness?

How could my colleagues and I have read about George Washington, Thomas Jefferson, and Abraham Lincoln and not be moved to act as they were moved to act?

In prison, I studied the American civil rights struggle. At a 1990 Yankee Stadium rally, I referred to the bond between black South Africans and black Americans as the children of Africa. Great Americans, such as Marcus Garvey, W.E.B. Du Bois, and Martin Luther King, Jr. reinforced that kinship.

How could we have admired John Brown, Sojourner Truth, Frederick Douglass, Marcus Garvey, W.E.B. Du Bois, Martin Luther King, Jr. and others and not be inspired to act as they did?

Dr. Du Bois was an early participant in the struggle for the emancipation of South Africa. At the 1900 Races Conference in London, he protested the exploitation of blacks in South Africa. He and his colleagues had maintained their opposition to minority rule here on the agenda of the NAACP since its inception in 1909.

While Marxists have criticized the parliamentary system of the West as undemocratic, I have revered such a system. I would judge the British Parliament to be the most democratic institution in the world, and I do admire its judiciary for its impartiality and independence. This is not to condone all their actions—especially some of the ways they have dealt with my people. I admire also the Congress of the United States, the country's implementation of the doctrine of the separation of powers, and the independence of its judiciary.

In 1990, I warned the United States Congress that we would have peace in our country only after the apartheid system was ended.

In a 1993 interview with the ANC magazine *Mayibuye*, I referred to the principal results of the ANC negotiations with the government: the termination of the state of emergency, the release of the political prisoners, the return of the exiles, an atmosphere of free political activity in most of the country and the revision or repeal of repressive laws. I anticipated the installation of a transitional executive council and elections for a constituent assembly which would create a new national constitution.

In my inauguration address on May 10, 1994, I encouraged South Africans to act as a united people in order to build a new nation. I interpreted my mission to be one of producing trust, binding the many wounds of the country, and promoting reconciliation.

While I believed that the liberation of South Africa would stimulate economic development, I did not want to exaggerate what would be the beneficial impact of liberation because I thought that it would take even generations to overcome the legacies of colonialism.

Consistent with the spirit of reconciliation in our Freedom Charter which affirmed that our country belonged to all who lived in it, we called upon our white compatriots to join us in establishing a new South Africa. Whites have participated in our policy decisions in the ANC, and they joined our military force. Some judges openly criticized the cruelty of apartheid. The kindness of several of my white guards in my last years in prison strengthened my conviction concerning the essential humanity of the whites who had imprisoned me for more than twenty-five years.

In 1960, Chief Albert Luthuli received the Nobel Peace Prize—a tribute to him as the leader of our moral struggle and an apparent affront to the National Party. In 1984, Archbishop Desmond Tutu was awarded the prize due to his opposition to racism. By his words and courage, he had fought racism and inspired a nation. I assumed that the Nobel Committee would not consider me because I was the founder of Umkhonto we Sizwe that conducted our armed struggle. But in 1993, they awarded the prize to F. W. de Klerk and me. I accepted it on behalf of all who had participated in our struggle.

While the relationship between President de Klerk and the ANC was at times very unsatisfactory, I thought that he made an indispensable contribution to the peace process. When we received the peace prize, I paid tribute to him for his courage in acknowledging the horrendous wrong of apartheid and for his understanding that all the people of South Africa should determine their future through the political process.

In the words of the prophet Isaiah: "We have risen up as on the wings of eagles. We have run and not grown weary. We have walked and not fainted."

THE POWER OF THE NEGATIVE

I did not determine on a particular day to dedicate my life to the liberation of my people. Rather, a thousand indignities created in me an anger, a spirit of rebelliousness, and a desire to overthrow the system that oppressed my people.

In my youth, I had an experience that helped me to learn how to relate to my opponents. I did attempt to ride a donkey. To unseat me, he ran into a thornbush which scratched my face—embarrassing me before my friends. I then understood that it is cruel and unnecessary to compel a person to suffer by humiliating him. Even as a boy, while seeking to defeat my opponents, I attempted not to dishonor them.

My father and mother had never attended school. My father officiated at the traditional rites concerning planting, harvest, birth, initiation ceremonies, marriage, and funerals. After a friend of our family proposed that I should go to school, my father decided that I should—perhaps, because of his own lack of education.

While South African law firms generally would not employ an African as an articled clerk, a Jewish firm did hire me. I have found that Jews are more liberal on racial and political issues than most whites possibly because historically they have been so victimized by prejudice.

It was painful to have to live a life of poverty even at times when I was not in prison. Still, although my poverty repelled many, it did inspire generosity and true friendship in a few.

Mantsebo Moshweshwe, the queen regent of Basutoland—which is now Lesotho—spoke to me in Sesotho in 1942 and learned that I knew only a few words. She questioned me in English as to what kind of lawyer and leader I would be when I could not speak the language of my people. This question embarrassed me but did enable me to realize my parochialism that had been influenced by the ethnic divisions encouraged by the white government. I then understood how unprepared I was to serve my people.

With great delight, I marched in August 1943 with 10,000 demonstrators in Alexandra Township in order to oppose the bus fare increase. I was impressed that the protest was able to compel the bus company to rescind the increase.

In 1944, our ANC Youth League Manifesto protested how two million white men dominated eight million Africans by segregating them in political, religious, economic, and social life. White men owned eighty-seven percent of the land while Africans had to struggle to exist on the remainder.

In the Manifesto, we maintained that the severity of the domination by whites generated in Africans a hatred of any impediment on their path to full and free citizenship and that their feelings would find expression.

The Manifesto presupposed that blacks in South Africa did know that they could not depend upon the white man to free them. They realized that they had to sweat for their freedom and to determine their destiny through the ANC.

In 1946, in opposition to the Asiatic Land Tenure Act and the Ghetto Act, the Indian community organized a two-year campaign in the Transvaal in which 2,000 volunteers went to jail. The campaign, patterned after Mahatma Gandhi's 1913 campaign, that challenged the immigration laws, became the exemplar for our protest in the Youth League because of its organization, militancy, and capacity for sacrifice.

In the 1948 election, I was stunned by the victory of the revived National Party with its apartheid platform over the United Party, led by General Jan Smuts, who had denounced apartheid as "a crazy concept, born of prejudice and fear." Nevertheless, I valued the judgment of Oliver Tambo, who stated that he liked this outcome since it allowed us to know exactly who our enemies were and where we stood.

When the Nationalist government used the Prohibition of Mixed Marriages Act, the Population and Registration Act, the Immorality Amendment Act and the Group Areas Act for the implementation of apartheid, the ANC reacted in 1949 by launching a campaign in order to transform itself into a mass organization.

Why did Africans hate the pass laws? Because these laws permitted the police to challenge Africans at any time. Was there a single African male—already segregated in his job, residence, and transportation—who was not subjected to this additional harassment? Thousands who could not produce a pass were imprisoned. These laws did disrupt family life by separating husbands from their wives.

For three decades, the ANC had conformed to objectives in its 1919 constitution: "to record all grievances and wants of native people and to seek by constitutional means the redress thereof." The ANC used a variety of tactics such as petitions, delegations to the authorities and the passing of resolutions to protest discrimination and the exclusion of Africans from government. The ANC pursued these tactics with the belief that the authorities would grant the rights it demanded.

In December 1949, because the government continued to ignore the petitions of the ANC and expanded its repressive tactics, our ANC Youth League was able to persuade an ANC conference to accept our radical "Programme of Action." It stated that Africans were entitled to self-determination and called for the use of boycotts, strikes, stay-at-homes, protest demonstrations, civil disobedience, and other peaceful but unlawful means to achieve our goals.

In our struggle, the boycott has been an effective method. But it should be used only as objective conditions require it. When it might not be prudent to utilize the boycott, another tactical weapon such as a demonstration, protest march, strike or civil disobedience may be appropriate.

When confronted with the choice between obeying a law that denied our right to protest or disobeying that law, we had to follow the dictates of our conscience, put our pursuit of the public good above the demands of this unjust law and engage in civil disobedience. Also, why were we legally or morally bound to obey laws that we did not help establish? Moreover, in seeking justice, why should we have looked to the courts that enforced laws which negated human rights?

On June 26, 1950, the ANC conducted the Day of Protest, a political strike, to protest the murder of eighteen Africans by the government on May 1 and to denounce the passage of the Suppression of Communism Act, which gave the government the power to ban an organization or individual that challenged its policies. I was very pleased with the degree of success of the campaign since we were fighting against such formidable odds.

Since I am a Christian, I do not believe in the materialistic theories of Marx, Engels, Lenin, and Stalin. However, I do approve of the Marxist conceptions that struggle is necessary for historical progress and that revolutions are required for fundamental changes. The ANC welcomed Marxists into its ranks because they supported national liberation movements.

Even though the Communist Party had no color bar and the idea of a classless society appealed to me, I did not become a member of the Communist Party. I was opposed not only to its philosophy of materialism but to its antipathy to religion. Nevertheless, I did develop friendships with communists who worked with the ANC. Then too, I was impressed with how communist countries supported Afro-Asian struggles against colonialism.

In my "Presidential Address" to the ANC Youth League in 1951, I alluded to our setbacks in the struggle because of our inexperience but argued that many of us developed due to our failures and that we should engage in more self-criticism in preparing for other campaigns. At a 1991 ANC conference, I repeated this recommendation.

Chief Albert Luthuli, the president of the ANC, questioned the value of moderate tactics when the government did not even respond to his petitions for thirty years and when our people had reached the point where they had almost no rights.

Our people had to understand that we could not wait for a future parliament to produce the laws that would acknowledge our dignity as human beings. We were compelled to wage a determined struggle against opposition by a desperate regime to win even one battle for our political rights.

In 1952, I served as the national volunteer-in-chief in the Campaign for the Defiance of Unjust Laws, launched by the ANC and the South African Indian Congress. The volunteers defied the pass laws, violated the curfew, and held sit-ins at "Whites Only" railway compartment waiting rooms and post office entrances. Before the campaign, usually a stigma was attached to being imprisoned. But the campaign removed the stigma and fear of prison. Africans had come to regard going to prison as a badge of honor.

Because of the Defiance Campaign, the conscience of the European public became more aware of the suffering of the African people. More than 8,000 volunteers were imprisoned for civil disobedience of the apartheid laws but none of them committed a violent act. In our trial after the campaign, the judge suspended all the sentences imposed upon my nineteen colleagues and myself because we had led a disciplined and nonviolent campaign. This campaign induced the formation of the Liberal Party and the Congress of Democrats, and led to discussions at the United Nations on the policies of apartheid.

As ANC Transvaal President in 1953, I maintained that the racist policies of the government had aroused the righteous indignation of men of conscience. I warned those in power that if they continued to resort to brutal methods, the clash between the forces of freedom and the forces of reaction was inevitable.

At a 1953 ANC meeting, I quoted Pandit Nehru, "There is no easy walk to freedom anywhere, and many of us will have to pass through the valley of the shadow of death again and again before we reach the mountain tops of our desires."

In 1954, the Law Society of the Transvaal submitted to the Supreme Court an application to have my name removed from the roll of accredited attorneys. It denounced my activities in the Defiance Campaign as "unprofessional and dishonorable." This application, however, had the effect of generating offers of assistance from many Afrikaner lawyers—including even some supporters of the National Party—who did recognize the prejudice in the application. Their reaction indicated that at times even in racist South Africa, individuals could make legal judgments in terms of professional solidarity and not just color. The Supreme Court did determine that it was not dishonorable for me as an attorney to join with my people in their struggle for political rights even if my activities violated the laws of the country.

My opposition to discrimination has been grounded in my sense of duty to my people and my profession. As a lawyer, in protesting injustice, I believed I was supporting the dignity of an honorable profession.

In 1955, I urged the ANC to use the government's attacks on the people's organizations and the Bantu Education Act as well as all other discriminatory measures as rallying points to achieve a united front.

In trying to persuade a tribal chief to oppose the imposition of the Bantu Authorities, I told him that I believed he was putting his own interests before those of the community and that if I were in a similar position, I would attempt to put the interests of my people before my own. When, however, the chief stiffened at the moral rebuke, I regretted my approach. This experience did teach me that, in discussions, there is no distinct advantage in adopting a morally superior tone toward one's opponent.

The demands in our 1955 Freedom Charter implied that we aimed to engage in a national campaign of struggle in order to defeat the economic and political policies of the Nationalist government.

The Freedom Charter called for the abolition of apartheid laws and all discriminatory practices—including the pass laws and the laws that disrupted families—and for the end of the restriction of ownership of land on a racial basis. The society described in the Charter would not allow forced labor, child labor, compound labor, the tot system (paying laborers in part with wine), contract labor, and farm prisons. The free society would demolish slums and construct new suburbs, seek to end adult illiteracy by a mass education plan, and end the color bar in economic, political, educational, and cultural life.

Severe restrictions had made it illegal for some leaders of the ANC to meet with each other. In December 1956, almost all the banned and unbanned leaders were arrested and then transferred to the Johannesburg Prison. While awaiting trial, we were happy to have the opportunity to exchange ideas and experiences for two weeks.

We were pleased that our arrests provoked demonstrations around the world. In protests throughout South Africa, signs proclaimed, "We Stand by Our Leaders."

A freedom fighter should aim not for his own glory but for the liberation of millions of people. Even as he subordinates his family to the family of the people, he must subordinate his own personal feelings to the liberation movement.

In 1959, when there was resistance to the Bantu Authorities in Zeerust, the government jailed, tortured, and murdered scores of innocent people. In response to this repression, a number of branches of the ANC were formed in Zeerust—one with about 2,000 members.

In our Treason Trial, Chief Luthuli explained the policy of the ANC on nonviolence by drawing the distinction between pacifism and nonviolence. When violently attacked, pacifists do not engage in self-defense but men and nations, committed to nonviolence, sometimes have to defend themselves.

I testified that the ANC was not opposed to whites but did resist white supremacy and its unjust laws. I informed the court that we consistently preached racial harmony and condemned racialism.

In 1953, the Liberal Party had proclaimed its belief in the essential dignity of every human being. But I criticized it for, in effect, supporting the apartheid regime because it would rely upon only constitutional means in pursuing its goals and it repudiated the principle of "one person-one vote." It held, therefore, that the black majority had to obey a constitution that prevented them from participating in government. By its allegiance to the constitution, the Liberal Party accepted the slavery of the people, low wages, mass unemployment, and wretched housing. In my 1960 court testimony, however, I stressed that the Liberal Party had altered its positions, was working closely with the ANC, and had accepted many of its policies.

In March 1961, our All-in African Conference did propose that the government summon a national convention of elected representatives irrespective of race, color or creed to form a nonracial democratic constitution for South Africa that would eliminate the policies of racial oppression. The conference resolved that if the government did not call the convention, we would conduct demonstrations throughout the country on the eve of the establishment of the Republic and would call on all Africans not to cooperate with it. The conference asked other nations to apply sanctions against the Republic.

In our leaflet announcing a national three-day stay-at-home protest beginning on May 29, 1961, we did explain that the government rejected our demands for a national convention in order to construct the constitution for a democracy, universal adult suffrage, decent wages, the abolition of the pass laws, and an end to minority white domination.

To suppress the stay-at-home campaign, the government quickly adopted strong-arm measures such as calling up the army, arming the European civilians, deploying the police in the African townships and other areas, banning meetings and jailing more than 10,000 innocent Africans under the pass laws. The stringent nature of these measures proved that the government considered our Movement as the most powerful opponent to its policies.

An atmosphere of crisis permeated the celebrations by the

government that marked the inauguration of the Republic on May 31, 1961. The country even resembled a restless military camp. This panic-stricken display of force was an indication of the power of the liberation movement.

In a letter to newspapers on June 26, 1961, I explained that I would not surrender to a government I did not recognize and that, for the sake of our noble cause, I had to leave my wife, children, mother, and sisters, give up my profession, and go underground, living as an outlaw in my own land. I affirmed that freedom could be achieved only through militant action, hardship, and sacrifice and declared my intention to continue fighting for freedom for the rest of my life.

In the letter, I did urge blacks to withdraw their cooperation from the Nationalist government and to seek to undermine the economy of the country. I revealed our intention in the ANC to appeal to all nations to end their economic and diplomatic relations with South Africa.

We in the ANC summoned the international community to participate in our struggle by imposing comprehensive and mandatory sanctions that could force the Pretoria regime to terminate the apartheid system and could minimize the loss of life that would otherwise have occurred to reach this goal.

An objection against our appeal for sanctions was that they would hurt our people. Still, I contended that our people had to tighten their belts and be willing to make sacrifices for the greater good of achieving their freedom.

When the government banned demonstrations, closed other channels of peaceful communication, and escalated the use of violence—even beating the people in their homes during the stay-at-home—the ANC's leaders decided to respond to the violence by adopting violent tactics while continuing strikes, civil disobedience, and mass demonstrations. The ANC would have committed a crime against its people if it did not expand its tactics.

I regarded nonviolence not as a moral principle but only as a strategy. In order for nonviolent resistance to be effective, your opponent must comply with the same rules as you do. Gandhi could be successful in dealing with the British partly because ultimately they were realistic and prudent. But the Afrikaners in South Africa proved to be quite different from the British. Against such an opponent, nonviolence could not be effective. When the Afrikaners continued to use violence against peaceful protests, it was no longer moral for us to use an ineffective strategy.

In November 1961, my colleagues and I did establish the Umkhonto we Sizwe (MK), the Spear of the Nation, as the multiracial military wing of the ANC against the violence of the apartheid regime. We hoped that this organization would cause the government to dismantle apartheid and would thus help us to avoid a civil war between blacks and whites which would have involved a great loss of life and much bitterness. We knew that it had taken more than fifty years to efface the scars of the Anglo-Boer War.

We founded Umkhonto we Sizwe as a defense against the reign of terror of the apartheid regime. If the oppressor uses violence, the oppressed ought to respond with violence. An African proverb states that you are unable to avert an attack by a wild beast with only bare hands. One can use violence in self-defense and still be a good Christian. Didn't Christ drive the money-changers from the temple?

As the first commander-in-chief of Umkhonto we Sizwe, I helped to organize a campaign of selective sabotage of empty government buildings, electric power stations, and rail and telephone lines. This campaign was intended to discourage the investment of foreign capital in the country. It would also channel the anger of our people and thus reduce the number of outbreaks of terrorism.

Members of Umkhonto we Sizwe would take precautions to avoid killing or injuring people, focus on the destruction of buildings, and not be armed on their operations. We did not believe in assassination. Because it aimed to avoid the loss of life, it would provoke less bitterness than terrorism, guerrilla warfare or open revolution. We judged that sabotage was the option which, at the time, best provided hope for future race relations. Nevertheless, we did prepare for guerrilla warfare if sabotage were to fail.

If we had not responded with armed struggle to the reign of terror by the regime when nonviolent forms of resistance proved to be ineffective, then we would not have been men of moral integrity. We would have surrendered to a government of minority rule and betrayed our cause. We believed that we had a moral obligation to engage in armed struggle.

When I was indicted in 1962 for inciting African workers to strike and for leaving the country without the valid travel documents, I decided to use the trial as a showcase to explain the ANC's moral opposition to racism. As a representative of freedom, justice, and democracy, I intended to denounce the oppressive government that repudiated these values. In its own court, I would put the state on trial.

I testified that I did what the philosopher Bertrand Russell did. His conscience caused him to disobey an unjust law. He was convicted and sentenced for protesting his government's nuclear weapons policy. Because of the morality of his cause and his obligation to humanity, he violated the unjust law and suffered the consequences of his disobedience.

In my concluding statement, I stressed that I fought against white domination and black domination. I expressed my hope that we would become a democratic society and professed my willingness to die, if necessary, to achieve that ideal.

Before the sentence, I told the judge that my hatred for the dreadful conditions imposed on my people was more powerful than my fear of the terrible conditions I might have to endure in prison. I emphasized that, after completing my sentence, my hatred of racial discrimination would move me to resume the struggle for the removal of the injustices.

I told my lawyers that if the judge asked me why he should not declare the sentence of death, I would tell him that I was prepared to die. I would not appeal the sentence. I was certain that my death and the deaths of comrades could be sources of inspiration and that we might best serve the cause as martyrs.

The recollection of our martyrs had encouraged our people to overcome divisions in their ranks and to remain committed to the struggle.

One cannot truly understand a nation unless one has been inside its jails. We should judge a nation not by how it treats its highest citizens, but its lowest ones. South Africa treated its imprisoned citizens like animals.

In prison, my hatred for the system of apartheid increased while my anger toward whites decreased. I hated the system that placed us in opposition to each other but I loved even my enemies.

As political offenders, we were denied privileges that were granted to those convicted of murder or rape. Prison did test character, revealing some men to possess a spiritual strength and others to be less than they had seemed to be.

In an isolation cell for several days, I received only water that had been boiled in rice. This and my other experiences in prison enabled me to realize that the spirit, when it is fortified by strong convictions, can then empower the body to survive deprivation.

By challenging the injustice of our conditions in prison, we tried to preserve our humanity. We viewed our opposition to these conditions as part of the campaign against the injustice of apartheid. We had to struggle to obtain the basics in prison such as proper food, long trousers, and study privileges. It took almost three years to be allowed sunglasses for work in the lime quarry.

While my colleagues and I experienced many deprivations in prison, the enforced isolation did give us time to think and study. I was able to engage in correspondence studies for my bachelor of laws degree. For many of my years in prison, I participated in political discourses, even while working in the quarry. Prison conditions tended to temper our debates and helped my colleagues in the ANC and me to understand more what united us with members of the Pan Africanist Congress and others than what divided us.

In the classic Greek plays I studied in prison, I found the notions that character could be judged by how one confronted difficult situations and that a hero was a person who did not break even under the most challenging circumstances.

As a member of our prison drama society, I was asked to portray Creon, the king of Thebes, in *Antigone*. I did consider Antigone to be a freedom fighter and a symbol of our struggle because she rebelled against an unjust law on the grounds that the moral law was higher than that of the state.

The brutal oppression by the apartheid system inflicted a deep and abiding wound on my people. Still, it also had the effect of producing men with extraordinary courage, wisdom, and generosity in the liberation movement. It may have taken such severe oppression to create such character. I learned the meaning of courage from these comrades who were willing to endure torture and risk their lives for an ideal.

In a 1976 message from prison, I did appeal to Africans, Coloureds, Indians, and democratic whites to submerge their differences and close ranks so that they could form a solid wall of resistance to apartheid. In the ANC, we cherished the value of unity as the foundation of our struggle.

Bantu Education, designed by the government to support apartheid, produced such indignation in a generation of black youth in the 1970s that they rebelled against the system and helped expose its moral bankruptcy.

On January 31, 1985, I was offered my freedom for the sixth time. President P. W. Botha made the offer that required me to repudiate violence as a political instrument. In rejecting the offer, I believed that if I were to leave prison and return to an apartheid society, I would be morally compelled to resume the activities that had caused my imprisonment. As long as there were pass laws, the ban on the ANC, and other apartheid restrictions, I could not agree to my release. I asserted that while I cherished my life and freedom, I cared more for the freedom of the people. Because I was their representative in prison, I would not sell my birthright or theirs to secure my freedom.

In 1985, my cell in Pollsmoor Prison separated me from my colleagues. Still, I considered this isolation as an opportunity freeing me, without opposition from my colleagues, to initiate discussions with the government to avoid more violence and war. Moreover, if my negotiations were not successful, my colleagues could maintain that I had acted as an individual and not as a representative of the ANC.

People gave their lives for the demand of "one person, one vote." There could not be any compromise over this demand.

In 1985, I did warn that if the leaders of the government persisted in their refusal to meet with us to discuss political equality and indicated that we had to remain subjugated by whites, then we would continue to use violence.

Given the contributions of the Communist Party of South Africa to our Movement, I was unwilling in 1989 to accede to the government's demand that we end our association with it. How could the government have its treaties with the Marxist states of Angola and Mozambique and refuse to talk to the South African Marxists?

The Harare Declaration, initiated by the ANC and adopted by the Organization of African Unity (OAU) on August 21, 1989 in Harare, Zimbabwe and by the General Assembly of the United Nations, denounced apartheid in South Africa and contained several of our demands. It called upon the Pretoria regime to negotiate with the ANC and the other liberation movements. It stipulated that prior to any negotiations, the regime should release all political prisoners unconditionally, remove the bans and restrictions on all proscribed individuals and organizations, withdraw all the troops from the black townships, end the state of emergency, repeal all legislation limiting political activity, and stop all the political trials and political executions.

Why were President de Klerk and his government willing

to begin negotiations with the ANC? Not because they had a change of heart. Rather, it was due to the reality of our armed struggle and the internal pressure from the youth, the trade unions, and the religious and professional organizations—all reinforced by the economic sanctions from the international community.

On December 13, 1989, I met with President de Klerk and informed him that he should remove the ban on the ANC and other political organizations, release the political prisoners, permit the exiles to return, and end the state of emergency. On February 2, 1990, he informed Parliament that the time had come for negotiation and then started to dismantle apartheid by unbanning the ANC, the PAC, and the SACP and thirty-one other organizations, liberating political prisoners who had been sentenced for nonviolent activities, suspending capital punishment, and removing some of the restrictions imposed by the state of emergency.

On February 11, 1990, the day of my release from Victor Verster prison, I did protest how apartheid had wrecked the economy and had produced conditions that generated political turmoil. I lamented the fact that apartheid had destroyed the family life of millions and had left them without homes and jobs.

At a mass rally at Cape Town's City Hall, I repeated what I had told a judge at my trial in 1964. I maintained that I was prepared to die, if necessary, to achieve a democratic society.

In another speech in Cape Town, I stressed that the heroic sacrifices of the people had helped make it possible for me to be free. I also commended the members of the ANC for their sacrifices for our cause.

Four generations of freedom fighters from different racial and religious backgrounds, an army of the people, developed their commitment to the cause and a comradeship in combat experiences and political struggles.

I chose to return to my house that had four rooms. Many in the ANC had advised me to move to a grand house nearby that my wife had secured. I rejected their advice as long as I could because I thought that it would have been inappropriate for me to live in an expensive house and that a leader should live like the people.

Because I wanted our negotiations with the government to take place, I still supported the armed struggle. I did continue to call for the maintenance of international sanctions until we achieved our political rights. The economic and diplomatic sanctions highlighted the despotic nature of the government and provided tremendous inspiration for our Movement.

Who contended that sanctions had to be continued until the government made fundamental and irreversible changes in its policies? The ANC but also the majority of South Africans, the Organization of African Unity, the Frontline States, the Non-Aligned Movement, and the General Assembly of the United Nations. When the European Community unilaterally decided to lift its ban on the import of gold coins, steel, and iron from South Africa, I stated that this decision rewarded the jailer for allowing a little more light into our hellhole.

In a 1992 message to the Jewish community, I asserted that the message of Passover had universal human significance and that Moses' demand, "Let my people go," inspired us in our pursuit of democracy and justice.

We never intended violence to be an ultimate solution. If the government were to negotiate in good faith, we would be ready to suspend the armed struggle. On August 6, 1990, the ANC and the government signed the "Pretoria Minute," that contained dates for the completion of the process of granting certain types of indemnity and for the release of the political prisoners. The government would also re-examine the Internal Security Act, and we suspended but would not terminate the armed struggle.

In the ANC, we condemned any kind of violence by blacks against blacks. We denounced as criminal the hijacking and burning of vehicles and the harassment of innocent people. The government referred to this strife to try to justify further oppression. We urged all our people in Natal to unite against those responsible for the violence. Reports of the violence there caused my deepest suffering in my last years in prison. Further, I condemned the perpetrators of violence against our Indian compatriots as enemies of the liberation movement.

In 1990, our plan in the ANC was for an economy which would be based mainly on free enterprise but we were also considering the option of state participation in sections of the economy like mining, the financial institutions, and monopoly industries. We intended not to authorize the Anglo-American Mining Company to retain about seventy-five percent of all the shares on the Johannesburg Stock Exchange. Most of the resources of the country had been owned by a few whites. Several areas of the economy were nationalized, including the railroads, airways, health services, and electric industries.

In my 1990 address at the United Nations, I affirmed that the ANC regarded it as an inviolable principle that humanity must oppose racism by all means at its disposal.

We have empathized with the stand of black leaders in the United States who protested the ways that African-Americans were denied their constitutional rights.

Whether racialism comes from a white or a black man, I repudiate it as barbaric. In the ANC Youth League, while we wanted to eliminate white domination, we recognized that our democracy would have to include different racial groups. In my 1960 court testimony, I rejected as ultra-revolutionary the brand of African nationalism that had the slogan, "Hurl the white man into the sea." In prison, I preached nonracialism. My pledge has been to work toward a democracy in which all South Africans would live together in peace and harmony on the basis of equality.

In my 1964 trial, I had testified that the ANC had fought against racialism for half a century. Our Freedom Charter had rejected racialism. In 1969, the ANC included non-Africans as members and in 1985, they were on its national executive committee. In New York in 1990, I reaffirmed that the ANC and the Mass Democratic Movement (MDM) had condemned racialism. Our people had become more aware of the need for the solidarity of all democratic forces—notwithstanding race, party affiliation, religious belief, and ideological conviction.

In 1990, I criticized President F. W. de Klerk for not using his powerful and efficient army and police force to suppress the violence in Natal between the supporters of the ANC and the members of the Inkatha Freedom Party that caused the deaths of 5,000 people—Zulu against Zulu. I charged that he had been using the differences between these organizations to try to crush the ANC, which he regarded as the greatest threat to white supremacy. The IFP had become a tool of terrorism for his regime.

In a 1990 address to the South African Youth Congress, I protested that the South African police had used violence to stop a peaceful demonstration and seemed to be cooperating with armed right-wing vigilantes who were shooting innocent people. The government did not control its police, who were trained to interpret every demand by blacks as a declaration of war.

At a 1990 town meeting in New York, I contended that the government of South Africa should not be given any credit in the United States for rectifying its mistakes. The government should never have banned the ANC, imprisoned my comrades and me or imposed the state of emergency. After thousands of our people were killed, the government acknowledged that the system of apartheid was evil.

I expressed my gratitude to the United States Congress in 1990 for their anti-apartheid legislation as well as to millions of American supporters for helping to make it possible for me and other political prisoners to be released from prison and to share in transforming South Africa into a united, nonracial, and democratic country. The Congress had empowered us to participate with all people of conscience in the struggle for democracy and human rights throughout the world.

My recommendation to the United States and Great Britain was not to help Mr. de Klerk against the right wing. I asked them to allow the ANC to negotiate with him. If they were to

assist him, they would have undermined his position among
whites because the right wing could then have claimed that
such assistance proved that he was a puppet of these Western
powers.

In my address to the United States Congress, I asserted that
the fundamental rights to freedom, equality, and the pursuit of
happiness must, if necessary, be secured with the weapons of
war.

I told the Congress that we went to jail since it would have
been immoral for us to be silent while an obscene apartheid
system sought to reduce an entire people to a condition worse
than that of the beast of the forest. To permit fear and a drive
toward self-preservation to regulate our conduct would have
been an act of treason against our people and our conscience.

Thousands in our Movement have gone to jail but they do
not harbor bitterness because they can see that their sacrifices
have not been pointless. The goals of the Movement are being
realized.

In Stockholm in 1990, Oliver Tambo offered to appoint me
as president of the ANC to succeed him. I refused his offer,
insisting that we should wait for an election. In this way, we
could conform to the principles of the ANC.

In 1990 and 1991, I condemned the South African Defence
Force and the police for firing into crowds of demonstrators
and strikers, killing scores of innocent people.

On my 1991 visit to Cuba, I referred to the 1988 battle of
Cuito Cuanavale in Angola as a turning point in our struggle
to free the continent and our country from apartheid. Cuban
volunteers, the Angolan army, and fighters from the South
West Africa People's Organization (SWAPO) defeated South
African troops. The defeat significantly reduced Pretoria's
ability to destabilize its neighbors and also contributed to its
decisions to withdraw its troops from Angola and to recognize
Namibia's independence.

Pandit Nehru warned that while nationalism has its value,
it can cause one to distort the truth about one's country. In my
youth, I had believed in a restricted form of nationalism but

experience compelled me and my colleagues in the ANC to abandon our exclusiveness and, in the spirit of the All-India Congress, to interpret our struggle in a global context with a realization of interdependence and a spirit of cooperation. We had come to understand that no people anywhere could be truly free as long as their brothers elsewhere were subject to foreign rule.

In the 1994 election, the ANC did receive 62.6 percent of the national vote. Some of my colleagues were disappointed that we did not win the two-thirds of the vote which would have empowered us to write a constitution without input from the other parties. But I was relieved at the result because we would not be accused of creating an ANC constitution instead of a South African constitution, and we would have a greater opportunity to cooperate with the other parties in forming a government of national unity.

8

Archbishop Desmond Tutu

Apartheid proved to be as evil as Nazism and communism. Not content with denying blacks the right to vote, this system uprooted more than three million of them from their homes and dumped them in the arid, homeland resettlement camps, thereby producing reservoirs of cheap labor.

How ironic, tragic, and evil that the apartheid government, which celebrated "Family Day," forced blacks into migratory labor which destroyed their family life! Even the white Dutch Reformed Church, knowing that a happy and stable family life forms the necessary foundation of a sound and healthy society, eventually condemned the migratory labor policy as a cancer in our society.

This system of institutionalized violence punished political dissenters with prison sentences, banishments or detentions without trial.

Apartheid produced an educational system that spent on a white child ten times the amount it spent on a black child. As a result of this short-sighted policy of discrimination and waste of human resources, South Africa has had to endure a desperate shortage of skilled workers.

Instead of viewing every person as created in the image of God, apartheid exalted a biological quality, skin color—a total irrelevancy—to the status of determining the value of a person.

Apartheid was un-Christian because it did not treat people

as persons who had been created by God, redeemed by Jesus Christ, and sanctified by the Holy Spirit. The government was guilty also of blasphemy by dealing with persons, who were "God-carriers" and His representatives, as if they were things.

Our Biblical faith provides the basis for our conviction that every person has infinite worth in the eyes of God. Rejecting the dignity of a person, as apartheid did, was like spitting in the face of God. In opposing apartheid, the main inspiration for some of us was not a political motive but our faith.

In claiming that God created us for separateness, apartheid contradicted the Gospel of Jesus, which affirms that God has created us for interdependence as well as harmony. Apartheid was sinful in causing disunity, enmity, and alienation.

In 1980, I recommended to Prime Minister P. W. Botha that the government should take four actions to demonstrate that it was prepared to make fundamental changes: commit itself to a common citizenship for all South Africans in a unified South Africa; abolish the pass laws; immediately cease all the population removals; and establish a uniform educational system.

If apartheid was to be dismantled, the government also had to release all the political prisoners and detainees, permit the exiles to return home, and prepare for the establishment of universal suffrage.

Why should we have settled for the crumbs of concessions from the master's table? We wanted to be there participating in the determination of the menu.

My Nobel Peace Prize affirmed that, despite the criticisms of our Movement, the world understood that we were striving for peace and approved of our methods. The prize served as a source of encouragement for the victims of apartheid. How appropriate that this award was made on Human Rights Day!

Our goal was the liberation not only of blacks but also of whites from the bondage of apartheid. We knew there was no separate freedom. Whites could not be free until blacks were free. Whites who sought security by possessing a formidable arsenal of weapons can now find security in an open and just society.

We can demonstrate that we are children of God by not having a desire for revenge. In the Old Testament, there is the law, "An eye for an eye," but Martin Luther King asked us to consider what would happen if we believed in that law. Very soon, all of us would be blind.

In 1983, I asserted that because blacks had been subjected to many decades of oppression, exploitation, and deprivation, it was a miracle of God's grace that they still talked to whites, wanted to avert a bloodbath, sought a nonracial South Africa, and could state their commitment to a ministry of justice and reconciliation.

In order to be authentic, our struggle also had to address the concerns of the movement for the liberation of women. St. Paul affirmed, "There is neither Jew nor Gentile, slave nor free, male nor female, but we are all one in Christ."

Women should be members of the ordained ministry. Their distinctive talents are essential for a truly human existence, and their ordination would increase the effectiveness of the Church.

Faithful to its mission, the Church was in the forefront of our struggle, condemning all that oppressed God's children. It worked for justice in addition to preaching the necessity of reconciliation since justice is essential to reconciliation.

I reminded President P. W. Botha of the Biblical basis for religious leaders to address the sociopolitical and economic situations. To cite two examples, Elijah challenged Ahab, the king of Samaria, about the seizure of Naboth's vineyard after his murder, and Nathan reprimanded David for having Uriah killed.

So that reconciliation could occur, the agents of apartheid had to admit that they damaged our people by evicting them from their homes, dispensing inferior education, and denying them their human dignity and fundamental rights. These agents had to be willing to make whatever reparations were possible.

When they asked for forgiveness, we had to forgive.

Without justice, we could not achieve peace. God's Shalom, peace, encompasses not only justice and righteousness but also wholesomeness, participation in decision making, fullness of life, laughter, joy, compassion, sharing, and reconciliation.

The divine mission of Jesus was one of reconciliation. The South African Council of Churches (SACC) has prayed and worked for the unity of churches and for a fellowship which would include everyone in a new South Africa.

The South African Council of Churches viewed itself as an agent of divine mercy. Throughout the nation, it encouraged the unemployed to be involved in self-employment and self-help projects and yet was criticized for delaying the bloody revolution by means of these projects. Whatever the reaction, we continued to do what we believed was right.

African and Black Theology must include a concern with liberation. In Africa, liberation is not seen as an alternative to personal salvation in Jesus Christ. Rather, it is understood that if you take the Gospel of Jesus seriously, you will then be engaged in the liberation struggle.

I am convinced that God provided me with direction in this struggle against injustice, and that the government could not do anything to prevent me from doing God's will.

In the South African Council of Churches, our belief has been that our ultimate loyalty should be to God and His Son, Who provided us with our mandate, and not to any human authority. The criterion for the evaluation of our statements and actions should be the Gospel of Jesus and not the laws of the apartheid government.

Attempting to prevent further criticism of apartheid by the Church, some stressed the need for the separation of church and state. But to advocate such a separation is to ignore the tradition of the Hebrew prophets, who emphasized the social, economic, and political implications of religion, and to deny the teaching of Jesus, Who stated that all of life—the secular as well as the sacred—belongs to God.

When some South African Christians condemned apartheid as repugnant to the Christian conscience, they were criticized for mixing religion with politics. However, when the Dutch Reformed Church here had attempted for years to provide a scriptural basis for the Nationalist Party's policy of apartheid, there had been no protest about mixing religion with politics.

Because of its persistent emphasis on liberation, there is no more revolutionary book than the Bible. Whites brought the Bible to us, and we blacks have been using it to interpret our predicament and anticipate our future.

Even many who admitted that apartheid was contrary to the Gospel of Love were members of racially divided churches. Although white ministers did serve black congregations, black ministers were rarely appointed to white congregations.

Our Christian faith summons us to realize that, through our common baptism, we are united in the Body of Jesus Christ, Who has broken down all the barriers that separate us, such as race, culture, sex, status, etc. Redeemed by Him, we are one humanity. Only by blacks and whites being together can we be truly human.

A person becomes a person only through other persons. We are created for friendship, fellowship, and community. If we seek exclusive self-sufficiency instead of interdependence, we violate a fundamental law of our being, and things go horribly wrong. Not even the most powerful nation can decide to be completely self-sufficient.

In the establishment of His Kingdom, God intends us to be His co-workers and to assist each other to become even more human. The life of Jesus challenges us to labor for the poor and the oppressed.

As servants of God in days of crisis, we Christians have to practice intense faith and hope. Our actions must be hallowed by prayer, the sacraments, worship, and meditation that seeks to derive its inspiration from the Holy Spirit.

To state the evident, since I am a Christian religious leader, then, by definition, I repudiate communism and Marxism as atheistic and materialistic. My mission has been to work for the expansion of the Kingdom of God.

We are created by God, like Him, and for Him. Since God is infinite, we have been made for the infinite, and only God can satisfy our hunger for the infinite.

Because God is the source of all truth, and truth cannot be self-contradictory, there can be no conflict between the facts of science and religious truths. As a Christian, I glory in the discoveries of science about God's creation.

As the "Rainbow People of God," we worked to establish a society in which everyone would possess the rights to work, a stable family life, free education, and freedom of movement, association, thought, and worship. Our citizens would have freedom from ignorance, hunger, and fear.

In order to elevate the morale of our people, I assured them that since the foundations of the universe are moral, apartheid was destined to collapse. Their faith has created an abundant harvest. Blacks and whites together are victors. My belief that absolute moral principles govern our lives has also directed my subsequent work.

The Truth and Reconciliation Commission (TRC) sought to foster the process of rehabilitation by providing many of the victims of apartheid with a chance to emerge from anonymity to tell the nation how they were damaged. In this manner, we acknowledged the reality of their personhood and helped to restore their consciousness of their dignity.

Our Human Rights Violations Committee of the TRC held hearings to assist the commission in deciding which persons had suffered heinous violations of their human rights and thus qualified as victims according to the law. The Reparations and Rehabilitation Committee of the TRC then presented its recommendations to President Mandela concerning the nature and size of the reparations for these victims. In establishing the process, the National Party had ensured that the decisions of the Amnesty Committee, headed by a judge, were not subject to review by the rest of the commission but only by a court of law.

Those who committed the atrocities of apartheid were also victims. In the process of dehumanizing their brothers and sisters in the human family, these representatives of apartheid dehumanized themselves.

If it were not for the requirements of theology, we on the commission would have viewed the perpetrators of atrocities as demons. Although we condemned their horrendous acts, our religious faith directed us to have compassion for them and to hope they would repent and change.

My belief is that we cannot say with certainty that anyone is in hell. The account of the repentant thief on the cross who received a promise of paradise from Jesus reveals that, by responding to the grace of a loving God, anyone may repent even at the eleventh hour and be forgiven.

Given all of the privileges whites enjoyed and the powerful forces shaping their thinking, it was not surprising that many of them had racist attitudes and supported apartheid. But one can marvel that a significant number of whites not only did not conform to the persistent pressures of the racist culture but participated in the struggle to abolish apartheid. Some of these whites made an essential contribution to the struggle as they endured ostracism, harassment, detention, and torture.

If I were white, I would have needed an abundance of grace to oppose a system which was the source of such substantial privileges. Still, our white supporters did include the United Democratic Front—a rainbow coalition—the women of the Black Sash, church leaders, the young whites in the End Conscription Campaign, trade unionists, and the Detainees' Parents Support Committee.

In emphasizing the necessity for forgiveness, we have to understand that forgiveness does not require that the victims forget the atrocities. On the contrary, it is essential that they recall them in order to prevent their recurrence. Forgiveness does not involve condoning the acts of oppression. Neither does it mean being sentimental. But forgiveness does involve an attempt to comprehend the conditioning that motivated the perpetrator.

Nelson Mandela, who was the most revered head of state in the world, deserves much of the credit for the fact that South Africa has survived and is now free of the unrest and carnage that have marred Bosnia, Kosovo, the Middle East, and Northern Ireland. For many of our citizens, Mandela has been a heroic exemplar of forgiveness and reconciliation.

Forgiveness is a rational approach that generates harmony but anger, resentment, and desire for retaliation are corrosive of community. While it is difficult to ask for forgiveness or to grant it, South Africa will have no future without confession, forgiveness, and reparation.

When I testified in court, I asked P. W. Botha, the former president, to state that he was sorry about how the policies of his government had caused so much pain. But he stubbornly reacted to my appeal only with anger. After being convicted and given a suspended sentence and a fine, he received an acquittal on the basis of a narrow technicality. His appearance in court aroused in me not anger, but pity.

In a speech to Parliament on February 2, 1990, President F. W. de Klerk announced that political organizations which had been proscribed since the 1960 Sharpeville Massacre— including the African National Congress, the Pan-Africanist Congress and the South African Communist Party—could function again as legal entities. We are indebted to him for this courageous initiative that allowed for power sharing and prevented a blood bath.

When F. W. de Klerk appeared before the TRC in 1996, he offered an apology for apartheid, but carefully qualified it. He did not understand that apartheid by its nature was evil. His inability to present an apology without reservations indicated that despite his 1993 Nobel Peace Prize, he lacked generosity of spirit—one of the qualities of greatness.

Once amnesty was granted, victims did not have the right to institute civil claims against the perpetrators. Therefore, it was necessary to provide reparation measures to compensate the victims for the loss of this right and allow for healing and reconciliation.

After listening to the testimonies of the victims, the TRC did recommend that there be urgent interim relief, in addition to the individual reparation grants, to provide for scholarships, occupational training, medical assistance, housing subsidies or the erection of a tombstone. The government and the civil society have to act upon these recommendations and develop programs in order to secure justice for the victims.

The TRC had some success. Many police of the apartheid regime applied for amnesty which required that they make a full disclosure. The revelations by these perpetrators about their violations of human rights served as responses to critics who had maintained that the publicized accusations by the victims were untested. Then too, the TRC provided a public forum for many of the victims to express their willingness to forgive. Moreover, the information from the many hearings allowed the TRC in about fifty cases to conduct exhumations and provide for decent burials. The families of the deceased might thereby experience a healing and obtain closure.

The TRC had its weaknesses. We were unable to motivate the majority of whites to assume a positive role in the process of truth telling and reconciliation. Nor could we persuade the old South African Defence Force (SADF) to cooperate fully with us. Those major figures of the SADF who applied for amnesty did so because policemen who had applied indicated they had worked with them in the joint operations. Since the mid-1980s, police activities had become more militarized.

Our principal goal in the TRC has been to promote unity and reconciliation. Still, the majority of white South Africans have yet to embrace the new dispensation. Yes, they have lost exclusive political control but they have most of the economic power. They should set aside their resentment and contribute their skills and resources to make democracy work.

Everyone in South Africa should make a contribution to the

process of reconciliation by respecting human rights, having no tolerance for racism, and working to form a more inclusive society.

Until recently, the Dutch Reformed Church had presented Biblical arguments in support of apartheid. One of the more significant contributions to the process of reconciliation was the DRC's public apology for harassing and denouncing as heretical those who had prophetically denounced apartheid. While my church, the Anglican Church, condemned apartheid in its public statements, it conformed to apartheid in practice.

The greatest threat to reconciliation is the poverty of the masses of blacks. Whites must realize that unless they assist blacks in obtaining access to adequate housing, clean water, electricity, affordable health care, and good jobs, we will not achieve reconciliation.

Hostility and conflict plague so much of human existence! But God's intention is to direct us to a harmony and unity in Jesus so that all will belong to His family and no one will be an outsider.

True peace is such a splendid blessing for a nation. I would offer certain recommendations to world leaders involved in conflicts with other leaders. Talk with your adversary. Alter the way you describe him. Imagine becoming his friend and start acting to foster this friendship. In your negotiations, do not have too many preconditions, be flexible, be prepared to make compromises consistent with your principles, and try to arrange for all to emerge from negotiations as winners.

In 1998, Dublin and Belfast audiences were receptive to my message that because the nightmare in South Africa had ended, one could be hopeful about almost any situation. On the basis of our experience in South Africa, I told them that when those opposed to the peace negotiations increased their attempts to prevent the implementation of the Good Friday Agreement, then those who seek peace should intensify their determination and vigilance.

For the preservation of our freedoms in South Africa, we

depend on our new constitution, not on a parliament. In the constitution, we have a covenant that respects human rights. Our highest court, the Constitutional Court, has demonstrated that it will reject any law from the legislature that contradicts the constitution.

My vision of a new South Africa includes a nonracial and genuinely democratic society in which the rule of law and a Bill of Rights protects individual liberty. Neither segregation nor integration will be enforced. Through His free will, God created us to be free and when we are free, we are able to set others free to be themselves.

I was confident that we would be free. Whenever the desire for freedom and self-determination has been awakened in a people, they will never be satisfied with anything less than freedom and self-determination.

Our freedom was inevitable since the God of the Exodus, the merciful liberator God Who has a special concern for the powerless and takes the side of the oppressed, would ensure that our just cause would triumph. In uprooting the unjust and freeing the exploited, God also frees those enslaved by their sinfulness. God leads His people out of bondage—whether it is spiritual, political, economic or social. St. Paul asked, "If God be for us, who can be against us?"

Jesus' resurrection proved that right will be victorious. An essential message of Easter is that even as life triumphed over death, so too freedom and justice will overcome tyranny, and that reconciliation, compassion, and peace will prevail.

THE POWER OF THE NEGATIVE

Ultimately, the suffering produced by apartheid's "final solution"—resettlements involving starvation and a migratory labor system so destructive to family life—caused me to call for economic sanctions on the government.

We wanted the international community to apply as much political, diplomatic, and economic pressure as possible upon the government to secure the negotiations to begin dismantling apartheid. The opponents of economic sanctions did not offer us an effective nonviolent alternative.

My earnest attempts to encourage President Reagan and Prime Minister Thatcher to support our struggle by imposing economic sanctions on South Africa had been unsuccessful. President Reagan's program of "constructive engagement" presumed that if the United States did continue its economic relationship with South Africa, it would be in a better position to alter apartheid. But, eventually, the United States imposed some sanctions which, together with prayers throughout the world, helped cause the collapse of apartheid.

I issued several warnings, including one in 1976 to Prime Minister John Vorster and another in 1980 to Prime Minister P. W. Botha, that the government had to make real changes leading to power sharing or I thought our oppressed people, in their anger and hatred, would resort to desperate means.

Some of the progress in our liberation movement was due to the fact that the government used repression. The regime believed that its severe measures would stifle the spirit of the people but they produced the opposite effect.

Because the apartheid laws contradicted the imperatives of the Gospel, we Christians had a moral obligation and even a religious duty to agitate for the revocation of these laws by all peaceful means.

We had to "Render to Caesar" but God's Kingdom includes Caesar's domain since God's jurisdiction is universal. God's honor was involved, and therefore, we distinguished between legality and morality and called for the disobedience of unjust laws. In a situation of oppression, to choose not to disobey would be to choose to side with the oppressor.

The so-called right wing did not offer any opposition since it did not aim to dismantle apartheid. A real opposition would have proposed a radical alternative to the bankrupt and barren policies of apartheid.

The reason that I opposed the injustice of the government was not because I liked doing it but because I believed I was doing God's will. If I tried to keep quiet, God's word, as the prophet Jeremiah said, would have burned like a fire within me. The government could have had me killed but that would not have been the worst thing for me as a Christian.

When thousands of children in the township of Soweto in 1976 marched to protest a decree that ordered an increase in the use of the Afrikaans language in the schools, they were expressing their rejection of the whole apartheid system of legalized inferiority, oppression, injustice, and exploitation.

I affirmed that the white community should agree to share political power and to accept a redistribution of wealth and an equitable sharing of the resources of our land. I did contend that it would be prudent for them to agree to a decline in their standard of living by giving up something voluntarily rather than engaging in a bloody confrontation and risking the loss of everything.

Because I have witnessed the effects of violence in other countries, I have worked more intensely for peace in South Africa. In 1966, my family and I were in Jerusalem for two months, and before the Six-Day War, we saw the escalating violence between the Jews and Arabs. Before the overthrow of Haile Selassie, I was in Addis Ababa and saw the rioting in the streets. Prior to the exclusion of Asians from Uganda, I was there and later experienced the fear and evil that plagued the land. In the Sudan, I saw the impact of seventeen years of civil strife upon people and their property. On my visit to Nigeria and the former Biafra, I saw the tragic results of the civil war on the souls of defeated Biafrans and on property.

It was a privilege to address the General Assembly of the Presbyterian Church in Belfast. But what I saw there shook me to the core of my being. In Britain, we saw on television pictures of the screaming children in Vietnam being burned by napalm. No, I did not want any violence for the people of South Africa.

By providing us with an object lesson on how not to solve our political and racial crisis, God demonstrated his love and mercy for South Africa. That object lesson was Rhodesia, where there was a bloody liberation war—with 20,000 deaths, devastation, bitterness, and hatred—before the creation of an independent Zimbabwe in 1980.

I opposed not only those who upheld the institutionalized violence of apartheid but those who relied on violent methods to attempt to overthrow it. We should not imitate the system we condemned as immoral.

In the Supreme Court in Pretoria, and on other occasions, I indicated that I did not support the methods of my friends in the African National Congress because in 1961, they moved away from a complete commitment to nonviolence after the Sharpeville Massacre. However, I supported their objectives to establish a nonracial, democratic South Africa. In 1987, I visited the exiled ANC leaders in Lusaka, Zambia to persuade them to suspend the armed struggle. Then they could use the suspension to pressure the government to begin negotiations with them.

While I opposed the ANC policy of armed struggle, I had not completely endorsed pacifism. I believed that there could come a time when an armed struggle would be appropriate. Christian theology allows for the use of force as a last resort. To cite two examples, violence was used legitimately against Adolf Hitler and Idi Amin.

For all those who planned to take action against the South African Council of Churches, I stressed that the Church had existed for nearly 2,000 years even while tyrants persecuted, arrested and killed Christians. The tyrants became the flotsam and jetsam of forgotten history whereas the Church remained as an agent of justice, peace, love, and reconciliation.

As the salt and light of the world, the Church, through the power of God, must aim to transform situations of hate, fear, suspicion, brokenness, separation, bitterness, harshness, and insensitivity. It has to convince persons, who are treated as mere statistics, that they are of immense value to God. In the midst of grasping and selfishness, the Church must be a sharing community, using its resources for the sake of the marginalized ones—the least of the brethren of Jesus.

In order to be free to function as the prophetic voice of the powerless and to denounce all forms of injustice, the Church has had to maintain a critical distance from the state. It could then determine whenever the state forfeited the allegiance of its subjects.

The Church must resist the persistent temptation to pursue power, prestige, and privilege and to forget that the Master was born in a stable and His birth was announced first not to the high and mighty but to shepherds.

Suffering is inevitable in the life of the Church. A Church that is not marked by the cross and that does not suffer cannot be the Church of Jesus. The Church must be prepared to share in the suffering of Jesus—especially through demonstrating its solidarity with the poor—in order that it can participate in His resurrection.

Taking up one's cross is not optional but rather essential to Christian leadership and discipleship. Leadership, authority, and power, understood in terms of the life and message of Jesus, involves service, suffering, and, when necessary, even giving up one's life for others.

As representatives of God, we officials of the Church had an obligation to walk through the slums to show our solidarity with those who were victims of the government's policy of resettlement. We also had to attend the treason trials with the families of the detained as well as those horrific funerals.

We could never have achieved liberation without sacrifice and suffering. Through our suffering, we were also sharing in the suffering of Jesus, and therefore, were preparing to share in His glory. In order to participate in Easter, we had to share in Calvary.

In a 1987 sermon, I felt the need to affirm that we could be called to be martyrs. What happened to St. Paul and St. Peter might happen to us since we could be forced to suffer and even die for the faith.

Steven Biko, the founder of the South African Students Organization (SASO) and the Black Consciousness movement (BC), died in prison at the age of thirty-one as a result of several beatings by the police. Steven was equally committed to the liberation of blacks and whites. He lived his life for his friends and enemies, and his death, tragic as it was, proved to be a consummation of his life. He knew, as Jesus proclaimed, that unless a seed die in the ground, it cannot yield grain and that the greatest love a person can have for his friends is to lay down his life for them.

In our struggle, we knew that God is not an Aristotelian unmoved mover Who knows only Himself. He is moved by the agony of His people. He rescued them from their misery in Egypt and led them to the Promised Land.

Because God willed freedom and justice, He delivered the Israelites from the despair and pain of slavery and regarded these disorganized slaves as His own chosen people.

God does not sanctify the status quo whenever it is defined by injustice, exploitation, and oppression. From the history of Israel, one can conclude that He is a God of surprises as He uprooted unjust powerful rulers to establish His Kingdom.

In freeing the Israelites from their bondage in Egypt, God demonstrated His absolute control over the forces of nature by turning the rivers of Egypt into blood, converting the light of day into darkness, and directing the path of the locusts. The God of the Exodus was the God Who had created everything out of nothing.

Since the Israelites had been strangers and aliens in Egypt, they had a moral obligation to be compassionate, particularly to the stranger and the alien. They had been liberated so that their lives could manifest this liberation, and they could be God's representatives for the sake of the world.

Even after the Israelites were delivered from the Pharaoh, they had to travel in the desert and to live on a diet that made them long for the fleshpots of Egypt. Total liberation has its price. We knew that before we achieved our freedom, there would be bannings, imprisonments, detentions without trial, deaths in detention, exile, disunity, and treachery.

Jesus taught us the new law of love so that, like Him, we could be caring persons and be even more concerned for the good of others than for ourselves. Jesus made it possible for us to be free from all that makes us less than God intends us to be. To experience that freedom, we must be willing to live out the implications of the law of love.

I pray that in the Church we imitate the generosity of Jesus Who, though spiritually rich, became materially poor for us so that by means of His poverty, we might become spiritually rich.

Jesus scandalized the religious leaders of His day by dining with social outcasts. He even declared that the despised ones —the sinners and tax collectors—would precede the proper ones into the Kingdom of God. As the divine physician, He proclaimed that He came to heal those who were spiritually ill.

The death of Jesus was the death of death since it was the beginning of the resurrection life. What initially seemed to be a shameful and meaningless defeat did prove to be a splendid victory that gave meaning to all history.

St. Paul asserted that we believers are fellow-workers with God. Our task is to replace the evil, darkness, oppression, and chaos with their glorious opposites. We serve as the agents of an invincible Power.

We will merit heaven or deserve hell depending on whether we have performed certain secular actions such as feeding the hungry, clothing the naked, and visiting the sick and those in prison. In this sense, Archbishop Temple could maintain that Christianity is the most materialistic of the major religions. Then too, according to the Christian faith, God uses ordinary material things in the sacraments as vehicles for His grace.

Jesus warned that only prayer and fasting could drive out some demons. I have preached that the demons of injustice, oppression, and exploitation could not be exorcised except by prayer and fasting. I, therefore, appealed to members of my diocese and province to fast corporately every Friday and to pray especially on that day for our Republic of South Africa.

Where do the most meaningful theologies originate? Not in a university seminar but in a situation where they have been hammered out on an anvil of adversity. Black Theology and Liberation Theology examine issues which profoundly affect our lives.

Black Theology arose within the context of black suffering caused by white racism. In the light of Christian revelation, Black Theology tries to understand why blacks have suffered so much, not at the hands of pagans, but at the hands of white Christians who profess their allegiance to the same Lord and Master. Black Theology seeks to liberate the white man by awakening him to the degradation into which he has fallen by dehumanizing the black man, and to arouse the black man to seek the glorious liberty of the sons of God.

The principle of transfiguration states that the persecutor Saul could become the greatest missionary for the very truth he had rejected and that Peter, who three times had denied that he knew his Master, could abandon his fear and become the prince of the apostles who boldly proclaimed his faith in Jesus. This principle of transfiguration is also operative when the cross, an instrument of execution, is a source of life and blessings for

Christians.

In Jesus' parable about the Pharisee and the publican at prayer in the temple, the Pharisee, who fasted and gave tithes, thanked God that he was not like the publican and other sinful men, whereas the publican acknowledged his sinfulness and asked for God's mercy. Since the publican humbled himself, he was the one who was more acceptable to God.

Healthy differences of opinion can enhance the life of the Church. We ought to cherish love and unity, not uniformity. Our maturity will be determined by how well we are able to disagree even as we continue to promote the greater good of the other.

Reconciliation in South Africa could not be achieved only by our forgiveness. It would require confrontation, a call for repentance by the perpetrators of the injustice, and a redress of the unjust system. Reconciliation has its preconditions. In order to achieve reconciliation between God and man, it took the death of His Son Who overcame the powers of evil.

On the Truth and Reconciliation Commission (TRC), we have witnessed some outstanding examples of the willingness to forgive. Amy Biehl, a Fulbright scholar at the University of the Western Cape, had been involved in the anti-apartheid student campaign at Stanford University. In August 1993, as she was driving with friends to Gulgulethu Township, youths stoned her car. After chasing her and her passengers, they stoned and stabbed her. Rather than seek any revenge for her death, her parents decided to support the amnesty process for her killers and established the Amy Biehl Foundation to assist Gulgulethu's youth.

Our people were tear-gassed, attacked by police dogs and batons, detained, tortured, banned, imprisoned, and sentenced to death or exiled. Despite their pain, nearly all the victims before the TRC demonstrated an extraordinary magnanimity by their capacity to forgive. I did marvel at their nobility and generosity of spirit.

Nelson Mandela was imprisoned for twenty-seven years.

Some would say, "What a waste!" This is not my view. Like nothing else could, his many years of suffering strengthened and purified his soul, endowed him with a credibility and an authority, and proved that he was a true leader. He lived and suffered for others.

We have a democratically elected government that had a president who was imprisoned as a terrorist and which consists of political parties which had been locked in a life-and-death struggle. Why did God choose our nation for such a radical transition? Perhaps, to prove that if, in spite of our history, it could be done here, then no other people should despair of a solution.

Our purpose on the TRC was to aim to help heal the nation. It may well be that we have been successful to the extent that members of the TRC had also been traumatized by apartheid in so many ways. Hence, it was not difficult for us to identify with the victims who testified.

At the first TRC meeting, we agreed to go on a retreat. We had a day of silence in the presence of my spiritual counselor in order that we might become receptive to direction from the transcendent Spirit. We had a second retreat on Robben Island where Mandela and his colleagues had been imprisoned. As we visited cells, we became keenly aware of the suffering that had won our freedom.

In January 1997, while the TRC held its hearings, I learned that I had prostate cancer. My illness did cause me to value time more and to be more congenial toward my colleagues on the TRC. I even referred to my illness to lessen the tension at our meetings. Due to my illness, I have appreciated more the love of my wife Leah, the playfulness of my grandchildren, the commitment of my colleagues, and the beauties of nature. My illness has also helped me develop a deep gratitude when I reflect on my opportunities to be involved in the struggle, to witness the advent of freedom, and to serve on the TRC.

Why does God use such weak and vulnerable creatures as ourselves to attain His goals on earth for justice, wholeness, and reconciliation? The reason, according to St. Paul, is that our weakness makes it quite clear that God should receive the glory.

In 1992, the Azanian People's Liberation Army (APLA) bombed King William's Town Golf Club, killing four whites. Beth Savage, whose family were opponents of apartheid, was among those injured. She had to undergo open-heart surgery and remained in an intensive-care unit for months. Because of shrapnel in her body, she had to be cared for by her family. This remarkable woman told the TRC that her experience had empowered her to empathize with others who had to undergo trauma.

The TRC did not seek retributive justice. Our concern was not to punish. Our goal was restorative justice—to heal the perpetrator and the victim and to rehabilitate the relationship between them.

In Rwanda, most of the Hutus and the Tutsi were Christian, lived together, intermarried, and spoke the same language. In 1994, Hutus massacred 500,000 Tutsi. In 1995, we visited a church filled with corpses from the massacre. After learning of this genocide, one could not regard racism as the cause of every human evil. While colonial overlords had provoked the Hutus by favoring the Tutsi, blacks massacred blacks.

The TRC aimed to promote forgiveness. To forgive is to reject the desire to retaliate. This rejection frees the victim. Some of the victims testified about the sense of relief they experienced after forgiving. If the perpetrators confessed and expressed their contrition, they helped their victims to forgive but many of the victims realized that they should not wait for confessions before they did offer forgiveness. Otherwise, in some cases where perpetrators refused to confess, the victims would be permanently doomed to victimhood. When Jesus was hanging on the cross, He asked His Father to forgive His executioners, pleading that they did not know what they were doing. He did not wait for a confession.

On our flight to Nigeria, we encountered severe turbulence.

I became anxious because we did not have a white pilot and did wonder if the Nigerian pilots could control the situation. But what a shock it was when I realized that I was so brainwashed, I had spontaneously accepted one white assessment of blacks! This incident helped me to deepen my understanding of the power of conditioning. In evaluating the agents of apartheid, we ought to consider the impact of the pressures that might have conditioned them. Without condoning the human rights violations, we should try to be more generous in judging the perpetrators. As we better understand that we too have been influenced by conditioning and that we all are capable of great evil, we will be more compassionate toward them.

In order to achieve a genuine reconciliation, the perpetrator must acknowledge the wrong he has done. There has to be a full exposure of any degradation. While a truthful approach does involve the risk that it could worsen the situation, it is a necessary condition for real healing.

In the TRC we have sought the truth about the atrocities to our people. This exposure has prepared the way for restitution, forgiveness, reconciliation, and peace.

Sources

1. Frederick Douglass

B   Blassingham, John W., et al., eds. *The Frederick Douglass Papers. Series One: Speeches, Debates, and Interviews, 1841-1895.* New Haven: Yale University Press, Five Volumes, 1979-1992.

F   Foner, Philip S., ed. *Frederick Douglass on Women's Rights.* New York: Da Capo Press, 1992.

G   Gates, Henry Louis, Jr., ed. *Frederick Douglass, Autobiographies: Narrative of the Life of Frederick Douglass, an American Slave; My Bondage and My Freedom; Life and Times of Frederick Douglass.* New York: The Library of America, 1994.

Pages 1-4. slaveholders, G, 231, me, G, 232, 233, belief, B, IV, 229, 230, Bible, G, 298-301, 600, 601, cause, B, I, 21, 22, 33, 267, II, 104, 118, III, 165, character, B, I, 137, 138, 144, 146, 183, 221, 266, 314, II, 51, 91, 92, 243, 251, come, B, I, 221, II, 57, 85, 232, 233, V, 358, 359, 477, right, B, IV, 307, master, B, I, 93, 111, 273, 345, 346, 372, 404, II, 3, 255, III 7, G, 420, 421, earnings, B, I, 184, G, 337, captive, B, I, 328, weak, B, I, 3, 17, 98, 109, 128, 144, 188, 314, II, 32, them, B, I, 31, 91, 94, 95, 136, 137, 160, 275, 276, 280, 311, 321, 373, 403, 409, 418, 476, 477, II, 3, 10, 254, 255, III, 9, 99, 280, 281, G, 401, 402, 403, 420, liberty, B, I, 276, 297, G, 402, 403, 426, free, B, I, 16, 61, 87, 99, 314, 400, 401, II, 495, 507, 543, III, 281, G, 237, 544, death, B, I, 40, 41, 135, 184, 343, 376, Testament, B, I, 190, II, 262, 267, 439, 462, III, 222, 279, G, 426, men, G, 330, judgment, B, I, 210, II, 92, III, 12, 103, 230, 330, G, 189, resolution, B, IV, 87, souls, B, III, 300, legislators, B, III, 98, 99, 128, 129, 297, 516.

Pages 5-9. presidency, B, I, 256, II, 14, 15, 189, me, B, I, 37, brethren, B, I, 30, God, B, I, 35, 44, 51, 109, 138, 187, 188, 282, 283, 328, 472, 473, 479, 480, II, 27, 269, 355, 382, 383, III, 128, G, 407, conscience, B, III, 21, 22, abolition, B, I, 24, 25, 143, 144,

147, 148, II, 15, 16, 29, 329, 379, 425, III, 37-39, 241, 337, IV, 363, slaves, B, I, 137, 143, 144, 309, 311, 470, read, B, I, 40, 283, 470, 478, 479, III, 137, 321, 338, movement, B, I, 160-162, 176-178, 190, 192, 233-236, 240-243, 329, 330, Ireland, B, I, 77, 274, II, 382, 383, overthrow, B, III, 21, 527, evil, B, I, 42, 66, 92, 93, 137, 184, 292, 293, 325, 354, 374, G, 698, 699, and slavery, B, II, 149-151, 437, 524, it, B, II, 165, 166, 211, IV, 406, 407, practice, B, III, 244-248, former, B, V, 411-413, writings, G, 398, us, B, I, 176, II, 113, 115, 168, 396, 453, IV, 262, 393, 394, 480, 565, lawless, B, V, 74, 75, New Bedford, G, 896, 900, interpretation, B, I, 33, 79, II, 144, 145, 278, III, 172, G, 704, Independence, B, II, 347, 356, 357, III, 176, 352, IV, 121, 122, 153, G, 391-393, 704-706, protect the Negro, B, II, 144, IV, 83, 98, 99, 119-122, 178, G, 391, 392, 704, 705, 834, slave, B, I, 129, II, 4, 427, person, B, III, 147, 167, to slavery, B, III, 474, of slavery, B, III, 526, 527, peace, B, III, 451, IV, 316, classes, B, III, 545, 546.

Pages 10-14. family, B, III, 551, conduct, B, I, 123, serfs, B, IV, 413, 441, 442, V, 100, 101, 624, G, 815, 816, crushed, B, IV, 433, 434, 436, 437, V, 536, 537, 540, 543, G, 918, 919, 921, friendships, B, V, 55, 56, will, F, 107, of the Negro, B, II, 213, IV, 208, other, B, IV, 613, persuade, G, 903-906, freedom, F, 105, 109, 116, 119, 132, 165, 174, 178, 179, G, 906, things, B, V, 351, 352, government, B, II, 451, V, 352-355, F, 51, 80, 82, 95, 121, 137, 148, 163, 178, 179, G, 907, obey, B, IV, 147, 173, 396, F, 51, 57, 58, 78, 92-94, 105-107, 111, 120, 123, 136, 137, needs, F, 110, over right, B, IV, 173, F, 139, 175, G, 907, estates, F, 64, understanding, F, 49, 51, malice, F, 93, violence, F, 79, lampposts, F, 55, 87, 179, test, F, 80, this right, F, 123, excluded, B, II, 249, goals, F, 115, government, B, IV, 173, masters, B, IV, 522, 523, 565, G, 932, color, B, V, 66, 67, death, B, IV, 206, V, 80, Anglo-African, B, V, 536, fathers, G, 832.

Pages 15-19. brotherhood, B, III, 507, 508, mankind, B, II, 71, slaveholders, B, IV, 317, V, 51, friends, B, V, 458, bondage, B, I, 124, 219, III, 49, IV, 157, 174, 200, 201, 239, 240, V, 456, learn to read, B, II, 256, G, 37, 38, effects, G, 24, form, G, 54, 64, 65, 587-591, me, G, 702, evil, B, II, 61, righteousness, B, I, 42, 77, 310, 374, 467, 474, II, 11, 21, 24, 25, 27, 103, 270, 333, 530, III, 223, 283, 313, V, 373, G, 429, churches, B, I, 104, 301, force, B, III, 201, Moses, B, III, 317, V, 25, 26, authentic, G, 251, respect, B, II, 417, 458, 459, IV, 110, G, 451, states, B, IV, 363, G, 439, 722, 723, 734,

738, 739, law, B, II, 391, 417-420, 459, 460, destroy, B, IV, 115, 359, 399, 400, 424, G, 736, development, B, III, 145, 169, IV, 110, 111, G, 734, 735, institutions, B, I, 187, 262, II, 153, III, 434, us, B, III, 434-435, nobility, F, 113, spirit, B, IV, 437-439, war, B, V, 537, government, B, IV, 158, country, G, 771.

Pages 20-23. president, B, IV, 158, 159, institutions, B, IV, 164, 165, nation, B, IV, 167, congressmen, B, IV, 168, suffering, B, IV, 317, 330, 331, 398, 403, extent, B, V, 50, adversity, B, IV, 546, 565, V, 95, 530, friendships, B, V, 40, others, B, III, 204, Tubman, F, 159, 167, helpless, B, V, 558, potatoes, B, V, 558, 559, success, B, V, 549, 550, respect, B, I, 55-59, 166, 167, 206, 209, II, 108, 109, justice, F, 59, one's progress, F, 166, effectively, F, 118, overcome, F, 127, 134, conflict, B, V, 555, inventions, B, V, 560, mind, B, V, 138, defense, B, III, 92, harmony, F, 144, denies, B, V, 575, Constitution, B, IV, 341, V, 241, 242, real progress, B, V, 628, victorious, B, IV, 546.

2. Booker T. Washington

Harlan, Louis R., et al., eds. *The Booker T. Washington Papers.* Urbana: University of Illinois Press, Fourteen Volumes, 1972-1984. Volume One contains *Up from Slavery.*

Pages 25-29. usefulness, VII, 191, 192, X, 459, laws, IX, 254, 324, 325, 409, hand, I, 75, IV, 57, V, 62, foundation, I, 76, IV, 62, 381, 407, 508, V, 192, 218, 261, 355, 539, VII, 342, X, 119, XIII, 350, history, I, 74, 332, IV, 440, V, 574, VII, 190, 439, IX, 237, harmony, I, 45, 74, 153, V, 229, VII, 188, X, 468, XII, 287, XIII, 74, 328, 498, crime, IV, 195, 196, Negroes, X, 600, ourselves, VII, 188, prejudice, VIII, 400, 468, society, III, 478, X, 48, property, I, 108, 303, IV, 92, V, 374, 503, VII, 117, 191, IX, 95, 96, X, 50, 296, 443, 466, 600, XIII, 121, 122, up, I, 125, 126, 303, IV, 72, 92, 93, 196, 197, 235, 374, 409, 509, V, 537, 583, IX, 376, X, 34, 35, XII, 414, hatred, X, 33, 34, thyself, II, 446, IV, 124, 125, XII, 176, another, IV, 180, power, V, 84, library, IV, 103, V, 189, training, VI, 534, have, III, 347, V, 342, X, 48, 49, civilization, I, 74, 252, II, 194, IV, 215, 383, 384, 483, 484, V, 520, 678, 709, VI, 115, 204, VII, 93, 114, VIII, 307, 310, IX, 108, X, 404, XIII, 363, 468, life, III, 93, V, 544, IX, 327, 328, done, IV, 435, grandchild, X, 406, 407, 410, race, I, 244,

246, years, I, 317, XII, 285, 286, week, III, 478, IV, 195, 234, V, 347, VI, 471, XII, 285, 286, industry, IV, 92, 138, V, 38. anyone, III, 89, 90, 315, V, 63, X, 258.

Pages 30-34. color, III, 234, 235, IV, 212, V, 584, life, III, 316, 528, IV, 190, VI, 533, X, 581, helpfulness, VI, 136, League, III, 305, 316, V, 454, VIII, 113, heart, II, 430, 432, VIII, 306, lives, II, 191, 192, 194, III, 185, 187, 200, 477, 510, IV, 61, 312, 369-371, 373, 481, V, 35, 57, 63, 276, 326, 330, 578, 581, 610, 618, 644, 678, VI, 194, VII, 235, 471, VIII, 473, 550, IX, 64, 381, 383, 421, X, 61, skills, V, 534, articles, I, 152, VI, 556, XII, 352, XIII, 226, 350, supply, IV, 91, 92, V, 328, conferences, III, 209, V, 100, 348, helpful, I, 105, III, 316, V, 305, 330, 532, 533, 536, 612, 613, 624, VI, 472, VII, 349, VIII, 82, 237, X, 405, governments, I, 68, 88, 116, 325, IV, 509, V, 504, VI, 143, 300, VII, 92, VIII, 132, XIII, 518, property, III, 187, 399, 409, 411, IV, 383, 521, 524, V, 35, 58, 277, 279, 351, 504, 601, 602, VI, 246, VII, 171, 172, X, 334, correction, III, 286, 320, IV, 92, 193, V, 614, skill, I, 73, III, 478, IV, 102, 198, 222, 356, 407, VI, 301, VII, 117, soil, I, 261, rights, III, 478, produces, VIII, 311, cause, VII, 289, XIII, 325, 467, satisfaction, I, 353, 354, effort, I, 328, love, VI, 41, race, I, 311, IX, 373, X, 430, 431, more useful, I, 252, 336, II, 434, III, 129, 130, 144, 146, 230, 235, VI, 193, IX, 683, 684, X, 23, be useful, IV, 197, 409, VII, 96, VIII, 442, IX, 254, 255, 376, X, 26, 35, development, V, 155-157, features, I, 149, V, 361-363, 575, 576, XII, 67, destroyed, VII, 189, 190, man, XIII, 20, 140, 360, City, III, 319, 324, IV, 190, 191, VI, 322, 323, courts, VIII, 143, X, 221.

Pages 35-39. reap, IV, 72, 186, 187, 221, 382, V, 190, 217, 356, 374, 375, 584, VI, 204, X, 405, lynching, III, 362, 364, V, 90, 91, VI, 217, 218, VIII, 83, 84, 133, X, 408, politics, V, 356, 359, 379, 380, VI, 143, VII, 172, 173, 189, VIII, 83, 133, X, 352, cost, VI, 218, compensation, IV, 221, conveniences, III, 515, VI, 471, obey it, X, 409, crime, XIII, 155, 270, protection, I, 76, 104, V, 191, VI, 555, VII, 191, IX, 243, sent it, IX, 478, 481, advance the Negro, IX, 551, 552, race, VII, 198, support, IX, 454, respects, IV, 179, 181, 197, V, 57, 335, attitude, VIII, 529, self, III, 396, IX, 211, American Negro, II, 442, V, 34, VI, 77, 78, VII, 470, VIII, 82, IX, 145, 229, 239, Alabama, III, 412, children, III, 202, us, I, 121, IV, 491, 492, races, VII, 439, country, I, 350, IV, 389, 407, 490, V, 350, 351, miserable, IX, 127, resentment, I, 74, 433, III, 411, V, 98, IX, 183, 184, 207, XIII, 98, 121, 122, 141, 226, 227, University, VIII, 116, X, 90, place, IX, 88, 89, serve, X, 303, others, IX, 326, 327, actions, VIII, 549, 550, own race, VIII, 388, intense, III, 219, 286, IX, 185, 186, 322, 323, 326, 533, 638, X, 599, 600, parishioners, IV 234, VI, 140, 141, vicious, VIII, 442, state, IV, 384.

Pages 40-44. race, IX, 328, enterprises, IX, 73, 74, Christlike, VI, 556, 557, VII, 95, 439, lives, X, 52, South, I, 258, 263, IV, 357, V, 87, 352, VI, 216, community, I, 364, 385, IV, 539, VI, 204, good, I, 373, machinery, I, 455, remove, XIII, 365, helpfulness, XIII, 370, independent, I, 434, star, I, 223, IV, 93, 198, V, 605, VI, 116, VII, 290, 470, X, 380, 464, elsewhere, I, 222, labor, III, 31, 32, 284, 373, IV, 191, V, 346, 579, conditions, IX, 638, life, I, 420, them, I, 419, 420, practice, I, 415, mother, I, 403, 404, student, I, 416, effort, I, 232, slavery, I, 405, self-reliance, I, 260, it, II, 93, 94, 499, V, 578, VI, 556, land, II, 279, conceited, I, 301, language, IV, 311, unlearn, XII, 358, 359, country, XII, 36, candor, VI, 276, 277, year, VIII, 315.

Pages 45-50. giving, VIII, 315, people, III, 552-553, V, 502, 503, schools, X, 51, community, III, 481, 482, benefits, I, 419, race, I, 418, 419, Institute, VIII, 126, 130, administration, VII, 297, Bibles, XI, 89, usefulness, III, 130, V, 36, flourishing, XII, 150, complaining, VIII, 355, IX, 262, doubled, XI, 108, 110, restrictions, VII, 91, 92, 115, 470, X, 36, 403, poverty, XII, 357, 358, lives, II, 397, virtue, II, 397, achieved, XII, 358, time, II, 503, III, 25, V, 584, 617, smooth, I, 234, possess, I, 419, character, I, 419, XIII, 78, kingdoms, I, 419, XIII, 78, prejudice, IX, 154, XII, 425, way, VII, 469, X, 49, property, X, 88, 452, education, III, 509, superficialities, VII, 289, 290, debt, III, 218, VI, 188, permanent success, XIII, 348, country, V, 601, mistakes, IV, 284, our success, XIII, 351, goals, V, 378, 536, 537, 602, VI, 170, potential, VII, 188, X, 600, 601, flattery, VII, 288, strengths, V, 363, 373, work, V, 73, 74, Institute, V, 73, 74, VII, 469, 488, VIII, 417, feelings, V, 628, efforts, I, 232.

3. Marcus Garvey

C   Clarke, John Henrik, ed. *Marcus Garvey and the Vision of Africa*. New York: Vintage Books, 1974.

H   Hill, Robert A., et al., eds. *The Marcus Garvey and Universal Negro Improvement Association Papers*.

Berkeley: University of California Press, Nine Volumes, 1983-1995.

HB Hill, Robert A. and Barbara Bair, eds. *Marcus Garvey: Life and Lessons, A Centennial Companion to the Marcus Garvey and Universal Negro Improvement Association Papers.* Berkeley: University of California Press, 1987.

J Jacques-Garvey, Amy, ed. *Philosophy and Opinions of Marcus Garvey.* New York: Atheneum, Two Volumes, 1969.

Pages 51-54. in Africa, J, II, 119, wealth, HB, 46, 47, 211, H, II, 187, III, 211, 214, 274, 317, 389, 562, 591, 592, VII, 123, 188, 204, 882, races, HB, (Introduction), liii, lvi, H, I, lii, lxxxvii, II, 30, 118, 411, 473, 588, III, 79, 80, 151, 175, 312, 317, 404, 581, 596, 600, VII, 10, 281, 297, 473, IX, 129, 208, 536, J, I, 11, 52, Canada, HB, xv, 37, 38, H, I, xxxvi, 8, 9, II, 28, 236, 302, 348, 352, 368, 479, III, 213, 273, 299, 529, VII, 49, 50, 62, 147, 157, 193, Destiny, HB, xxxi, H, I, 65, II, 299, III, 312, IX, 131, J, II, 37, 38, 302, of Africa, HB, 98, 206-208, H, I, lix, 62, 65, 117, III, 313, 560, communities, HB, 98, 99, 208-210, H, I, lix, 62, 65, 66, 104, 117, 332, IX, 518, organizations, HB, 321, 322, condition, HB, 207, race, H, I, 162, II, 98, self-reliance, HB, 68, 345, H, III, 10, 407, Corporation, HB, xxii, lxi, 340, H, I, lxiv, 339, II, 63, 222, III, 3, 98, 268, 269, 275, VII, lxii, 371, 702, 714, 782, 795, 816, 930, men, HB, 184, 185, H, I, xl, God, HB, 203, 204, H, III, 583, VII, 701, IX, 136, J, II, 38, 62, 81, 325, in Africa, C, 251, H, III, 23, 24, 79, 310, VII, 120, 226, 227, 279, 281, 882, IX, 383-385, to Africa, H, VII, 850, 851, 855, 859, 883, 894, railroads, H, III, 589, 590, slavery, HB, 50, J, I, 94, 95, II, 141, 576, products, J, II, 333, him, H, I, 333, II, 31, 131, 187, III, 407, justice, H, I, 303, III, 9, peoples, H, VII, 667.

Pages 55-59. rights, C, 332, 345, 346, J, I, 95, world, H, I, 506, III, 27, South, HB, 305, H, III, 174, VII, 564, 571, 682, 758, 789, order, HB, 240, 241, 244, of Africa, H, I, lxix, lxx, lxxiv, 315, II, 50, 94, 411, 482, 500, 502, III, 83, VII, 473, J, I, 14, 93, Ireland, H, I, lxxiv. II, 499, 538, races, H, I, lxxvi, III, 586, disloyal, HB, liv, J, II, 35, 36, again, C, 157, HB, 4, 20-22, 160, 161, 193, 269, J, I, 14, 77, II, 19, clubs, HB, 202, 209, 264, 265, country, C, 156, HB, xxxix, 3, 7,

9, 13, 14, had, H, III, 369, 370, 390, 553, VII, 198, 199, children, H, I, 378, 379, 553, III, 390, VII, 198, 199, existence, H, VII, 655, continue, HB, 95, J, I, 64, II, 24, 25, achieved, H, III, 579, IX, 132, independence, H, VII, 594, themselves, H, VII, 155, human rights, HB, xxvii, envy, H, I, 134, 135, Indian, HB, lvii, lx, 117, 118, H, VII, 130, 684, J, I, 5, 21, 22, destiny, H, VII, 105, J, I, 89, 90, 91, II, 118, man, C, 49, H, II, 258, III, 26, 381, 561, J, I, 91, II, 118, our rights, H, I, 504, II, 94, 616, III, 296, 414, 577, 581, 589, dead, HB, 314, 315, Christian, H, III, 428, hut, H, VII, 387, 388, conscience, H, VII, 27, barbarians, H, II, 415, destroyed, J, I, 2, explain, HB, 228, 279, souls, H, I, 41, ourselves, HB, 280, groups, C, 84.

Pages 60-65. Christ, H, III, 155, 212. superiority, HB, 131, H, II, 47, III, 33, 406, 561, 597, 605, VII, 98, 138, IX, 190, lowly, J, II, 31, love, J, I, 27, position, C, 84, culture, H, I, 64, 65, 109, 110, 115, 181, 182, righteous, J, II, 179, term, H, VII, 574, 696, 710, 711, mercy, J, II, 337, antagonism, C, 248, felt, H, II, 116, 480, III, 213, 283, 294, VII, 224, 225, 388, 389, 881, fear, H, III, 149, 150, 155, 275, 281, service, HB, 106, 107, 327, 328, H, I, xc, II, 156, III, 312, VII, 473, souls, C, 295, J, II, 223, 335, free, H, I, 42, nation, H, I, 5, 6, 54, 55, 68, 104, 115, VII, 47, 129, 283, Indians, II, I, lvii, 5, 166, succeed, H, II, 127, freedom for Negroes everywhere, H, I, 5, 6, III, 151, 598, Corporation, H, II, 586, III, 50, actions, H, I, lxxxviii, serve, H, I, 141, J, I, 65, 101, II, 319, rights, H, I, 49, II, 57, III, 373, VII, 99, 175, protest, HB, 244, emancipation, HB, 46, corrupt, C, 190, H, II, 258, 282, III, 579, J, II, 218, 219, enemies, H, I, 161, 162, future, C, 344, H, II, 235, VII, 28, 951, 952, 1006, climb, H, VII, 79, consciousness, HB, 156, H, I, xxxviii, 179, class, HB, 153, H, I, xxxviii, 197, 198, III, 529, 530, justice for Negroes everywhere, H, VII, 130, noble cause, H, 70, 78, 171, 201, program, H, I, 6, country, H, II, 414, 500, West Indies, H, II, 121, 453, 454, III, 274, 275, 297, 403, 405, IX, 129, 536, liberation of the race, H, I, 333, 376, 416, II, 45, 46, 121, 122, 253, 254, 417, 501, III, 150, 403, VII, 96, obstacles, J, I, 97, percent, H, II, xxxi, 79, 86, 87, 99, 103, 104.

Pages 66-71. members, H, II, 293, 300, 301, 303, their race, H, I, lxxvi, 303, II, 8, 47, III, 295, sin, J, I, 18, leader, HB, 107, Palace, H, II, 415, Motherland, H, III, 319, our cause, H, II, 134, 255, 501, III, 588, 589, of Africa, H, VII, 1006, slavery, H, II, 477, 478, freedom, H, II, 557, purity, H, I, lxxxi, lxxxii, any race, HB, 335, 350, H, II, 50, VII, 281, 762, 763, offended, H, III, 427, them, H, III, 594, 595, new members, H, III, 166, ventures, HB, 96, H, II, 464, VII, 415, throughout the world, H, VII, 229, myself, H, VII, 61, 220, justice, H, VII, 10, 13, and Africa, H, VII, 73, virtue, H, VII, 51, country Africa, H, VII, 197, determination, H, VII, 281, 702, classes, H, VII, 515, trouble, H, VII, 213, Africans of the world, H, II, 206, are, H, II, 478, 479, country, H, II, 412, 413, 456, III, 155, nation, H, I, 10, 11, protect them, H, VII, 686, do, H, I, lxxxv, lxxxvi, VII, 593, death, H, II, 31, 115, 116, 127, 128, 130, 177, 220, 223, 253, 255, 282, 555, III, 8, 152, 154, 405, 409, 550, 578, IX, 130, 131, parts of the world, H, III, 24, sacrifices, HB, 156, for them, H, VII, 67, 68, progress, H, II, 587, destiny, H, II, 228, VII, 68, top, H, I, 4, efforts, J, I, 78, UNIA, HB, 108, 109, misfortune, H, VII, 127, life, J, I, 62, 88.

4. W.E.B. Du Bois

D   Du Bois, W.E.B. *Black Reconstruction in America, 1860-1880.* New York: Atheneum, 1992.

F   Foner, Philip S., ed. *W.E.B. Du Bois Speaks: Speeches and Addresses, 1890-1919, 1920-1963,* Two Volumes. New York: Pathfinder Press, 1970.

H   Huggins, Nathan, ed. *W.E.B. Du Bois Writings: The Suppression of the African Slave Trade, The Souls of Black Folk, Dusk of Dawn, Essays and Articles.* New York: The Library of America, 1986.

W   Walden, Daniel, ed. *W.E.B. Du Bois: The Crisis Writings.* Greenwich: Fawcett Publications, 1972.

Pages 73-77. obligation, F, I, 3, 37, 111, treatment, F, I, 142, H, 1137, 1192, imperialism, F, I, 143, II, 53, H, 673, 690, W, 235, 334, 335, back, F, I, 143, them, F, II, 192, 193, himself, F, I, 202, speeches, H, 372, 1031, 1040, it, D, 100, F, I, 261, 283, 284, helpers, D, 112, 113, 238, 716, F, II, 96, 193, H, 1032, 1033, South, D, 223-230, 351, H, 377, 384, 385, 387, 388, vote, D, 577, 713, H, 1029, ignorance, H, 686, 687, civilization, F, I, 125, H, 372, W, 16, 77, duties, F, I, 176, labor, F, I, 4, 146-148, segregation, F, II, 24, 221, H, 695, 720, 721, laws, F, I, 200, education, F, II, 22, 23, W, 301-303, graduates, D,

694, F, II, 80, 81, H, 399, W, 301-303, Negro, F, I, 128, 129, 223, II, 23, H, 399, 698, 731, 732, socialism, F, I, 8, II, 1, 108, 200, 304, 307, 309, 310, 312, H, 774, 789, 1113, 1187, W, 112-114, 371, 393, individual, F, I, 84, 85, H, 825, 826, activity, F, I, 43, 82, 130, 131, H, 403, 822, him, F, II, 52, H, 484, 620, 1224, W, 205, habits, F, I, 43, 136, II, 72, 81, 113, H, 842, 853, 855, 856, allow, F, I, 132, 133, 140, H, 604, 773, 788, 842, 847, 854, 858, 861, 1017, W, 75, 76, 129, 136, 137, 139, 141, 142, 151, 174-176, 184, wasted, F, II, 105, H, 861, 871, 874, W, 67, world, H, 437, 438, have, H, 691, States, F, II, 191, H, 620, 861, 871, 874, thirty, F, II, 223, "defense," H, 1110-1111.

Pages 78-82. vote, H, 1155, 1156, power, H, 679, 696, 760, 761, 770, 771, 776, W, 33, 56, siege, H, 770, 771, Negroes, F, II, 54, 158, H, 736, 931, 933, 936, 1093, character, F, I, 142, H, 638, colonialism, F, I, 6, II, 53, H, 649, few, F, II, 161-178, shortcomings, F, II, 162, 163, H, 755, 757, W, 248-250, ventures, F, II, 13-20, H, 757, W, 301, 306-308, 310-328, life, F, II, 73, 326, socialism, F, II, 195, H, 1245, 1246, W, 31, 32, 36, 424-428, ones, F, II, 159, ourselves, F, I, 81, and voters, F, II, 85, H, 701, 788, 1242, 1245, 1246, 1252, W, 31, 75, 103, 115, 116, 186, hands of the workers, F, I, 171, 200, II, 34, 36, 38, 210, 211, H, 481, 789, 1247, strength, F, I, 235, million voters, F, II, 302, W, 196-200, issue, F, II, 269, welfare of the workers, F, II, 320, means of living, F, II, 73, 273, 276, 277, 305, H, 419, 842, books, F, II, 273, life of the world, F, I, 190, rights, F, II, 219-222, 225, 227, W, 261, 262, starve, F, II, 223, 246, 247, 274, revolt, F, II, 184, emancipation, F, II, 196, decent living, F, II, 311, H, 1303, state, F, I, 143, II, 230, 249, H, 763, 775, 789, 1088, W, 360, 361, Council, H, 1096-1099, 1105, 1302, 1303, silence, H, 1104, 1105, children, F, I, 235, 236, H, 965, 1170, W, 339, 340, 344-351, their race, H, 958, 959.

Pages 83-88. over the world, F, II, 287, 288, 310, worker, F, II, 258, W, 380, race in America, F, I, 58, H, 749, Party of the United States, F, I, 8, H, 775, 1305, W, 368, 371, servants, F, II, 87, regardless of race, F, I, 81, II, 196, H, 788, 825, 826, 1131, can, F, I, 84, 142, II, 181-184, H, 545, 639, 820, 825, inner life, F, I, 25, H, 566, 567, thrift, H, 562, 563, 566, whites, H, 638, problems, H, 582, Russia, H, 575, W, 67, 120, 260, me, H, 572, 573, problem in the United States, F, I, 37, H, 596, 597, my life, H, 1137, W, 57, 58, 60, 61, legislation, H, 727, narrow, H, 392, 393, 398, W, 303, disfranchisement, H,

1160, W, 346, 347, abolished, H, 733, together, H, 732, W, 68, 256, whites, H, 740, 741, W, 26, 257-259, equality in America, H, 889, 895, officers, H, 735, vision, F, II, 13, W, 305, 306, Negro race, F, II, 18, hope, H, 494, skins, H, 538, 539, 541, 544, development, H, 402, W, 56, democracy, H, 395, improve, H, 1158, W, 25, 70, comprehend, H, 474, his soul, F, I, 147, 170-172, 174, 175, 224, II, 5, H, 621, 695, 698, 700, 777, 1131, 1132, 1245, 1251, W, 14, 15, 20, 71, found, H, 1131, 1132, W, 55, activities, H, 679, 696, 761, 770, 771, 776, W, 33, 56.

Pages 89-93. justice, H, 1247, 1257, W, 31, perpetrate, H, 679, 680, South, F, I, 39, improvement, F, I, 177, my soul, H, 759-761, "news", H, 648, other, H, 648, discrimination, H, 640, extinction, H, 714, unity, F, II, 204, number, H, 1166, 1167, generation, H, 707, Du Bois, H, 629, 630, expedient, W, 104-107, century, H, 1198, protestors, H, 1231, 1232, of segregation, H, 778, 783, 1248, line, F, II, 84-86, H, 780, 1245, 1246, 1252, World War I, H, 781, color, H, 711, 777, 788, 1242, dangers, F, II, 195, 198, 199, 200, racial segregation, F, II, 252, 253, guilt, F, I, 24, 89-92, II, 276, work, F, II, 73, 276, 292, H, 423, 792, 1114, 1116, to America, F, II, 88, crucified, F, II, 74, dignity, F, II, 315, self-defense, F, II, 313, violations, F, II, 194, disarmament, F, II, 244, 245, 290, 303, H, 621, 775, 789, 1088, totality, F, II, 314, nation, F, II, 283.

5. Malcolm X

M   Breitman, George, ed. *By Any Means Necessary: Speeches, Interviews, and a Letter by Malcolm X.* New York: Pathfinder Press, 1970.

B   Breitman, George. *The Last Year of Malcolm X: The Evolution of a Revolutionary.* New York: Pathfinder Press, 1967.

H   Breitman, George, ed. *Malcolm X on Afro-American History.* Second Edition. New York: Pathfinder Press 1970.

S   Breitman, George, ed. *Malcolm X Speaks.* New York: Grove Press, 1966.

C   Carson, Clayborne. *Malcolm X: The FBI File.* David

Gallen, ed. New York: Carroll & Graf Publishers, Inc., 1991.

F Clark, Steve, ed. *Malcolm X, The Final Speeches, February, 1965.* New York: Pathfinder Press, 1992.

Y Clark, Steve, ed. *Malcolm X Talks to Young People: Speeches in the U.S., Britain, and Africa.* New York: Pathfinder Press, 1991.

E Epps, Archie, ed. *Malcolm X: Speeches at Harvard.* New York: Paragon House, 1991.

I Gallen, David, ed. *Malcolm A to X: The Man and His Ideas,* New York: Carroll & Graf Publishers, Inc., 1992.

P Golson, G. Barry, ed. *The Playboy Interview.* New York: Wideview Books, 1981.

A Malcolm X and Alex Haley. *The Autobiography of Malcolm X.* New York: Ballantine Books, 1973.

L Perry, Bruce, ed. *Malcolm X: The Last Speeches.* New York: Pathfinder Press, 1989.

Pages 95-98. Islam, C, 235, P, 39, 40, A, 218, man, E, 23, 24, 27, 28, A, 83, 98, 108, 109, 123, 124, 125, 130, 131, 153, 252, 458, rights, S, 19, 20, P, 40, 52, immorality, A, 410, see, M, 158, 159, A, 289, minds of our people, M, 26, 46, 159, B, 55, 56, 59, 88, 89, S, 38, 39, C, 233, E, 34, 140, 141, L, 133, brothers, M, 37, 38, 39, 40, 156, 159, B, 106, S, 73, C, 38, 289, 480, 481, 497, F, 182, 251, 252, 258, I, 58, 105, A, 416, L, 17, 130, 133, 157, legal, M, 37, 56, 160, S, 43, 49, 116, 203, 224, C, 317, L, 175, community, M, 61, B, 109, C, 497, F, 104, 105, Y, 70, E, 174, A, 221, blacks, M, 46, 48, B, 48, S, 42, 70, C, 256, F, 105, all of our people, F, 84, 252, constructively, S, 196, Y, 99, for themselves, S, 168, 169, F, 93, 94, Y, 14, L, 166, 167, movement, F, 55, 60, 93, 94, L, 128, 129, 171, selfhood, M, 53, rediscover themselves, M, 54-56, E, 142, L, 37, of themselves, M, 160, S, 196, slavery, S, 173, 174, Y, 11, L, 43, free, I, 59, nonviolent, M, 22, him, H, 46, E, 59, 134, destroying this country, S, 58-60, 71, 93, 162, 163, 165, C, 74, 184, 289, 316, A, 334, 338, 351, 352, 362.

Pages 99-101. all people, M, 158, 170, 171, S, 24, 25, 58, 59, 112,

162, 177, C, 237, 345, 356, F, 37, 63, 83, 84, 185, A, 338, L, 115, 147, democracy, A, 275, earth, A, 220, 266, 285, 286, 368, 369, blacks, M, 151, 152, S, 96, 144, A, 371, 413, L, 14, will, M, 152, S, 195, is, S, 13, F, 24, 25, 66, 67, 81, 105, L, 13, my people, E, 164, 165, in this country, S, 118, attitude, M, 13, 58, 59, 164, B, 45, 47, 48, S, 21, 22, C, 176, 262, 292, E, 34, A, 375-377, whites, M, 4, 11, 29, 30, 41, 66, 67, 101, 155, 170, 180, B, 106, 107, S, 8, 22, 43, 76, 77, 135, 153, 164, 210, 224, C, 239, 262, 276, F, 46, 183, 263, Y, 22, E, 34, 171, 173-175, A, 366, L, 39, 88, states, M, 12, S, 7-9, 50, 56, 57, E, 68, men, M, 179, agenda of the General Assembly of the United Nations, M, 7, 8, 24, 27, 85, 86, B, 116, S, 34, 35, 53, 54, 83, 84, 130, C, 40, 290, 296, 305, 335, F, 62, 104, 169, 170, Y, 45, E, 12, 33, 143, 144, 173, 174, A, 179, 350, L, 89, 178, 180, 181, victims, B, 116, S, 81, F, 177, E, 143, A, 179, attention of the General Assembly of the United Nations, M, 87, S, 54, 76, 81, C, 40, 78, 79, A, 361, abroad, M, 177, 178, S, 76, 77, 217, there, M, 104, 105, B, 63, 64, S, 63, 210, 211, being, B, 24, S, 197, A, 424, one, E, 45, A, 356, 366.

Pages 102-107. noise, A, 8, 391, manhood, H, 3, myself, A, 35, 36, 38, 159, 270, punchy, A, 24, education, P, 48, 49, A, 391, 392, alive, A, 172, 174, 176, 177, 179, 180, 181, slavery, A, 162, 176, 177, 197, 212, 213, arguments, A, 184, criminals, B, 8, A, 212, 252, 262, 287, 296, freedom, A, 379, exemplary Muslims, A, 261, 262, help, A, 163, prison, A, 258, ancestors, A, 199, NAACP, L, 172, 173, best Muslims, A, 233, live, C, 253, Y, 68, public, A, 233-235, grew, C, 225, of the NOI, A, 282, me, A, 290, and the NOI, C, 252, 253, 260, prophet, F, 103, 104, 278, A, 212, 214, 245, 294-299, 365, 446, myself, S, 216, 226, F, 103, 104, 278, 279, A, 306, L, 86, 87, mine, E, 174, have, M, 6, 10, racism, M, 26, 27, 36, S, 5, 6, 51, 73, C, 34, 175, F, 56, 94, 95, Y, 38, L, 51, 105, 167, 168, borders, S, 215, rules, H, 8, brothers, S, 66, one, H, 43, S, 65, 66, F, 100, demanding, H, 6, 7, S, 52, E, 159, development, S, 132, to us, M, 23, 90, 102, S, 132, 133, vote, M, 92, right, Y, 75, L, 168, 169, toward us, M, 11, S, 113, Y, 21, E, 171, L, 56.

Pages 108-112. here, M, 125, cemetery, A, 417, mistakes, M, 29, since, S, 201, F, 87, L, 119, 120, rights, C, 41, 42, A, 427, world, S, 150, forward, H, 70, S, 139-142, L, 176-178, Restitution, F, 266-268, P, 51, murdered, S, 52, 53, 76, 79, 150, 151, C, 238, F, 272, Y, 24, P, 40, L, 76, 77, 179, exist, M, 166, S, 49, 200, F, 58, Y, 40, 41, E, 136, 137, A, 366, "death," M, 182, C, 184, 309, Y, 20, 21, 25, A,

394, Louis, M, 155, A, 350, 361, 366, 377, 394, stand, M, 147, them, S, 110, A, 271, 272, 374, L, 61, our people, A, 273, L, 26, another, A, 362, 363, offensive, F, 265, 266, communities, M, 159, 160, B, 64-66, S, 19, 212, C, 24, 261, nerve, A, 415, Lion, A, 269, interests, A, 381, Congo, M, 147-150, 162, S, 94, 95, 149, 220, F, 49-51, 91-93, Y, 77, 78, L, 162-165, organizations, M, 111, person, S, 99, assets, M, 23, it, S, 204, moderate, A, 423, 424, L, 87, ground, A, 417, Allah, F, 231, A, 210, 378, 381, 428, 429.

6. Martin Luther King, Jr.

CC   Carson, Clayborne et al., eds. *A Call to Conscience: The Landmark Speeches of Dr. Martin Luther King, Jr.* New York: Warner Books, 2001.

K   Carson, Clayborne and Peter Holloran. *A Knock at Midnight: Inspiration from the Great Sermons of Martin Luther King, Jr.* New York: Warner Books, Inc., 1998.

P   Carson, Clayborne et al., eds. *The Papers of Martin Luther King, Jr.* Volume I, *Called to Serve, January 1929-June 1951.* Volume II, *Rediscovering Precious Values, July 1951-November 1955.* Volume III, *Birth of a New Age, December 1955-December 1956.* Volume IV, *Symbol of the Movement, January 1957-December 1958.* Berkeley: University of California Press, 1992, 1994, 1997, 2000.

FBI   Friedly, Michael and David Gallen. *Martin Luther King, Jr.: The FBI File.* New York: Carroll & Graf Publishers, Inc., 1993.

G   King, Martin Luther, Jr. "A Comparison of the Conceptions of God in the Thinking of Paul Tillich and Henry Nelson Wieman," Ph.D. dissertation in systematic theology, Boston University, 1955.

M   King, Martin Luther, Jr. *The Measure of a Man.* Philadelphia: Fortress Press, 1988. First published by the Christian Education Press, Philadelphia, in 1959.

L   King, Martin Luther, Jr. *Strength To Love.* New York:

Harper & Row, Publishers, 1963.

F   King, Martin Luther, Jr. *Stride Toward Freedom: The Montgomery Story*. New York: Harper & Row, Publishers, 1958.

T   King, Martin Luther, Jr. *The Trumpet of Conscience*. New York: Harper & Row, Publishers, 1967.

C   King, Martin Luther, Jr., *Where Do We Go From Here: Chaos or Community?* New York: Harper & Row, Publishers, 1967.

W   King, Martin Luther, Jr. *Why We Can't Wait*. New York: Harper & Row, Publishers, 1963.

H   Washington, James Melvin, ed. *A Testament of Hope: The Essential Writings of Martin Luther King, Jr.* San Francisco: Harper & Row, Publishers, 1986.

Pages 113-115. minister, P, I, 1, 44, 45, 144, 363, II, 254, 255, K, 17, W, 95, optimism, P, I, 360, inspiration, F, 135, 136, W, 73, P, IV, 330, criticism, P, II, 137, 138, personality, F, 100, dimensions, K, 121-133, M, 36-38, 41, 42, 48-50, 54-56, L, 67, 69, 71, 73- 77, Easter, P, I, 281, 294, 360, II, 19, 188, 253, 525, III, 200, 261, 262, 327, 328, IV, 191, 330, K, 15, 18, 136, FBI, 371, CC, 34, 40, 54, G, 242, 275, 298, 299, F, 69, 70, 106, 136, 138, 158, 171, 172, L, 48-50, 64, 94, 101, 104, 105, 107, 141, 142, W, 59, 61, 66, T, 75, H, 9, 13, 14, 20, 40, 88, 141, 252, 261, burdens, K, 109, L, 114, 115, 124, truth, P, III, 419, K, 34, L, 132, H, 10, rewarded, P, II, 166, 229, power of freedom, P, I, 280, 281, CC, 129, K, 46, 87, 88, M, 18, L, 19, 90, 95, T, 72, 77, C, 97, 180, H, 118, 119, humanity, H, 119-121, 144, total freedom, H, 104, immoral, P, III, 338, W, 6, 19-21, 139-141, 143, T, 6, H, 21, 96, 100, 177, 338, guilt, C, 69, 70, 72, 73, 83, H, 64, 71, 270, 314, 316, citizenship, F, 197, H, 117, 147, 159, ideals, P, I, 117, III, 337, 338, 345, 373, 418, 472-474, IV, 186, 333, CC, 62, 63, K, 31, 32, 89, FBI, 235, 443, F, 20, 21, 33, 201, 205, L, 92, 104, 130, 131, 137, W, 85, C, 83, 97-100, 122, H, 37, 85, 121, 147, 357, 358.
Pages 116-118. completed, P, IV, 271, 272, W, 6, C, 11, H, 6, 136, 137, 162, 354, blindness, K, 32, F, 139, 192, L, 28-31, 131, professional association, FBI, 525, W, 87, 88, C, 5, 8, 88, 89, H, 148, society, P, IV, 440, W, 158, justice, W, 158, 159, 162, 163,

world history, III, 73, 108, 136, 151, 198, 200, 221, 224, 230, 273, 276, 294, 326, 425, 426, IV, 293, 296, 297, 355, CC, 9, F, 60, 84, 85, 164, L, 23, 134, 138, 139, W, 61, C, 44, H, 16, 17, 23, 25, 26, 38, 86, 103, 148, 149, heart, P, I, 267, II, 127, 441, III, 278, 305, 306, 326, 327, IV, 81, 82, 121, 213, 319, 320, CC, 52, 67, K, 47, G, 149, F, 87, 104, 105, L, 35, 36, 37, 40, T, 72-74, H, 8, 9, 13, 19, 46, 47, 82, 88, 125, 335, spirit, P, I, 282, II, 326, III, 342, M, 48, F, 106, L, 23, 54, 73, C, 181, T, 69, H, 20, 138, 364, happy, P, IV, 252, 253, abusive, CC, 186, G, 147, C, 37, T, 34, H, 247, fear of integration, P, I, 205, 206, G, 149, F, 105, 156, 157, 215, L, 35, 36, 39, 40, H, 20, 92, holiness, K, 34, 35, G, 275, L, 39, H, 11, friend, P, III, 266, IV, 320, 321, 366, K, 49, 51-53, 95, F, 106, 139, L, 37-41, C, 63, 64, 191, H, 17, 19, 20, 87, 88, 109, 139, 148, 242, 243, darkens life, P, IV, 306, L, 114, obstacles to integration, P, III, 271, 284, 306, 307, 345, 368, 369, 380, 442, 450, 476, 494, 495, F, 33, 34, 198, W, 26, 27, 33, C, 31, 129, 131, 143, 153, 158, H, 22, 96, 100-104, 107, 109, 110, 124, 142, 172, 213, 310, 319, 320, 343, 344, responsibility, P, I, 234, 272, 273, 283, III, 344, IV, 162, 190, 306, 436, CC, 32, K, 48, 49, F, 85, 219, 220, L, 28, 95, 133, W, 37, C, 190, 191, H, 8, 12, 18, 25, 87, 123, 124, 140, 148, 225, 242, 317.

Pages 119-123. God, P, III, 207, 208, 221, 282, 323, CC, 35, F, 39, 40, H, 6, 50, 51, 137, way of life, C, 63, H, 38, 334, nonviolent, P, IV, 120, F, 102, H, 17, integrationist, P, II, 32, 190, K, 45, 179, F, 216, L, 36, H, 103, 110, opponent, P, IV, 294, CC, 66, F, 102, H, 7, 8, 18, oppression, K, 32, L, 70, W, 22, C, 126, 129, H, 20, respect, P, III, 261, 305, 418, IV, 120, CC, 32, 53, 130, F, 87, 102, 171, 221, H, 7, 200, 230, segregation, F, 191, C, 169, 170, H, 146, 162, someday, W, 57, 58, H, 348, Bill, FBI, 336, W, 33, C, 17, 18, 58, H, 56, 97, poverty, C, 10, 81, 82, worse, C, 13, 17, H, 314, 354, program, H, 350, ends, L, 131, T, 70, 71, H, 45, 102, 109, 214, issues, W, 9-11, 83, H, 183, happen, F, 211, 222, loan associations, F, 222, W, 167, C, 36-38, 50, 137, H, 60, 61, 246, white, C, 48, 49, 52, cause, F, 10, C, 11, 28, 69, 95, T, 8, 9, H, 316, army, C, 94, H, 218, centuries, W, 22, 23, 25, C, 47, 48, country, W, 25, 90, C, 125, equality, CC, 197, C, 31, 41, 48, 49, 52, 54, 55, Improvement Association, P, III, 115, 185, 186, 198-200, 278, 284, 285, 305, 325, 418, 431, 478, 484, K, 56, 96, F, 87, 184, 212, 213, L, 6, C, 61-63, H, 7, 65, 77, 83, 84, 86, 103, 139, 148, 218, 365, repression, C, 27, 56, 57, 59, 61, H, 68, 359-365, 383, urban life, T, 9-11, military power, C, 133.

Pages 124-128. deprivation, P, III, 415, L, 127-129, K, 6, 7, 26, 27, 87, C, 171, representation, F, 190, 191, 222, H, 92, its power, FBI, 449, H, 264, 265, compassion, C, 183, T, 71, well-being of the poor, C, 86, H, 272, nation, K, 213, L, 53, C, 178, T, 69, segregation, K 71, 72, 209, FBI, 451, 452, F, 169, L, 46, 130, W, 93-97, 129, 135, H, 89, 101, 228, 344-346, 356, 357, races, P, I, 194, II, 232, IV, 187-189, K, 72, 73, F, 205-211, L, 11, 47, 131, 140, C, 96, 99, H, 406, 407, problems of the poor, P, I, 384, II, 17, 290, III, 114, IV, 296, 477, K, 146, M, 14, F, 35, 36, 91, 116, 117, L, 89, 97, 121, 122, 137, 138, W, 24, 65, 95, C, 124, H, 37, 38, 282, children, F, 84-89, W, 90, 91, boycott, F, 76-80, 85-87, Christianity, P, II, 206, III, 318, 416, 425, IV, 317, 475, K, 29, 44, FBI, 135, 229, 296, 306, 448, M, 14-15, L, 96, C, 186, 187, H, 109, 214, principles, P, II, 167, F, 93, L, 99, 100, T, 33, H, 241, humanity, P, I, 359, 435, 436, II, 9, L, 98, housing, C, 50, 137-140, 150, 151, H, 396, 397, American life, W, 146, 147, C, 90, H, 219, alive, C, 78-80, opportunity, W, 150-152, H, 314, 315, 367, 368, facilities, C, 195, 196, character, P, I, 122-124, nobility, H, 22, excellence, K, 170, 171, H, 259, 260, 265, 266, percent, W, 22, C, 111, 127, nonexistence, K, 208, 209, 220, 221, FBI, 235, 448, F, 140, 196, 224, L, 34, C, 171, 191, T, 68, H, 39, 209, 215, 243, 269, 280, totality, P, II, 247, III, 342, F, 106, L, 23, 34, C, 190, H, 138, 209, 242, other persons, M, 42, L, 54, 72, C, 180, H, 122, 210, nations, L, 122, countries, C, 184, T, 62, 63, survival, W, 168, 169, C, 184.

Pages 129-133. new world, T, 50, integrated society, K, 223, W, 98, 99, T, 77, H, 104, 105, 111, 219, 277, 375, cooperation, P, IV, 274, H, 339, victory, P, III, 432, CC, 173, F, 9, 219, C, 16, H, 39, 124, 163, 349, the world, H, 376, man, W, 92, H, 356, commitment, K, 185, 186, H, 267, sins, P, I, 51, 52, 274, II, 166, IV, 295, M, 17, 18, 21, F, 99, L, 135, 136, H, 35, 36, transformation, P, IV, 355, F, 95-97, L, 138, H, 38, him, F, 104, 105, 137, 138, L, 36, 37, order, P, III, 200, 340, IV, 438, H, 135, 350, changes, F, 100, 101, C, 19, H, 135, 190, prevail, P, III, 453, 496, F, 54, 197, K, 210, W, 89, H, 104, 142, 270, free, W, 31, 61, maladjustment, P, I, 389, III, 286, L, 14, 15, H, 14, 15, 89, 250, shame, P, IV, 294, 296, 341, 355, 474, K, 28, FBI, 114, 381, F, 51, 52, 91, 212, 221, L, 6, 40, 128, W, 84, C, 46, T, 74, H, 48, 60, 87, 103, 164, 356, resistance, P, II, 485, L, 58-60, C, 128, personality, P, III, 416, M, 30, K, 56, 57, 97, F, 37, 113, 117, 194, 195, 205, L, 62, 63, 128, 130, 131, W, 85, C, 97, 98, H, 119, 142, 147, law, F, 117, 149, 216, 218, 223, 224, W, 86, 87, H, 49, 110, 149,

164, 165, 357, right to protest, H, 50, 282, affluent society, W, 83, power, P, III, 475, IV, 127, 299, CC, 30, K, 96, 217, M, 23, 26, F, 113, 162, 170, 174, 175, 191-193, L, 139, W, 82, 113, 122, 123, 126, 154, 155, C, 90, 95, 128-130, H, 7, 44, 86, 99, 146, 147, 188, 374, area of life, L, 22, 23, C, 100, 101, H, 51, 118, 123, 124, unity, P, III, 237, 239, F, 150, H, 76, 78, inception of the boycott, P, III, 123, 237, 302, 318, IV, 270, 439, F, 43, 44, 110, W, 24, H, 76, 78, plans, P, III, 239, F, 49, H, 78, joined the boycott, P, III, 239, F, 55, H, 78, support of the boycott, P, III, 239, F, 55, H, 78, participate in the protest, P, III, 239, F, 54, 55, H, 78, 79, opportunity, F, 63, continue the boycott, F, 108, H, 79.

Pages 134-139. precision, P, III, 240, F, 75-77, H, 79, join the protest, P, III, 240, F, 126, 127, win, P, III, 240, F, 112, H, 79, arrest, P, III, 240, 304, 305, F, 126, 128, H, 79, nation, P, III, 120, 188, 240, 305, F, 135-140, H, 76, 79, 83, protection, F, 140, 141, H, 323, determination, P, III, 238, H, 76, momentum for the protest, P, III, 133, 240, 279, 305, F, 142, 143, 149, 150, H, 84, methods, P, III, 240, 305, H, 79, tolerance, P, III, 24, 295, F, 56, 61, 153-157, cause of freedom, F, 146, H, 76, resisted, F, 213, 214, C, 129, 130, campaigns, F, 102-104, 156, H, 8, 13, 19, 87, races, W, 91, H, 361, 375, another, P, III, 261, 278, 447, K, 33, 47, F, 102, 103, 163, 214, 220, 221, L, 6, 36, H, 8, 12, 83, heal, P, IV, 120, 121, 297, CC, 191, K, 97, FBI, 336, W, 14, 28, 30, 132, H, 38, 39, 109, 214, 249, 334, 348, 349, racism, W, 81, 82, 132, C, 91, H, 350, 383, 387, corrected, W, 88, 168, H, 183, basis, F, 103, 106, W, 30, them, W, 34, 35, campaign, W, 34, 35, 48, H, 344, arrested, W, 69-73, lives, W, 29, 101, 102, 104, C, 108, H, 126, 170, 337, anvil, W, 38, year, W, 41, 43, 46, 47, 125, 144, unity, W, 126, demands, T, 5, H, 127, Bill, C, 1, 2, retaliated, W, 91, 92, C, 17, 64, T, 58, H, 69, 102, 164, 363, skills, P, III, 307, 419, C, 55, 56, H, 57, violence, C, 23-32, pioneer, W, 99, bear, CC, 192, K, 97, C, 64, 65, T, 74, H, 250, capacity, C, 109, reconciliation, P, III, 188, K, 137, 138, 164, L, 83, W, 3, 4, defeat, C, 138, sympathy, K, 108, 109, L, 82, condition, L, 109, reality, FBI, 371, L, 142, H, 397, branch, P, III, 345, H, 183, banks, CC, 176-180, C, 143-146.

Pages 140-144. mankind, K, 113, 219, FBI, 452, 453, M, 26, F, 95, L, 29, 140, C, 183, T, 67, 68, H, 39, 275, Vietnam, FBI, 500, F, 199, H, 364, 408, self-determination, CC, 142, 149, 183, K, 180, 181, 219, 220, FBI, 501, 502, C, 182, 183, 188, T, 22, 23, H, 233, 234,

235, 241, 315, 326, 408, peace, CC, 144, 145, FBI, 385, 407, 502, T, 24, 25, H, 233, 234, 408, exemplars, C, 35, T, 22, 29, H, 237, 241, objector, CC, 155, 156, H, 239, 240, consensus, K, 221, 222, H, 276, 277, noble lives, L, 20, 21, education, C, 155, H, 311, 370, nightmare, C, 45, reconstruction, W, 77, C, 223, alliances, C, 50, 51, rights, C, 138, H, 65, 387, spirit, P, II, 254, CC, 194, 195, L, 57, 74, C, 133, 186, T, 43, H, 240, 315, control, T, 15, 48, 49, 53, 54, H, 68, communities, K, 217, FBI, 549-552, 556, 557, 568, H, 65-68, 274, schools, C, 38, 130, 135, 136, 162, 164-166, 189, 199, 200, T, 14, 60, 61, H, 65-67, 70, 247, 248, 409, affirmation, H, 314, known, F, 134, 135, L, 107, 141, H, 40, 42, God, L, 86, Jesus, P, I, 266, 267, 428, 429, F, 105, L, 33, 141, worst, L, 33, redemption, L, 14, H, 10, oppressor, P, IV, 341, 342, K, 97, FBI, 333, CC, 96, F, 87, 103, 179, 216, 217, L, 40, W, 19, 80, T, 75, H, 18, 41, 47, 219, 221, 222, 225, nation, L, 83, 141, C, 47, H, 41, seed of freedom, P, III, 419, 478, 494, IV, 87, K, 33, FBI, 338, CC, 55, 56, 70, F, 216, L, 132, H, 10, 52, 143, 149, 207, love, P, IV, 330, FBI, 391, F, 134, 135, L, 116, H, 355, live, CC, 66, 67, K, 111, FBI, 333, 391, F, 178, W, 44, 52, 57, H, 355, 356.

7. Nelson Mandela

C   Clark, Steve, ed. *Nelson Mandela Speaks: Forging a Democratic Nonracial South Africa.* New York: Pathfinder Press, 1993.

J   Johns, Sheridan and R. Hunt Davis, Jr., eds. *Mandela, Tambo, and the African National Congress: The Struggle against Apartheid, 1948-1990, A Documentary Survey.* New York: Oxford University Press, 1991.

M   McCartan, Greg, ed. *Nelson Mandela: Speeches 1990.* New York: Pathfinder Press, 1990.

H   Mandela, Nelson and Fidel Castro. *How Far We Slaves Have Come: South Africa and Cuba in Today's World.* New York: Pathfinder Press, 1991.

L   Mandela, Nelson. *Long Walk to Freedom: The Autobiography of Nelson Mandela.* New York: Little, Brown and Company, 1994.

N   Mandela, Nelson. *No Easy Walk to Freedom*. London: Heinemann Educational Books, 1965.

S   Mandela, Nelson. *The Struggle is My Life*. New York: Pathfinder Press, Second Edition, 1990.

NYT Mandela, Nelson. "Excerpts from Remarks by Mandela to Newspaper Editors and Writers," *The New York Times*, June 20, 1990, p. A 20.

K   Mandela, Nelson. Town Meeting. The Koppel Report, WABC, "Nightline," June 21, 1990.

CFR Mandela, Nelson. Interview with Charlayne Hunter-Gault at the Council on Foreign Relations, June 22, 1990.

UN Mandela, Nelson. Address to the United Nations, June 22, 1990.

USC Mandela, Nelson. Address to the United States Congress, June 26, 1990.

I   Mandela, Nelson. Inaugural Address. May 10, 1994.

Pages 145-151. industries, M, 5, H, 21, L, 87, S, 13, 14, trades, J, 24, L, 87, S, 179, citizenship, J, 321, L, 87, S, 14, Indian community, L, 90, species, L, 97, and non-whites, J, 22, M, 5, L, 98, 99, 106, 132, year, S, 180, demands of our people, J, 23, 41, L, 102, 120, 140, 211, N, 34, 51, 83, S, 31, 35, 44, 57, 67, masses, J, 22, M, 5, L, 99, 106, S, 147, owned, J, 22, elections, J, 23, M, 5, L, 165, S, 79-81, 86, weaken the ANC, L, 106, 107, 166, N, 48, S, 65, 79, pass, J, 24, S, 180, areas, J, 22, facilities, J, 23, Movement, L, 116, S, 35, supremacy, L, 145, N, 26, S, 38, 65, 66, 101, system, M, 25, 26, S, 219, townships, J, 22, white community, L, 200, education, J, 322, L, 200, organizations, J, 32, fighters, L, 295, 308, 353, 354, charge, S, 64, dehumanize us, C, 30, 37, UN, opulence, C, 37, terrorization of non-whites, J, 96, 212, S, 97, 154, 190, regulations, L, 162, leader, C, 67, 69, L, 18, 19, council, S, 150, countries, M, 15, 19, 34, 36, 43, H, 21, S, 2, 24, 85, 150, 173, 174, 197, Nationalism, L, 65, 94, N, 82, S, 91, 174, society, S, 22, 23, crushed us, L, 111, policy of the ANC, C, 101, 137, 218, J, 6, M, 67, H, 23, L, 150, S, 55, 150, NYT, stability, M, 17, 67, belief, J, 81, 82, 175, M, 67, H, 22, L, 151, 152, S, 50, 51, pride, J, 82, M, 67, 68, L, 152, 497, N, 39, S, 51, it, J, 82,

83, M, 68, L, 152, 153, S, 51, 52, 55, 173.

Pages 152-158. travel, J, 83, M, 68, 69, S, 52, mothers, J, 83, M, 69, S, 52, training, J, 84, M, 69, 70, S, 53, recreation, J, 84, M, 70, S, 53, liberty, M, 70, 71, S, 53, 54, children, N, 26, happiness, S, 23, protest, J, 105, L, 197, 198, 235, 258, 264, S, 113, 114, another, N, 80, 84, S, 87, 93, oppression, C, 114, M, 14, H, 26, L, 120, 225, 320, 468, 469, S, 164, 174, detained, J, 6, 7, 32, L, 206, 207, S, 5, 125, 126, days, S, 154, 155, reprisals, J, 9, L, 238, 239, S, 123, 209, education, J, 102, 106, 211, M, 27, 66, L, 130, 200, 321, S, 60, 68, 83, 86, 125, 155, insignificant, S, 60, 106, 126, 191, 209, country, S, 126, struggle, S, 161, 270, evolution, L, 407, 408, colleagues, L, 426, 427, 449, prison, L, 441, transformation, M, 34, demonstrations, M, 33, L, 149, S, 115, 223, countries, M, 54, 55, Botha, J, 170, M, 16, S, 176, brutality, L, 480-482, S, 210, servants, J, 226, M, 20, 24, L, 79, 218, 219, 510, 528, S, 215, citizens, J, 175, M, 28, L, 495, groups, CFR, family, J, 226, M, 20, L, 493, S, 214-216, released, J, 165, M, 49, L, 341, 342, 437, 441, N, 27, S, 191, loyalty, C, 53-56, J, 214, 226, M, 19, 43, 52, L, 40, 254, 531, S, 195, 197, 218, African people, S, 115, supported us, C, 250, J, 170, ordered, J, 174, 175, 214, 227, M, 9, 21, L, 455, 494, 495, S, 150, 195, 216, majority of the people, M, 59, H, 25, 26, NYT, CFR, USC, Cape Town, CFR, decide, CFR, others, UN.

Pages 159-166. self-determination, C, 80, 141, H, 22, 23, K, UN, that, CFR, enemies, K, freedom, S, 228, nation, S, 231, K, whole, UN, South Africa, M, 34, L, 501, Buthelezi, M, 36, K, prisoners, L, 503, S, 216, 217, disadvantaged, M, 64, joyful, C, 37, NYT, CFR, K, domination, C, 38, 39, 258, adopt, CFR, members of the ANC, NYT, UN, sunset, CFR, system, C, 36, CFR, happiness, C, 42, act, C, 41, kinship, L, 508, did, C, 42, in 1909, C, 262, judiciary, C, 248, L, 263, 320, 321, S, 176, ended, C, 40, constitution, C, 212, 214, reconciliation, L, 540, I, colonialism, C, 169, CFR, years, C, 178, J, 27, 41, 175, 228, 284, M, 22, 45, L, 248, 254, 469, 490, S, 45, 137, 217, CFR, struggle, C, 233, L, 247, 494, 532, 533, process, C, 158, 179, 210, L, 533, fainted, K, oppressed my people, L, 83, them, L, 9, education, L, 3, 5, 6, 11, 12, prejudice, L, 62, few, L, 68, serve my people, L, 73, increase, L, 75, remainder, S, 13, expression, S, 12, through the ANC, S, 15, 16, sacrifice, C, 223, L, 90, 91, stood, L, 97, organization, L, 98, 99, wives, L, 83, S, 180, demanded, J, 9, 21, N, 81, S, 152, 153, 163, goals, J, 9, 21, 42, L, 99, 100, 110, 111,

121, 141, N, 19, 81, 82, 83, S, 2, 3, 28-30, 87, 88, 91, 92, 130, 154, 163, 182, appropriate, N, 62, S, 69-71.

Pages 167-172. human rights, J, 145, S, 137, 153, 154, odds, L, 102, 103, S, 31-33, movements, L, 104, 105, S, 91, 92, colonialism, J, 173, L, 17, 65, 105, 453, N, 82, S, 91, 92, 175, 176, recommendation, C, 102, J, 38, 39, no rights, S, 163, political rights, J, 40, N, 34, S, 25, 44, honor, J, 41, 42, M, 32, 33, L, 111, 112, 121, N, 20, 21, S, 34, apartheid, J, 25, 44, L, 111, 112, 115, 120, 121, N, 22, 83, S, 2, 34, 41, 92, 93, 163, inevitable, S, 39, desires, J, 27, 45, S, 42, country, L, 141, 142, S, 151, 152, profession, S, 151, front, S, 61, opponent, L, 159, 160, government, S, 55, cultural life, J, 82-84, M, 68-70, L, 152, 153, S, 51-53, weeks, L, 174, 175, Leaders, L, 175, feelings to the liberation movement, L, 198, members, L, 200, themselves, L, 204, 205, racialism, N, 83, 84, of its policies, J, 40, 41, N, 34, 35, 84, S, 43, 45, 93, Republic, S, 97, 98, 101, 144, domination, S, 106, 149, to its policies, S, 95, 107, 108, 119, power of the liberation movement, S, 128, my life, J, 103, L, 240, 241, 326, 523, S, 1, 6, 121, South Africa, J, 102, goal, J, 313, M, 7, 50, achieving their freedom, J, 174, CFR, tactics, C, 226, J, 109, 214, 215, M, 12, H, 23, N, 24, S, 36, 131, 162, NYT.

Pages 173-177. strategy, L, 137, S, 166, War, J, 138, 139, 227, M, 72, L, 246, 248, 294, 295, 315, 318, 451, S, 123, 162, 167, temple, C, 102, 103, 132, J, 173, 176, L, 236, 237, 453, 454, 468, S, 165, terrorism, L, 246, 248, 314, 318, 453, S, 122, 162, 167, 168, fail, J, 110, 146, 169, 176, 312, L, 169, 237, 247, 272, 315, 318, 319, S, 123, 165, 167, 168, 185, armed struggle, L, 455, S, 166, 185, 195, trial, L, 276, disobedience, S, 152, that ideal, M, 23, injustices, L, 290, S, 8, 158, 159, martyrs, C, 34, L, 326, the struggle, S, 192, 230, animals, L, 174, 175, enemies, L, 495, be, L, 396, S, 188, deprivation, L, 363, quarry, L, 355, us, L, 280, 292, 374, circumstances, L, 397, state, L, 397, an ideal, L, 542, our struggle, J, 175, 212, 213, 216, M, 31, 39, S, 68, bankruptcy, J, 104, L, 148, S, 191, my freedom, L, 454-456, S, 195-197, representative of the ANC, M, 9, 10, L, 457-459, demand, C, 33, 97, 103, 243, CFR, violence, J, 172, Marxists, M, 15, L, 476, executions, J, 305-306, M, 41, 72, S, 200.

Pages 178-183. community, C, 96, 259, 266, M, 41, L, 495, NYT, CFR, emergency, M, 6, 22, L, 484, 485, S, 211, jobs, J, 227, M, 21, S, 216, society, M, 23, L, 322, S, 9, 181, 217, cause, M, 19, L, 493, political struggles, C, 131, like the people, L, 497, 498, our

Movement, C, 27, 28, 32, 116, 165, 179, J, 228, M, 7, 23, 41, 50, H, 27, L, 495, 507, S, 217, NYT, hellhole, C, 96, 260, 273, K, justice, C, 159, armed struggle, C, 58, 62, 112, J, 169, M, 13, L, 510, 511, liberation movement, M, 7, 11, 26, 33, 35-38, 44, S, 219, 225, 226, industries, M, 27, 60-63, S, 232, NYT, disposal, UN, rights, CFR, K, equality, J, 160, 175, 228, M, 28, N, 19, S, 26, 93, 133, 184, 221, conviction, J, 8, M, 34, N, 84, S, 55, 60, 93, 181, K, regime, C, 18, 85, 89, 155, 175, 191, 194, 195, L, 502-504, 512, 513, 519, 520, CFR, K, declaration of war, C, 191, 192, 196, M, 45, 46, H, 25, L, 511, evil, K, world, C, 42, L, 508, powers, NYT, K, weapons of war, C, 36, conscience, C, 41, realized, C, 260, ANC, L, 500, innocent people, C, 12, 82, 86, 87, 106, 156, independence, C, 11, 274, H, 10, 20, 23, rule, J, 214, unity, L, 539.

8. Archbishop Desmond Tutu

C   Tutu, Desmond M. *Crying in the Wilderness: The Struggle for Justice in South Africa.* John Webster, ed. Grand Rapids: William B. Eerdmans Publishing Company, 1982.

H   Tutu, Desmond M. *Hope and Suffering: Sermons and Speeches.* John Webster, ed. Grand Rapids: William B. Eerdmans Publishing Company, 1984.

N   Tutu, Desmond M. *No Future Without Forgiveness.* New York: Doubleday, 1999.

R   Tutu, Desmond M. *The Rainbow People of God: The Making of a Peaceful Revolution.* John Allen, ed. New York: Doubleday, 1994.

W   Tutu, Naomi, ed. *The Words of Desmond Tutu.* New York: Newmarket Press, 1989.

Pages 185-190. labor, C, 107, H, 87, 96, 97, 104, 128, 155, 158, N, 15, 56, 99, 149, 228, R, 99, W, 41, 62, 75, our society, C, 76, 80, trial, H, 114, 115, R, 92, 163, 164, W, 41, 49, workers, N, 102, W, 63, person, H, 44, N, 91, W, 43, things, C, 49, 50, H, 29, 140, 141, 152, 155, 167, 187, N, 92, 93, 109, faith, N, 6, 92, 93, alienation, C, 54, H, 166, 167, W, 39, system, C, 56, 57, suffrage, R, 102, menu, H, 10,

Sources 229

45, Day, W, 85, 97, just society, C, 43, 87, 98, H, 32, 45, 77, W, 84, blind, R, 214, justice and reconciliation, H, 99, Christ, H, 165, W, 59, Church, N, 12, W, 59, to reconciliation, C, 36, H, 101, 164, W, 47, killed, R, 150, forgive, R, 222, sharing and reconciliation, W, 47, South Africa, H, 162, 164, right, H, 159, 179, struggle, H, 76, will, H, 22, 187, government, C, 64, H, 153, to God, C, 29, H, 154, 177, politics, H, 36, 37, future, H, 24, 155, 178, congregations, C, 117, human, H, 29, W, 72, self-sufficient, N, 35, W, 31, 65, 73, oppressed, H, 60, 78, 159, 177, Spirit, H, 66, of God, R, 154, infinite, H, 146, creation, H, 143, fear, C, 123, H, 119, 120, subsequent work, N, 86, 87, dignity, N, 30, 115, 165.

Pages 191-196. law, N, 114, 232, 234, themselves, N, 103, 196, 197, change, N, 83, 127-129, forgiven, N, 84, 85, torture, N, 164, 179, 251, 252, Committee, R, 102, perpetrator, N, 271, 272, forgiveness and reconciliation, N, 10, 151, 164, 184, reparation, N, 31, 35, 151, 155, 165, 273, pity, N, 223, 249, 250, blood bath, N, 36-38, greatness, N, 250, 251, healing and reconciliation, N, 55, 58, victims, N, 60, 62, 228, 229, 233, 273, closure, N, 164, 165, 192, 234, 235, militarized, N, 231, 232, 235, 236, 239, work, N, 165, 231, 232, society, N, 274, practice, N, 184, 185, 187, 275, achieve reconciliation, N, 232, 274, outsider, N, 264, 265, winners, N, 280, 281, vigilance, N, 261, 262, constitution, N, 16, 17, themselves, H, 45, 61, R, 267, self-determination, H, 29, R, 200, us, C, 44, 64, 89, H, 42, 155, R, 116, W, 26, prevail, C, 36, 83, H, 158, N, 86, 267, W, 91, government, H, 114, 128, R, 106, alternative, C, 53, 110, H, 116, 117, 129, W, 52, collapse of apartheid, N, 237, desperate means, C, 39, 56, 91, H, 35, 181, R, 72, effect, R, 200, peaceful means, C, 34, 48, 54, 114, H, 67.

Pages 197-206. oppressor, C, 34, 50, 54, H, 59, 170, W, 52, policies of apartheid, H, 119, Christian, H, 187, exploitation, C, 92, 93, everything, C, 44, 95, 109, H, 127, property, H, 33, people of South Africa, H, 33, in 1980, C, 96, R, 39, immoral, W, 48-50, with them, C, 20, R, 143, 152, 153, Amin, R, 129, love and reconciliation, C, 51, 52, Jesus, C, 31, H, 86, 100, subjects, C, 34, H, 86, shepherds, C, 114, H, 85, resurrection, H, 86, 187, life for others, R, 236, 237, funerals, W, 30, Calvary, H, 60, 74, faith, R, 132, for them, R, 15,19, 21, Land, H, 79, chosen people, R, 256, Kingdom, H, 177, nothing, H, 54, world, H, 55, 56, treachery, H, 52, 53, law of love, H, 58, rich, R, 120, ill, H, 138, history, R, 18, Power, R, 134, grace, H, 59,

SELECTED BIBLIOGRAPHY

Frederick Douglass

Foner, Philip S. *Frederick Douglass.* New York: Citadel Press, 1964.

McFeeley, William. *Frederick Douglass.* New York: W.W. Norton & Company, 1991.

Martin, Waldo E., Jr. *The Mind of Frederick Douglass.* Chapel Hill: The University of North Carolina Press, 1984.

Miller, Douglass T. *Frederick Douglass and the Fight for Freedom.* New York: Facts on File Publications, 1988.

Preston, Dickson. *Young Frederick Douglass: The Maryland Years.* Baltimore: The Johns Hopkins University Press, 1980.

Quarles, Benjamin. *Frederick Douglass.* New York: Atheneum, 1976.

Booker T. Washington

Franklin, Robert M. *Liberating Visions: Human Fulfillment and Social Justice in African-American Thought.* Minneapolis: Augsburg Fortress, 1990.

Harlan, Louis R. *Booker T. Washington: The Making of a Black Leader, 1856-1901.* New York: Oxford University Press, 1972.

Harlan, Louis R. *Booker T. Washington: The Wizard of Tuskegee, 1901-1915.* New York: Oxford University Press, 1983.

Mansfield, Stephen. *Then Darkness Fled: The Liberating Wisdom of Booker T. Washington.* Nashville: Cumberland House Publishing, 1999.

Marcus Garvey

Cronon, E. David. *Black Moses: The Story of Marcus Garvey and the Universal Negro Improvement Association.* Madison: The

University of Wisconsin Press, 1955.

Jacques-Garvey, Amy. *Garvey and Garveyism.* New York: Collier Books, 1976.

Lewis, Rupert. *Marcus Garvey, Anti-Colonial Champion.* Trenton: Africa World Press, Inc., 1988.

Stein, Judith. *The World of Marcus Garvey: Race and Class in Modern Society.* Baton Rouge: Louisiana State University Press, 1986.

W.E.B. Du Bois

Broderick, Francis. *W.E.B. Du Bois: Negro Leader in Time of Crisis.* Stanford, Calif.: Stanford University Press, 1959.

Lewis, David Levering. *W.E.B. Du Bois: Biography of a Race, 1868-1919.* New York: Henry Holt & Company, 1993.

Lewis, David Levering. *W.E.B. Du Bois: The Fight for Equality & the American Century, 1919-1963.* Volume II. New York: Henry Holt & Company, 2000.

Marable, Manning. *W.E.B. Du Bois: Black Radical Democrat.* Boston: Twayne, 1986.

Moore, Jack B. *W.E.B. Du Bois.* Boston: Twayne, 1981.

Rampersad, Arnold. *The Art and Imagination of W.E.B. Du Bois.* New York: Schocken Books, 1990.

Malcolm X

Clarke, John Henrik, ed. *Malcolm X: The Man and His Times.* New York: Collier Books, 1969.

Cone, James H. *Martin & Malcolm & America: A Dream or a Nightmare.* Maryknoll, New York: Orbis Books, 1991.

Gallen, David et al. *Malcolm X: As They Knew Him.* New York: Carroll & Graf Publishers, Inc., 1992.

Goldman, Peter L. *The Death and Life of Malcolm X.* Second Edition. Chicago: University of Illinois Press, 1979.

Karim, Benjamin, Peter Skutches & David Gallen. *Remembering*

Malcolm. New York: Ballantine Books, 1996.

Perry, Bruce. *Malcolm: The Life of a Man Who Changed Black America.* Barrytown, New York: Station Hill Press, 1991.

Wood, Joe, ed. *Malcolm X: In Our Own Image.* New York: St. Martin's Press, Inc. 1992.

Martin Luther King, Jr.

Ansbro, John J. *Martin Luther King, Jr.: Nonviolent Strategies and Tactics for Social Change.* Second Edition. New York: Madison Books, 2000.

Dyson, Michael Eric. *I May Not Get There with You: The True Martin Luther King, Jr.* New York: The Free Press, 2000.

Garrow, David J. *Bearing the Cross: Martin Luther King, Jr. and the Southern Christian Leadership Conference.* New York: William Morrow and Company, Inc., 1986.

King, Coretta Scott. *My Life with Martin Luther King, Jr.* New York: Holt, Rinehart and Winston, 1969.

Miller, William Robert. *Martin Luther King, Jr.: His Life, Martyrdom and Meaning for the World.* New York: Weybright and Talley, 1968.

Oates, Stephen B. *Let the Trumpet Sound: The Life of Martin Luther King, Jr.* New York: Harper & Row, 1982.

Phillips, Donald T. *Martin Luther King, Jr. on Leadership: Inspiration and Wisdom for Challenging Times.* New York: Warner Books, 1999.

Nelson Mandela

Benson, Mary. *Nelson Mandela: The Man and the Movement.* New York: W.W. Norton & Company, Inc., 1994.

de Klerk, F.W. *F.W. de Klerk: The Last Trek—A New Beginning, The Autobiography.* New York: Macmillan Publishers, 1999.

Meredith, Martin. *Nelson Mandela: A Biography.* New York: St. Martin's Press, 1998.

Ottaway, David. *Chained Together: Mandela, De Klerk and the Struggle to Remake South Africa.* New York: Times Books, 1993.

Sampson, Anthony. *Mandela: The Authorized Biography.* New York: Alfred A. Knopf, 1999.

Archbishop Desmond Tutu

de Gruchy, John W. *The Church Struggle in South Africa.* Grand Rapids: William B. Eerdmans Publishing Company, 1979.

du Boulay, Shirley. *Tutu: Voice of the Voiceless.* Grand Rapids: William B. Eerdmans Publishing Company, 1988.

Hulley, Leonard, Louise Kretzschmar and Luke Lungile Pato, eds. *Archbishop Tutu: Prophetic Witness in South Africa.* Cape Town: Human & Rousseau, 1996.

Kunnie, Julian E. *Bridges Across the Atlantic: Relating Black Theologies in the United States and South Africa Focusing on Social Analytical Methodologies and Utilizing James Cone and Desmond Tutu as Respective Symbolic Figures,* Th.D. dissertation. Graduate Theological Union, 1990.

Tlhagale, Buti and Itumeleng Mosala, eds. *Hammering Swords into Ploughshares: Essays in Honor of Archbishop Mpilo Desmond Tutu*: Johannesburg: Skotaville Publishers, 1986; Grand Rapids, Mich.: William B. Eerdmans Publishing Company, 1987; Trenton, NJ: Africa World Press, 1987.

Winner, David. *Desmond Tutu: The Courageous and Eloquent Archbishop Struggling against Apartheid in South Africa.* Harrisburg, PA: Morehouse Publishing, 1989.

INDEX

About the Author

John Joseph Ansbro received his Ph.D. from Fordham University and is professor emeritus of philosophy at Manhattan College where he was curriculum guidance supervisor of the faculty, chairman of the Interdisciplinary Arts Program, director of research in the Peace Studies Program, chairman of the department of philosophy, and founder and president of the Manhattan College Council on World Hunger. He taught Dr. King's nonviolence at Fordham University Graduate School in the Philosophical Resources for Contemporary Problems Program and was chairman of the Metropolitan Round Table of Philosophy. The recipient of several research grants, he is the author of *Martin Luther King, Jr.: Nonviolent Strategies and Tactics for Social Change* and forty articles in philosophical, educational, and civil rights journals in the United States, Europe, and Asia as well as numerous philosophical reviews.